THE DAVIDIC CHRONICLES

The Triumphs and Trials of Israel's Greatest King

Randy White

THE DAVIDIC CHRONICLES

The Triumphs and Trials
of Israel's Greatest King

All Scriptures are quoted from the King James Version.

ISBN: 978-1-961110-33-5

Library of Congress Cataloguing-in-Publication Data: LCCN: Pending

Dispensational Publishing House, Inc.
220 Paseo del Pueblo Norte
P.O. Box 3181
Taos, NM USA 87571
www.dispensationalpublishing.com

Ordering Information: Special discounts are available on quantity purchases by churches, associations, and U.S. trade bookstores and wholesalers. For details, contact the publisher at the address above or at our toll-free number: 1-844-321-4202.

Cover & interior layout by Ye Olde Typesetter, Show Low, Arizona USA

Biblical harp illustration by Adobe Stock.

Other illustrations generated by Dalle AI

Author's photo on the Sea of Galilee by Shelley White

First Printing, January 2025

1 2 3 4 5 6 7 8 9 10 11 12

TABLE OF CONTENTS

Chapter		Page

PREFACE

The life of King David is one of the most captivating stories in the Bible. His journey—from a young shepherd tending his father's flocks to Israel's most revered king—offers a timeless glimpse into the intersection of human frailty and heavenly purpose. Few figures in history have been so richly portrayed, with both their virtues and flaws laid bare for all to see. In David, we find a man after God's own heart (1 Samuel 13:14), whose faith and failures continue to speak to the realities of human existence.

This book, *The Davidic Chronicles: Triumphs and Trials of the Israel's Greatest King*, aims to provide a verse-by-verse exploration of David's life, not merely as a historical figure but as a man whose experiences echo timeless truths. It is a study of his victories and defeats, his integrity and lapses, and his unwavering reliance on God's promises. In David, we see a typological foreshadowing of the ultimate King, whose reign will never end.

My hope is that this work will deepen your understanding of David's life and its significance, both within the narrative of Scripture and in your own walk of faith. You will find a close examination of biblical texts, contextual insights, and reflections on how David's story informs our understanding of leadership, repentance, and God's faithfulness.

While this book examines the life of one man, it ultimately points us to the God who works through human history to accomplish His purposes. David's story reminds us that God's sovereignty is never hindered by human weakness and that His promises endure despite our failures.

The Davidic Chronicles

Whether you are a pastor, teacher, or student of the Word, I trust that this study will challenge, encourage, and inspire you. May it serve as a tool to better understand the Scriptures and the God who faithfully guided Israel's shepherd king.

Randy White

Taos, NM, 2025

Chapter 1:

INTRODUCTION TO THE DAVIDIC ERA:

Background on Israel's Monarchy and the Transition from Judges

Introduction

One could argue that David is the most famous king in history. He united Israel and Judah, conquered Jerusalem, developed one of the most prominent kingdoms of his time, is revered as an ideal Jewish king, is an ancestor of Jesus Christ, wrote some of the most touching poetry ever, and is a significant figure in the Bible and the Quran.

David's Transcultural Impact: A Comparative Analysis

David is not just a Jewish hero; he is a figure of monumental significance in multiple religious traditions and has been examined through countless cultural lenses over the millennia. His story reverberates far beyond the Hebrew Bible, finding echoes in the New Testament, the Quran, and various historical narratives and artistic expressions.

) David in the Bible and Christian Tradition

In the Bible, David emerges as a multi-faceted individual: a shepherd, warrior, poet, and king. He is a complex character who embodies both virtue and vice. On one hand, he showcases incredible faith and courage in confronting Goliath; on the other, he is flawed, as evidenced by his adulterous relationship with Bathsheba. Despite his imperfections, he is referred to as *"a man after God's own heart"* (1 Samuel 13:14). This description not only endears him to countless generations but also serves to illustrate the grace and forgiveness inherent in the Judeo-Christian tradition.

The Davidic Chronicles

Christianity venerates David not only as a historical figure but also as a prophetic one. He is considered an ancestor of Jesus Christ, fulfilling messianic prophecies. Many psalms attributed to David find their way into Christian liturgy, hymns, and theology, rendering him an enduring figure within the Christian tradition.

) David in Islamic Tradition

The Quranic portrayal of David, or Dawood as he is known in Islamic tradition, adds another layer of complexity. Though the narratives diverge in detail, the essence remains the same: David is a righteous servant of God endowed with divine wisdom and strength. He is considered one of the major Prophets in Islam, often mentioned alongside other esteemed biblical figures like Moses and Jesus.

The Quran attributes the Psalms (known as the Zabur) to David and mentions his ability to understand the speech of animals and birds, lending an almost mystical aura to his persona. His skill in metallurgy, described in the Quran, symbolizes the harmonious blending of divine gifts with human enterprise.

) The Universal Appeal of David

What makes David universally appealing is the profundity of his human experience—his struggles and triumphs, moral lapses, and redemptive arcs. His life serves as a mirror reflecting the complexities and ambiguities inherent in human existence, and perhaps it is this quality that makes his story resonate across cultural and religious boundaries.

Moreover, David's life offers a rich tapestry for exploring themes like leadership, morality, human error, repentance, and divine providence. His multifaceted character allows for diverse interpretations and lends itself to various forms of artistic and intellectual expression, from Michelangelo's sculpture to Handel's oratorio.

Contextualizing David: Israel's Historical and Theological Landscape

However, before we delve into the Davidic story, it is important to have a grasp of the larger biblical narrative in which David plays a significant role. Understanding the socio-political climate of Israel before and during David's time is crucial. This not only helps us gain a better understanding of David, but also allows us to position him within the biblical timeline.

The nation of Israel has its conceptual roots in the covenant God made with Abraham, as recorded in Genesis 12. In this covenant, God promises Abraham that he will be the father of a great nation and that his descendants will inherit the land of Canaan. This seminal event establishes the theological framework for the Israelite identity, and it becomes the foundational narrative that influences the nation's self-understanding throughout its history.

However, actualizing this divine promise was a lengthy and tumultuous 400 year process. The descendants of Abraham found themselves in Egyptian bondage, a period that profoundly shaped their collective identity and longing for a homeland. It wasn't until the leadership of Moses—a figure of monumental importance in both religious and political senses—that the Israelites were delivered from Egyptian slavery through a series of miraculous events, including the parting of the Red Sea.

Under Moses' guidance, Israel received the Law at Mount

Sinai, an event that can be seen as the constitutional moment for the emerging nation. The Law, encapsulated in the Ten Commandments and elaborated in the Pentateuch, set forth the religious and social laws, practices, and rituals that would define Israel's unique covenant relationship with God. Moses' role as a prophet and a lawgiver established him as a prototype for future leaders, guiding the ethical and spiritual dimensions of the nation.

After Moses' death, Joshua led the Israelites into the Promised Land, marking a transition from a nomadic existence to territorial settlement. Joshua's military conquests in Canaan and the distribution of the land among the twelve tribes were instrumental steps in establishing Israel as a political entity. Like Moses, Joshua acted as God's representative, leading the nation in both religious and secular matters.

The Period of the Judges: A Theocratic Society

For a period of over 500 years after the death of Moses and Joshua, the nation lived under the Torah and the priesthood in a largely successful theocracy. This period is recorded in the book of Judges and consists of 93 years of servitude and approximately 450 years of harmony. Few nations could claim such a peaceful and prosperous history. The nation was organized by tribes, with local authorities handling political matters while the Torah and the priesthood oversaw spiritual and moral affairs. Though there was a cycle of sin, servitude, supplication, and salvation (Judges 2:11-19), the nation spent more time in a peaceful and quiet society than in any other state. During this unique era, it can truly be said that God reigned over the nation.

The Demand for a Monarchy (1 Samuel 8)

Eventually, the "bottom up" political scene of the theocracy shifted. By 1 Samuel 8, the leaders asked the Prophet and Priest Samuel to appoint a king for them, stating that they wanted to be judged like all the other nations (1 Sam. 8:5). Despite Samuel's plea, warning them about the negative consequences of having a human king (1 Sam. 8:11-18), the people insisted on their request. God informed Samuel that it was not Samuel they had rejected, but God Himself, as they did not want Him to reign over them (1 Sam. 8:7).

The Anointing of Saul: A Complex Prelude to David

God permitted the people's request for a king, respecting their free will, although it was against His original design for Israel. In a divinely ironic twist, He chose Saul, a man who visually fit the cultural expectations of a king—tall and handsome (1 Sam. 9:2). Saul's reign, lasting 40 years, became a complex interplay of obedience and rebellion, serving as a cautionary tale for future monarchs and setting the stage for David.

A Promising Start

Saul's early years as king were marked by some significant successes. Saul's military successes provided a form of centralized leadership that, while effective in uniting the tribes against common enemies, marked a departure from the theocratic governance God had originally intended for Israel. Saul's willingness to heed prophetic guidance initially, particularly from Samuel, suggests a level of spiritual sensitivity that was needed for the role.

5

The Downfall: Disobedience and Pride

Despite these early successes, Saul's reign would be characterized by a series of failures—most notably, his incomplete obedience in the matter of the Amalekites (1 Sam. 15). His decision to spare King Agag and keep the best livestock was more than just a military misjudgment; it revealed a deeper flaw in his understanding of divine authority and obedience. This act resulted in God rejecting Saul as king (1 Sam. 15:23), and the anointing would soon pass to David (1 Sam. 16).

A Troubled Spirit and a Fateful Meeting

After God's spirit departed from Saul, he was plagued by a tormented mind, providing the context for his introduction to David. Saul's servants suggested finding a skillful musician to calm him. David, described as *"cunning in playing, and a mighty valiant man, and a man of war, and prudent in matters, and a comely person, and the LORD is with him"* (1 Sam. 16:18), was brought into Saul's court. This initial interaction was profoundly ironic: the one anointed to replace Saul was also the one providing him temporary relief from his divine torment.

The Unraveling of Saul and the Rise of David

The complicated relationship between Saul and David unfolded over years, characterized by Saul's increasing paranoia and David's growing popularity. It would take years after Saul's death for David to be recognized as king over all the tribes. Importantly, the period of Saul's decline served as a crucible for David, who was given a front-row seat to the perils of disobedience and the complexities of power. This learning period prepared David for the challenges he would later face, both internally and externally, during his own reign.

The Legacy of Saul: Lessons and Contrasts

Saul's life serves as a nuanced backdrop for understanding David. He embodies the pitfalls of human leadership disconnected from divine guidance, while simultaneously highlighting the complexities involved in leading a nation like Israel. His failures and successes provided David with critical life lessons, serving as both a warning and an instructional guide for the challenges that lay ahead.

God Uses A Flawed System to Accomplish His Purposes

The concept of a monarchy was not part of God's initial design for Israel, yet He permitted it, embodying a divine principle: God can bring about His purposes even through flawed systems and people. This is not unique to the time of Saul and David. For instance, consider the patriarch Jacob, who deceived his father Isaac to receive the firstborn's blessing (Genesis 27). Despite his flaws and deceitful methods, God still used Jacob, renaming him Israel and making him the father of the Twelve Tribes.

Similarly, during the period of Babylonian exile, God used King Cyrus, a pagan ruler, to facilitate the return of the Israelites to their homeland (Isaiah 45:1-4). In the New Testament, the Apostle Paul, formerly a persecutor of Christians, became one of Christianity's most effective evangelists and theologians after his conversion (Acts 9).

Returning to the monarchy, God's promise to David in 2 Samuel 7:15 stands out: *"And your house and your kingdom shall be established forever before you; your throne shall be established forever."* Though Saul's line ended, David's lineage is destined to be eternal. This underscores the idea that the Messiah, who will sit on the Davidic throne, will be a descendant of David.

Thus, the flawed system of a human monarchy, initiated by a disobedient populace and an impulsive king, becomes part of the divine mechanism for establishing an eternal throne. God's ability to work through imperfections manifests His sovereignty, attesting that even human errors and systems can be woven into His overarching, perfect plan.

What We Will Learn

In addition to learning about the events in the life of David, we will also study prophecy, poetry, and the account of one of the world's greatest individuals. This knowledge will deepen our understanding of the God who saves us, strengthen our Biblical worldview, and provide us with historical knowledge and personal insights that will guide us in making godly decisions for ourselves, our families, and our society.

Chapter 2:

DAVID'S ANCESTRY AND BETHLEHEM ORIGINS

Introduction

Having established the historical and theological backdrop that preceded David, we now turn our focus to David himself—specifically, his family lineage and early life in Bethlehem. In order to fully appreciate the monumental figure David would become, it is important to understand the modest origins from which he emerged.

Just like for Jesus, very little is known of David's early life. In fact, the first time he is introduced is when he is anointed King by Samuel, which we will look at in the next chapter.

Far from being born into privilege and power, however, David's ancestry and upbringing were humble and unassuming. Yet in the providential economy of God, these obscure origins served a divine purpose. David's background connects him to crucial biblical figures, including Ruth, Boaz, and Jesse. It also links him typologically to an even greater King who would one day be born in Bethlehem.

David's Bethlehem origins connect back to the Patriarchs through a lineage that includes some lesser known but important figures. We will trace this ancestry and its significance in understanding David's identity.

We will also consider David's upbringing as the youngest son of Jesse, a Bethlehem shepherd. In David's experiences as a humble shepherd boy, we find seeds of the leadership, trust, and insight he will later exhibit as king.

Finally, we will uncover typological connections between David and the ultimate descendant of his lineage, Jesus Christ. Their Bethlehem births bind them together in profound ways.

By stepping back to David's ancestral and early life context, we gain a foundational appreciation for the remarkable figure he would become through divine providence. His origins shaped the shepherd, poet, warrior and king he was destined to be.

David's Lineage in Ruth

The book of Ruth opens with tragedy striking Naomi's family. Due to a severe famine, Naomi, her husband Elimelech, and their two sons Mahlon and Chilion left Bethlehem for the land of Moab. There, Naomi's sons married Moabite women, Ruth and Orpah. However, in the span of ten years, Naomi's husband and both sons died, leaving her devastated and without an heir.

Upon hearing the famine had ended in Judah, Naomi decided to return home to Bethlehem. She encouraged her daughters-in-law Ruth and Orpah to stay in Moab and remarry within their own people. Orpah kissed Naomi goodbye, but Ruth clung to her mother-in-law, insisting:

> *"Intreat me not to leave thee, or to return from following after thee: for whither thou goest, I will go; and where thou lodgest, I will lodge: thy people shall be my people, and thy God my God."* (Ruth 1:16)

Ruth's steadfast commitment to accompany and care for Naomi, despite having no obligation as a widowed foreigner, showcases remarkable covenant loyalty. Her words, *"thy people shall be my people,"* speak of her conversion to Naomi's God, the God of Abraham, Isaac, and Jacob. Ruth's faithfulness to Naomi and her conversion to the Jewish faith laid the groundwork for her improbable incorporation into the messianic lineage.

Gleaning in the fields of Boaz

Once Ruth accompanied Naomi back to Bethlehem, they found themselves impoverished widows with no means of provision. Following the Torah's instructions to provide for the poor, Ruth went to glean leftover grain in the barley harvest (Leviticus 19:9-10, Deuteronomy 24:19).

In a divinely ordained happenstance, Ruth ended up gleaning in a field belonging to a man named Boaz, who was a relative of Naomi's late husband Elimelech. He noticed Ruth's diligence and loyalty to her mother-in-law and ensured she was protected and had sufficient grain. When Ruth returned and told Naomi she had met Boaz, Naomi saw it as the Lord's provision, sharing this insight:

"Blessed be he of the LORD, who hath not left off his kindness to the living and to the dead. And Naomi said unto her, The man is near of kin unto us, one of our next kinsmen." (Ruth 2:20)

Ruth's humble act of gleaning led her directly to Boaz, setting in motion the Lord's plan of redemption. Her faithfulness brought blessing as Boaz showed compassion through his position, foreshadowing his future role as kinsman-redeemer by marrying Ruth.

Boaz's kindness and protection of Ruth

When Ruth went to glean in Boaz's field, he demonstrated remarkable kindness and protection that went far beyond normal care for the poor. Seeing Ruth's character, he instructed his reapers:

> *"Let her glean even among the sheaves, and reproach her not: And let fall also some of the handfuls of purpose for her, and leave them, that she may glean them, and rebuke her not."* (Ruth 2:15-16).

Boaz showed further care by inviting Ruth to only glean in his fields, eat with his reapers, and drink the water they drew. He commanded the young men not to touch her or harm her. When Ruth asked why she found such favor in his sight, Boaz explained he knew of her love and care for Naomi after her husband's death.

At mealtime, Boaz personally handed grain to Ruth and told his reapers to intentionally leave extra handfuls for her to gather. The abundance Boaz intentionally provided her foreshadows the full redemption that will later come through their marriage.

Through a remarkable sequence of divinely guided events, the stage was set for Ruth's incorporation into the messianic family tree.

Their marriage and birth of Obed

As a close relative of Elimelech, Naomi's deceased husband, Boaz was qualified to act as a kinsman-redeemer for the family inheritance. This involved marrying Ruth to raise up a child to carry on her dead husband's name and line (Deuteronomy 25:5-10).

After Ruth lay at the feet of Boaz on the threshing floor, signaling her desire for him to redeem her, Boaz went before the city elders at the gate. When the one closer kinsman refused his right to redeem, Boaz declared:

"Ye are witnesses this day, that I have bought all that was Elimelech's...Ruth the Moabitess...have I purchased to be my wife, to raise up the name of the dead." (Ruth 4:9-10).

Boaz married Ruth, the Moabite widow, preserving Elimelech's inheritance. In God's providence, their son Obed was born to carry on the family lineage. The elders pronounced a blessing on the marriage:

"And let thy house be like the house of Pharez, whom Tamar bare unto Judah, of the seed which the LORD shall give thee of this young woman." (Ruth 4:12).

Tamar was the Canaanite daughter-in-law of Judah who disguised herself as a prostitute to bear his child, Pharez, after Judah failed to provide her a kinsman-redeemer. The allusion connects Boaz's legitimate kinsman redemption of Ruth to the unusual circumstances of Judah and Tamar that were pivotal in the messianic lineage.

Despite its unassuming beginnings, the marriage of Boaz and Ruth was integral in shaping the ancestry of the Messiah. God orchestrated Ruth's faithfulness and Boaz's redemption to continue the family line.

In the Rabbinic tradition, the wedding of Ruth and Boaz is often associated with Shavuot, which is one of the three major Jewish festivals (the other two being Passover and Sukkot). Shavuot commemorates the giving of the Torah at Mount Sinai, and it falls seven weeks after Passover, typically in late May or early June. It is traditional to read the Book of Ruth during Shavuot, both because the events in the book occur around the time of the barley harvest, which aligns with Shavuot, and because Ruth's acceptance of the Jewish faith is likened to the Israelites' acceptance of the Torah at Sinai.

In modern times, Jews celebrate Shavuot in a variety of ways. Some stay up all night studying Torah, a practice known as Tikkun Leil Shavuot. Many eat dairy foods, a tradition that may come from a verse in Song of Songs comparing the Torah to honey and milk. Synagogues often decorate with flowers and greenery, and it is traditional to read the Book of Ruth.

The Genealogy from Perez to David

Ruth 4:18-22 provides a succinct but crucial genealogy linking Perez to David:

> *"Now these are the generations of Perez: Perez begat Hezron, And Hezron begat Ram, and Ram begat Amminadab, And Amminadab begat Nahshon, and Nahshon begat Salmon, And Salmon begat Boaz, and Boaz begat Obed, And Obed begat Jesse, and Jesse begat David."* (Ruth 4:18-22)

This lineage traces back to Perez, the son of Judah and Tamar, who was one of the twelve sons of Jacob. Thus it connects to the patriarchs Abraham, Isaac and Jacob.

Other key figures are Ram, the father of Amminadab, who was the father of Nahshon, a leader of the Exodus generation. Salmon was the son of Nahshon and father of Boaz.

The span covers from Jacob who lived around 1900 BC, through the Exodus approximately 1440 BC, to the era of the Judges which preceded the kings.

The total generations from Abraham to David are fourteen. According to Matthew, it would be another 14 generations from David to Messiah. Furthermore, in Hebrew, the value of the name David, with its three letters, *dalet, vav,* and *dalet,* is 14.

David's Bethlehem Upbringing

The genealogy in Ruth 4:22 states that Obed was the father of Jesse, who was the father of David. Jessie is well documented in scripture as David's father and the grandson of Ruth and Boaz. However, David's mother is unnamed in the biblical accounts.

Although the Hebrew Bible does not explicitly name David's mother, her story is elaborated on in later Jewish texts, particularly in the Talmud and Midrash. According to these sources, Nitzevet was married to Jesse (also known as Yishai), and she was the mother of David and his brothers.

In the rabbinic account, Nitzevet is often portrayed as a righteous and strong-willed woman who endured great hardship. One well-known Midrashic story discusses how she was ostracized in her own home due to a complicated misunderstanding with her husband, Jesse. In this story, Jesse decides to separate from Nitzevet because he doubts the lineage purity of their children, suspecting they might not be of true Judahite descent. Nitzevet, aware of her righteousness and purity, finds a way to conceive David without Jesse knowing he is the father. Later, when David is anointed by Samuel, Jesse's doubts are resolved, and Nitzevet's integrity is restored in the eyes of her family.

The rabbis described Nitzevet as gentle, humble, and morally exquisite, qualities that she passed on to her youngest son. Her influence paved the way for David's faithfulness and courage.

These stories are not part of the biblical canon and should only be viewed as Jewish oral tradition. But while we cannot verify the account of Nitzavet, we certainly know that David *had* a mother! The Jewish traditional account gives us one possibility of who this mother might have been.

Family's livelihood as shepherds

The Bible portrays David's family, including his father Jesse, as shepherds from the tribe of Judah who cared for and raised sheep. They grazed their flocks near Bethlehem. Shepherding was a modest profession associated with quiet anonymity, yet it served as the unexpected background for Israel's greatest king.

As the youngest son responsible for tending his family's sheep, David had various duties, such as guiding, watering, finding pasture, keeping watch, protecting, rescuing, and counting the sheep. He mentions his experiences as a shepherd in several psalms, reflecting on the benefits of still waters and green pastures in his most famous work, Psalm 23.

This deep involvement in shepherding undoubtedly developed qualities such as courage, resourcefulness, comfort with solitude, proficiency with the slingshot and rod, and above all, trust in God's providence. These attributes prepared him for his future role as king. The humble obedience of the shepherd boy in small matters foreshadowed the confident leadership he would demonstrate on a national level.

David's Brothers

The Bible mentions several older brothers of David who were passed over when the next king was to be chosen. Jesse brought his first seven sons before the prophet (1 Samuel 16:10).

The eldest three named brothers were Eliab, Abinadab, and Shammah. David was the youngest, left in the fields tending sheep. His three oldest brothers are described as impressive in appearance and stature, especially Eliab, but God looked deeper than outward appearance (1 Samuel 16:7).

David's brothers clearly did not exhibit the same heart after God that distinguished David as a youth. Several of them later showed scorn and jealousy when David was brought into King Saul's court and experienced military success, accusing him of pride and evil motives (1 Samuel 17:28).

David's heart and character as a youth

From a young age, David exhibited traits that foreshadowed his future reign and aligned with God's standards for leadership. He had a deep love for God that showed in his prayer, praise, and trust. His courage in protecting the flock displayed nascent leadership. Psalms reflect his poetic gifts developed during long nights under the stars.

Though David faced lions, bears, giants, and enemies as a youth, God prepared and protected him. The foundations of courage, wisdom, skill, and faith established in obscurity empowered David for national influence. His patient refinement as a shepherd boy cultivated Israel's exemplary king.

Typology and Foreshadowing

There are several elements in David's early life and upbringing that foreshadow the life of Jesus, establishing a typological connection:

Bethlehem as birthplace of David and later Jesus

Bethlehem was the hometown of David's family and his birthplace, as affirmed in 1 Samuel 16. Centuries later, Jesus was born in Bethlehem as well, linking him to the prophesied messianic lineage of David (Micah 5:2). The shared birthplace connects the two definitive leaders of Israel.

Shepherd imagery connecting David and Jesus

David's experiences as a humble shepherd caring for his flock are echoed in Jesus' declaration, *"I am the good shepherd"* who lovingly leads, protects, and lays down his life for the sheep (John 10:11). This imagery ties the ultimate shepherd Jesus to Israel's prototypical shepherd king.

Rejection of older brothers, choosing of the unexpected

When God selected Israel's king, David's older brothers were passed over in favor of the overlooked youngest, foreshadowing Jesus as an unexpected messianic king descending from a humble background. In fact, one tradition with some merit even though seldom taught or adopted, considers Jesus to be the *youngest* brother, with Joseph having older sons from a previous wife who had deceased.

Link to David's future kingship and Jesus as Messiah

God's choice of David as the ideal leader prepared the way for the fulfillment found in Jesus, the perfect embodiment of kingship whose reign is eternal. The trajectory from shepherd to king in David's early life foreshadows Jesus' identity as the greatest Shepherd and King.

Conclusion

David's ancestry and upbringing in Bethlehem serve as foundational elements that shaped his trajectory towards becoming Israel's renowned king. Despite his humble beginnings as the overlooked youngest son of a shepherd, David's life was marked by God's favor and anointing from an early age. His experiences as a shepherd cultivated essential qualities of courage, leadership, and devotion that would be instrumental in his future reign.

However, the significance of David's early years extends beyond his personal development. His Bethlehem origins are intricately woven into God's redemptive plan across generations. The marriage between Boaz and Ruth, a faithful Moabite woman, played a vital role in incorporating her into the messianic lineage. The shared birthplace of David and Jesus further deepens the connection between these definitive leaders of Israel.

Moreover, David's early life foreshadows the coming of Jesus, the ultimate Messiah. The parallels between their experiences are striking. Bethlehem, the birthplace of David, also became the birthplace of Jesus, establishing a typological link between the shepherd king and the Good Shepherd who lays down His life for the sheep. David's selection as king, despite being the least likely choice among his brothers, anticipates Jesus as the unexpected and chosen Messiah, descending from humble origins.

Ultimately, David's journey from shepherd to king foreshadows the reign of Jesus as the perfect embodiment of kingship. Through David's obedient and faithful character, God prepared the way for the fulfillment found in Jesus, the ultimate Shepherd and King whose reign is eternal.

By exploring David's ancestry, upbringing, and the typological connections to Jesus, we gain profound insights into God's unfolding kingdom purposes throughout history. David's humble origins and his emergence as a shepherd, poet, warrior, and king were all part of God's providential plan.

As we reflect on David's remarkable life, may we be reminded of God's ability to use the unexpected, the humble, and the faithful to accomplish His purposes. Just as David's origins shaped him into the renowned king of Israel, may we find encouragement in knowing that God can use our own humble beginnings to bring about His divine plans.

In understanding David's ancestry and Bethlehem origins, we glimpse the intricate tapestry of God's redemptive work and gain a deeper appreciation for the remarkable figure David would become.

THE DAVIDIC CHRONICLES

22

Chapter 3:

DAVID'S ANOINTING BY SAMUEL

1 Samuel 16:1-13

Having explored David's crucial ancestral lineage and humble upbringing in Bethlehem, we now turn to the definitive moment that launched him onto the public stage - his anointing by the prophet Samuel as the next king of Israel.

While David's background and experiences as a shepherd boy shaped his character and prepared him for leadership, it was the divine appointment and empowerment he received through Samuel's anointing that marked the beginning of David's meteoric rise from obscurity to the throne.

The transfer of kingship from Saul to David did not happen all at once. Rather, it was a gradual process filled with uncertainty and danger. Samuel's clandestine anointing in Bethlehem initiated the long journey that would ultimately culminate in David becoming king over all Israel.

This pivotal moment is shrouded in secrecy, foreshadowing the years of hiding, rivalry, and conflict that would ensue between the two anointed kings - Saul and David. Through it all, however, God's choice of His next ruler became clear.

Samuel Sent to Bethlehem (1 Samuel 16:1-3)

Samuel's anointing journey began with a difficult assignment from God - travel to Bethlehem and secretly anoint one of Jesse's sons to be the next king over Israel.

This directly contradicted the current king, Saul, who

had been anointed by Samuel himself years prior. But Saul's utter disobedience in sparing the Amalekite king and livestock resulted in his rejection by God (1 Samuel 15).

Although the nation had rejected God's plan for governance, it was still under God's control. Despite Saul, the Benjamite, being chosen as King, the prophetic word had already stated that the Messiah would come from Judah (see Gen. 49:8-10). Therefore, God sends Samuel with anointing oil to Jesse, guiding the nation back towards its Messianic promise.

Understandably, Samuel felt apprehensive about this covert mission, fearing Saul may kill him if he discovered Samuel had anointed a replacement king.

But God reassured Samuel and gave him instructions to bring a heifer as a sacrifice, using worship as a public pretext for his travel to Bethlehem. This would disguise his true purpose - the solemn yet confidential task of selecting Israel's next monarch from among Jesse's sons.

The stage was now set for this clandestine meeting that would change the course of Israel's history.

Selecting the New King (1 Samuel 16:4-13)

Samuel's clandestine mission was to anoint one of Jesse's sons, but he did not yet know which one. Upon arriving in Bethlehem, he had Jesse present his sons before him one by one.

As Jesse's firstborn, Eliab, stood impressively tall and handsome before him, Samuel instinctively thought, *"Surely this is the Lord's anointed."*

But God immediately cautioned Samuel not to be swayed by mere outward appearance. For while man looks at the outer being, God looks upon the heart and motives that others cannot see.

This interaction established a key qualification - David's inward character would matter far more to God than any external traits. The search for Israel's next king would require discernment that reached deeper than surface perceptions. God had appointed a ruler based on faithfulness, not stature.

Samuel's discernment process took an unexpected turn. After reviewing seven of Jesse's sons, none were found to be the chosen one of God. Puzzled, Samuel asked Jesse, *"Are here all thy children?"* Jesse's response revealed the existence of an eighth son, the youngest, who was away tending the sheep.

This son, David, was not even considered significant enough by his own family to be presented before Samuel. Yet, he was the one chosen by God. While some may dismiss the oversight of David as merely cultural, it is peculiar that Jesse would fail to invite his youngest son to worship and sacrifice performed by Samuel, the High Priest of Israel and a prophet. It is worth delving deeper into this omission.

To gain a deeper understanding of the complexities surrounding David's background, rabbinic literature provides an intriguing perspective. In the Talmud, there is a discussion about Jesse's lineage. The narrative suggests that Jesse started to worry that he might not be considered a legitimate Jew because the marriage of Ruth to Boaz was forbidden by the Torah. Jesse became so convinced that he was outside the community of Israel that he decided to separate from his Jewish wife, Nitzevet.

25

According to Deuteronomy 23:3, she would have been prohibited from marrying him as he was a descendant of Moab. However, later on, Jesse wanted more children and decided to have children with his Canaanite concubine, since a Canaanite wouldn't be prohibited from marrying a Moabite. This concubine had a close relationship with Nitzevet, and together they devised a plan for Nitzevet to bear more children by disguising herself as the concubine. This resulted in the birth of David.

However, the older brothers, along with the community, believed that Nitzevet had an affair and gave birth to an illegitimate child. According to rabbinical teaching, David was ostracized throughout his childhood. It is only when Samuel calls for another person that David is brought forth. It is at this point that Jesse admits (according to the Talmud) that David is his own son.

It is important to note that this narrative from the Talmud is a rabbinical interpretation and not a part of the canonical biblical text. It aims to explain certain verses and provide a backstory to some of the more cryptic aspects of David's life and lineage. Whether one accepts this interpretation or not depends largely on one's theological perspective and how one views rabbinical literature in relation to the Hebrew Bible.

This Talmudic account can be used to shed light on the complexities surrounding David's early life and the potential reasons he might have been initially overlooked during Samuel's visit.

The potential ostracization David faced might find echoes in his own writings. First, Psalm 51:5 has an interesting phrase written by David who claims that, *"in sin did my mother conceive me."* The verse has become a Calvinist staple prooftext of their doctrine of total depravity, I have always suspected that there was something far more specific and physical to the testimony. Could David be giving testimony to the deceptive nature of his own birth?

Another biblical text that may shed light on the emotional turmoil and challenges David faced due to his perceived illegitimacy is Psalm 69. The Psalm, while prophetic of the Messiah, also encapsulates David's personal experiences, mirroring them onto the Savior's life. Thus, it holds truths about both David and the Savior.

In verse 4, David laments, *"They that hate me without a cause are more than the hairs of mine head."* This might echo the unjust treatment he received from those who wrongfully considered him an enemy. Verse 8 is particularly poignant: *"I am become a stranger unto my brethren, and an alien unto my mother's children."* This could very well reflect David's sense of estrangement from his own family, further compounded by the community's gossip and ridicule as suggested in verse 12: *"They that sit in the gate speak against me; and I was the song of the drunkards."*

David's emotional anguish is palpable in verse 20, where he expresses a broken heart and a desperate search for comfort and understanding, which he finds lacking. These sentiments, when juxtaposed with the Talmudic narrative, provide a profound understanding of the depth of David's early struggles, painting a picture of a young man grappling with identity, acceptance, and divine destiny amidst societal scorn.

The Davidic Chronicles

David Anointed as Future King (1 Samuel 16:12-13)

As the youngest son, David, was brought before Samuel, there was a palpable shift in the atmosphere. The shepherd boy, seemingly insignificant in the grand scheme of Bethlehem's societal structures, stood in sharp contrast to his elder brothers. Yet, in this young man, God saw the heart of Israel's future king.

Upon seeing David, the Lord's voice resonated within Samuel, declaring, *"Arise, anoint him: for this* is he." (1 Samuel 16:12). These words not only affirmed David's future role but also underscored the divine nature of kingship in Israel. It was not to be determined by human standards or prejudices, but by God's sovereign choice.

Following the divine directive, Samuel took the horn filled with consecrated oil, and with deliberate action and in the presence of David's brothers, Samuel anointed David. This act was transformative, not just symbolically, but spiritually. The text tells us that *"the Spirit of the LORD came upon David from that day forward"* (1 Samuel 16:13). This divine empowerment was a precursor to the challenges and triumphs David would face in the years to come, from confronting Goliath to leading Israel as its king. The anointing served not only as a seal of God's favor upon David but also as a source of strength and guidance in the trials and tribulations he would encounter.

With the anointing complete, and the future trajectory of Israel irrevocably altered, Samuel returned to Ramah. His mission was accomplished, but the narrative of David, the ostracized shepherd boy turned king, was just beginning. It's a narrative that reminds us of God's ability to see beyond societal expectations and human shortcomings, choosing and raising up individuals for His purposes based on the integrity of their hearts and their willingness to serve Him faithfully.

Conclusion

The anointing of David by Samuel in Bethlehem is not merely an isolated event in Israel's history but a pivotal moment that set in motion a series of divinely orchestrated events, leading to the establishment of a dynasty that would have lasting implications for Israel and the world. David, though initially an overlooked shepherd, was chosen by God, not by the standards of man, but by God's approval of what was in his heart.

David went back to the hills of Bethlehem, tending sheep. But his life—and the life of the nation—would never be the same.

THE DAVIDIC CHRONICLES

Chapter 4:

DAVID THE HARPIST

1 Samuel 16:14-23

Saul's Troubled Spirit (1 Samuel 16:14-16)

The Departure

The Biblical account immediately shifts from David's anointing to a pivotal moment in the life of King Saul, one that carries profound implications. In 1 Samuel 16:14, we are confronted with the stark proclamation, *"the Spirit of the LORD departed from Saul"* (v. 14). This event signifies a

31

significant turning point in Saul's reign, as the divine favor and guidance of God were withdrawn.

To grasp the gravity of this departure, we must first journey back to Saul's anointing as king in 1 Samuel 10:6-7. Here, we find a young Saul, upon whom the Spirit of the LORD came mightily. In this moment, he prophesied, and the people marveled. It was a divine confirmation of his anointed status as the king of Israel. The presence of God's Spirit was a symbol of God's favor and guidance.

David would later provide us with further insight into the importance of God's Spirit. In Psalm 51:11, he fervently prays, *"Do not cast me from your presence or take your Holy Spirit from me."* David's plea underscores the significance of the Spirit of God in the life of a leader. His prayer reflects a deep understanding of the consequences of losing the Spirit's presence.

It is essential to note that in the context of Saul's time, the Spirit of God was not understood to be the third person of the Trinity, as is often conceived in Christian theology. Rather, it was seen as the hand and presence of God Himself. The Spirit's presence signified divine favor, guidance, and empowerment. Therefore, its departure from Saul had profound implications for his leadership and relationship with God.

The Evil Spirit

Not only did the Spirit depart from Saul, but in its stead, *"an evil spirit from the LORD troubled him"* (v. 14). It's crucial to understand the word *"evil"* in the 17th-century context and the underlying Hebrew word to grasp the gravity of this situation and what it likely meant for Saul.

In the 17th-century English language, the term *"evil"* did not exclusively denote moral wickedness, as it does in modern usage. Instead, it often referred to something distressing, harmful, or calamitous. In this context, *"an evil spirit"* indicates a distressing or tormenting spirit rather than a morally malevolent one.

The Hebrew word used here for *"evil"* is *"ra'ah."* While it can refer to moral evil, it also carries the connotation of adversity, calamity, or distress. This is the situation we observe in the case of Saul.

What this likely meant for Saul was a profound inner turmoil, anxiety, and emotional suffering. It was a spiritual affliction that deeply troubled him and contributed to his mental and emotional instability. This distressing spirit would have had a debilitating effect on Saul's ability to rule effectively, further highlighting the consequences of his disobedience and God's withdrawal of divine favor.

It is interesting to note that Saul's servants recognized that the troubling spirit was from God. Their recognition suggests that they were aware of what Samuel had previously told Saul regarding his disobedience with Agag. This acknowledgment by Saul's servants further emphasizes the divine nature of the situation and the consequences of Saul's actions and how clearly those around him could see this.

Saul's servants recognized the power of music to calm the troubled mind of their king. In 1 Samuel 16:16, they suggest finding *"a man who is a cunning player on a harp"* to play soothing music for Saul when the distressing spirit troubled him.

A *"cunning"* player, as translated in the King James Version, referred to a skillful or proficient musician. In the 17th-century usage of the term the word did not have negative connotations as it may today. The Hebrew word behind this term is *"yada"* (עָדַי), which conveys the idea of knowing or being skilled at something. In this context, it implies a harpist who was highly skilled and experienced in playing the harp with expertise.

The recognition of music's soothing power was rooted in the conviction that music had the ability to influence emotions and bring comfort to a troubled mind. Saul's servants sought a skillful harpist who could use music as a therapeutic tool to alleviate Saul's distress, highlighting the significance of music in ancient times as a means of calming troubled souls.

In fact, scientists have a field of study concerning the physiological influence of music. In such study, they have proven that certain beats and rhythms in music can impact human physiology through a phenomenon known as *"rhythmic entrainment."* This means that our heart rate, breathing, and brainwave patterns can synchronize with the rhythms in music. For example, slow, steady rhythms in music tend to promote relaxation and slow breathing, while faster rhythms can increase excitement. Additionally, music can influence physical movement, making it easier to coordinate activities or maintain a steady pace during exercise. The *"music therapy"* recommended to Saul is very much in use today.

Saul Meets David (1 Samuel 16:17-18)

As Saul grappled with the tormenting presence of the distressing spirit, he sought a remedy, as suggested by his servants. In verse 17 of 1 Samuel 16, we witness Saul's agreement with their counsel. Recognizing the potential healing power of music, Saul expressed his consent to the idea, paving the way for a significant encounter that would change the course of his reign.

Verse 18 unveils the introduction of the young musician who would play a pivotal role in Saul's life and in biblical history. This verse provides a concise yet rich description of six noteworthy characteristics of the chosen musician, who would later be revealed as David, the future King of Israel:

1. **Skillful Playing:** David was described as one that is *"cunning in playing."* This phrase emphasizes his prowess as a skilled musician, proficient in playing the harp. His musical talents were a key aspect of his identity.

2. **Mighty and Valiant:** The mention of David as *"a mighty valiant man"* hints at unknown exploits to us, the reader, but that must have been known at least to the servant of Saul. This aspect of his character would become even more prominent in the years to come.

3. **Man of War:** While he was a musician at this point, he must have also been skilled in warfare, whether he had been in war or not. David's future as a warrior and leader is foreshadowed here. His courage and martial abilities would play a crucial role in his ascent to kingship.

4. **Prudent in Speech:** David's wisdom and prudence in speech were evident even in his youth. This characteristic would serve him well as he navigated

the complexities of the royal court and faced numerous challenges.

5. **Goodly Person:** David's physical appearance and demeanor were noteworthy. He possessed qualities that attracted attention and favor, which would become evident in various situations throughout his life.

6. **And the LORD is With Him:** Perhaps the most significant characteristic of all, the presence of the Lord with David. This divine favor and guidance would set David apart and ultimately lead him to fulfill his destiny as the renowned King of Israel.

In these few verses, we catch a glimpse of David's multi-faceted character, foreshadowing his extraordinary journey from a humble shepherd and musician to the iconic King of Israel, guided and anointed by the Lord Himself.

Incidentally, for those who are raising sons, this is a great list of things to instill in them, making them the *"renaissance men"* of the future. Each one of these six attributes can be *taught* and *caught* by guiding our sons from early days.

While our presentation of verse 18 has been wholly positive, there is a rabbinical tradition that is more negative. In this tradition, the servant who introduces David is Doeg the Edomite, who is not introduced into the Biblical text until 1 Samuel 21, but who plays an adversarial role with David. Some rabbinical scholars hold to a tradition that says that this servant wanted to inflict David with the same evil spirit. It is entirely speculation, but does give us a glimpse of how scripture passages can be understood in an entirely different light than we may first adopt.

David's Arrival In Saul's Court: (1 Samuel 16:19-20)

In 1 Samuel 16:19-20, we find an intriguing narrative that sheds light on the dynamics at play within Jesse's household. Jesse, the father of David, takes a prominent role in the unfolding events, being mentioned in both verse 18 and 19. This prominence raises questions about the reasons behind his involvement. Is it because David is young and not yet recognized, or does it indicate that Jesse himself is a well-known figure in the community?

This narrative also piques interest in light of rabbinical traditions that suggest David's mother may have been Nitzevet. As you remember from chapter 3, the tradition says that Nitzavet was long accused of giving birth to David through an affair with a man other than Jesse. Both the tradition and the Bible make it clear that Jesse is indeed the father.

It should be remembered that David had already been anointed as the future king by the prophet Samuel prior to these events. Yet, despite this divine anointing, he appears to have returned to his duties as a shepherd, as indicated in verse 19.

In verse 20, Jesse is mentioned for the third time, as he sends David to Saul with bread, wine, and a kid. The verse does not specify if this act was customary or held any special significance for the occasion. However, in 1 Samuel 10:27, there is a notation that a party failed to bring Saul a gift because they despised him. This suggests that bringing a gift to the king was likely a customary practice, and failure to do so might invoke the wrath of the king.

In essence, these verses provide a glimpse into the intricate tapestry of David's early life and the role of his family in the unfolding drama of Israel's history. It underscores the divine plan and guidance that would lead David from the obscurity of a shepherd's life to the throne of Israel.

David's Amazing Ministry To Saul (1 Samuel 16:21-23)

Bringing his gifts, David *"came to Saul, and stood before him."* This statement encompasses both the immediate action and the subsequent events that unfolded in the following days, weeks, months, and possibly even years. The Hebrew root for *"stood"* (סוֹקָּיַו [*wayyaqom*]) is also seen in the call of Samuel (1 Sam. 3:8), where the young prophet is instructed to respond with, *"Speak, Lord, for your servant hears."* The Hebrew word for *"hears"* is *"wayyaqom,"* indicating that Samuel was to be attentive and ready to listen to the Lord's message. In a similar manner, David now stood attentively as a servant of King Saul.

In verse 21, it is mentioned that David gained a position of significant trust. Saul loved him so much that David became Saul's armor bearer. The term *"armourbearer"* in the KJV refers to a specific role in ancient military contexts. An armourbearer was a trusted assistant or servant who had the responsibility of carrying and maintaining a warrior's weapons and armor. This role was crucial as the armourbearer ensured that the warrior was well-prepared for battle. Moreover, the armourbearer often stood by the warrior's side in combat, ready to offer support and assistance. The relationship between a warrior and their armourbearer was typically characterized by trust and loyalty, given that the armourbearer's role required a deep commitment to the safety and success of the warrior.

38

It is important to note that we do not have complete information regarding the frequency of David's service to the King in either his musical or armorbearer role. In the next chapter, despite being in the midst of war, David is not serving in a *"full-time"* capacity. Instead, he returns from the shepherd's fields. Our understanding of the full chronology of David's life during this early period is incomplete. However, what we know with certainty is that David's early introduction to Saul was very positive. It gave David full access to the King's life, and he even became a trusted confidant and bodyguard.Saul sent word to Jesse seeking permission to enlist David into service, stating, *"he hath found favour in my sight"* (v. 22).

The ministry of David, particularly in music, became essential to Saul and his kingdom. It is fascinating that when God sent the *"evil spirit,"* David was able to calm it by playing his harp. During this time, David may have been playing and possibly even singing some of the Psalms. These Psalms have brought comfort to countless people throughout history and continue to do so today. It is remarkable that David was given the opportunity to *"undo"* the work of God, thereby becoming an indispensable part of any ongoing success in Saul's kingdom as a shepherd musician.

Conclusion

In this chapter, we have delved into the transformative events that followed David's anointing as the future king of Israel. The departure of the Spirit of the LORD from Saul marked a profound turning point in his reign, symbolizing the withdrawal of divine favor and guidance. We've explored the significance of the Spirit of God in the context of Saul's time, understanding it as the hand and presence of God Himself, signifying divine favor and empowerment.

The arrival of an *"evil spirit"* troubled Saul, leading us to examine the 17th-century understanding of the term *"evil"* and its Hebrew counterpart *"ra'ah,"* which conveys distress and adversity rather than moral wickedness. This distressing spirit likely caused Saul frightening inner turmoil and emotional suffering, severely affecting his ability to rule effectively.

We also uncovered the recognition of music's soothing power in calming Saul's troubled spirit. Saul's servants sought a skillful harpist, described as a *"cunning player,"* highlighting the significance of music in ancient times as a means of alleviating distress.

In verse 18, we unveiled six remarkable characteristics of the young musician David, setting the stage for his extraordinary journey from a shepherd and musician to the iconic King of Israel, guided by the Lord's favor and presence.

Additionally, we explored the prominence of Jesse, David's father, in the narrative, raising questions about his involvement and potential connections to rabbinical traditions regarding David's mother, Nitzevet. We noted that despite his anointing as king, David returned to his duties as a shepherd, highlighting the divine plan at work.

Finally, we observed David's entry into Saul's court, where he became Saul's armor bearer and ministered to him through his musical talents. The significance of David's role in soothing Saul's troubled spirit and his potential singing of Psalms resonates with the comforting power of music that continues to impact people's lives today.

This chapter offers profound insights into the interplay of divine providence, human character, and the power of music in shaping the course of history, foreshadowing David's rise from obscurity to become the renowned King of Israel.

The Davidic Chronicles

Chapter 5

DAVID AND GOLIATH: A TALE OF FAITH *Part 1*
1 Samuel 17:1-24

The Challenge of the Philistine Champion (1 Samuel 17:1-11)

In 1 Samuel 17:1, we are introduced to a significant event in Israel's history as the Philistines gather their armies for battle. The mention of the Philistines is not unfamiliar, as they were a formidable adversary that had plagued the Israelites for a considerable time. The Philistines were a seafaring people, believed to have originated from the Aegean region. They settled along the coastal areas of ancient Canaan, particularly in the territories that are now part of modern-day Israel and the Gaza Strip. Their presence was a constant thorn in the side of the Israelites, often resulting in conflicts and clashes.

The location where the Philistines assembled for battle, known as Shochoh, holds significance in this narrative. Shochoh belonged to the tribe of Judah, marking it as part of Israelite territory. This gathering place was strategically positioned between two notable towns: Shochoh and Azekah. Both of these towns were located in the fertile Shephelah region, an area characterized by rolling hills and valleys. Ephesdammim, mentioned in the verse, is believed to be an additional name for this region. The Shephelah was a crucial battleground, and the positioning of the Philistine army between Shochoh and Azekah underscored their intent to challenge and possibly invade Israelite territory.

The mention of these geographical details not only sets the stage for the upcoming confrontation between David and Goliath but also emphasizes the ongoing conflict between the Israelites and the Philistines. This conflict had deep historical roots and would have been a matter of great concern for the Israelites, given the proximity of the Philistine forces to their homeland.

In 1 Samuel 17:2, the narrative shifts to the Israelite side of the conflict, where we find Saul and the men of Israel gathered in preparation for battle. Their chosen location for this critical confrontation is the valley of Elah.

The valley of Elah is a well-known geographical location in ancient Israel, situated in the region of Judah, not far from the Philistine territory. The name *"Elah"* itself is of Hebrew origin which means *"terebinth tree"* or *"oak tree."* These types of trees were common in the region and often used as landmarks.

The phrase *"set the battle in array"* in this verse conveys the idea of organizing the military forces for battle. In both Hebrew and English, it implies a deliberate arrangement and positioning of troops, weapons, and equipment in preparation for combat. The Israelites were making strategic preparations and aligning themselves to face the Philistine army in a formal and organized manner. This phrase underscores the seriousness and significance of the impending battle and the careful planning that went into it.

The valley of Elah's choice as the battleground and the meticulous organization of the Israelite forces highlight the gravity of the situation and the determination of Saul and his men to confront the Philistine threat. This location would soon witness a legendary encounter between a young shepherd named David and the imposing Philistine champion Goliath, a pivotal moment in the biblical narrative.

Verses 4-7 of 1 Samuel 17 provide a detailed description of the Philistine champion, Goliath of Gath, emphasizing the formidable nature of this giant warrior and his imposing equipment.

Goliath's physical stature is emphasized, with his height measured at *"six cubits and a span,"* at least nine feet in modern terms, and perhaps more than 11 feet tall. This colossal size sets him apart as a truly imposing figure on the battlefield.

His armor is described in meticulous detail. He wears a brass helmet on his head, which would provide protection for his skull and face, a crucial component of ancient battle attire. Goliath is clad in a *"coat of mail,"* indicating a suit of armor made of metal rings or scales. What makes this armor particularly remarkable is its weight, which is recorded at *"five thousand shekels of brass,"* equivalent to around 125 pounds. This weight underscores the sheer strength and power of Goliath, who can bear such a heavy load with ease.

Goliath's legs are also protected by brass greaves, which were shin guards made of metal. These would have shielded his lower legs from attacks during combat. Additionally, he carries a *"target of brass between his shoulders,"* likely a protective piece of armor covering his back.

The offensive weapon Goliath wields is a colossal spear. The staff of this spear is likened to a *"weaver's beam,"* a term used to convey its substantial size. The spearhead alone weighs an astounding *"six hundred shekels of iron,"* approximately 15 pounds. This spearhead would have been a deadly weapon, capable of causing significant damage in battle.

The attention to detail in describing his equipment serves to accentuate the challenge that the Israelites face as they prepare to confront this fearsome Philistine champion in the valley of Elah. Goliath's imposing stature and powerful weaponry create a sense of foreboding and heighten the drama of the impending battle.

In 1 Samuel 17:8, Goliath, the champion of the Philistines, addresses the Israelite army with a taunting question: *"Am not I a Philistine, and ye servants to Saul?"* This statement serves to emphasize the vast contrast between the two sides in the impending battle.

Goliath's words are meant to belittle the Israelites and their king, Saul. He essentially mocks them by pointing out that he, a single Philistine warrior, represents the entire Philistine nation, while the Israelite soldiers are merely servants of King Saul. This taunt aims to demoralize the Israelite troops and undermine their confidence.

From Goliath's perspective, he sees himself as the ultimate representative of the Philistine military might, standing alone against the entire Israelite army. This bold assertion not only underscores his immense physical stature but also the Philistines' confidence in his abilities. Goliath's challenge is a declaration of his superiority and a call for single combat, a common practice in ancient warfare. His goal is to avoid a full-scale battle and to settle the conflict through the outcome of this champion versus champion duel.

Goliath's statement is laden with arrogance and contempt, portraying the Israelites as weak and subservient to Saul, while positioning himself as the formidable defender of Philistine honor. This challenge

46

sets the stage for the dramatic confrontation that will follow, as a young David steps forward to accept Goliath's challenge on behalf of Israel, setting the scene for one of the most iconic battles in biblical history.

1 Samuel 17:9 states, *"If he be able to fight with me, and to kill me, then will we be your servants: but if I prevail against him, and kill him, then shall ye be our servants, and serve us."* In this verse, Goliath extends his challenge further, outlining the terms of the proposed duel between himself, representing the Philistines, and an Israelite champion.

Goliath's terms were as follows:

1. If the chosen Israelite champion is able to defeat Goliath in combat and kill him, then the Philistines will become servants to the Israelites.

2. Conversely, if Goliath prevails and kills the Israelite champion, then the Israelites will become servants to the Philistines.

This type of challenge, often referred to as a *"champion warfare"* or *"single combat,"* was not uncommon in ancient warfare. It was a way to avoid large-scale battles and the associated loss of life. Instead, two champions would represent their respective sides, and the outcome of their individual combat would determine the victor of the entire conflict.

The idea that the losers would become the servants was a common stipulation in such challenges. The idea was that the defeated side would submit to the victorious side and serve them as a form of subjugation or tribute.

While there are historical instances of champion warfare in various cultures, the biblical account of David and

The Davidic Chronicles

Goliath remains one of the most famous examples. In this specific case, Goliath's challenge was not only about personal combat but also about the honor and reputation of the entire Philistine army. It was a high-stakes confrontation with significant implications.

1 Samuel 17:10 presents Goliath's bold declaration to the Israelite army: *"I defy the armies of Israel this day; give me a man, that we may fight together."* In this verse, Goliath uses strong and provocative language to challenge and taunt the Israelites.

The key phrase here is *"I defy."* In this context, *"defy"* means to openly and contemptuously challenge or confront someone or something. Goliath is essentially expressing his contempt for the entire Israelite army. He is saying that he has no fear of them, and he sees them as weak and unworthy opponents. By challenging them to send out a champion to face him in single combat, he is not only questioning their bravery but also their entire military might.

Goliath's declaration is intended to demoralize and intimidate the Israelite soldiers. He is attempting to provoke fear and doubt among them by presenting himself as an invincible giant and by suggesting that none of them are courageous enough to face him in battle.

This kind of verbal taunting and psychological warfare was not uncommon in ancient warfare. Warriors often engaged in trash-talking and boasts to unsettle their opponents and gain a psychological advantage before a battle.

In the case of Goliath, his challenge sets the stage for the central conflict of the story: the unlikely hero, David, stepping forward to face this giant in the name of the God of Israel. Goliath's defiant words serve to highlight the extraordinary courage and faith that David demonstrates in the face of seemingly insurmountable odds.

1 Samuel 17:11 further emphasizes the impact of Goliath's challenge on the Israelite army. The verse states, *"When Saul and all Israel heard those words of the Philistine, they were dismayed, and greatly afraid."*

This verse paints a grim picture of the Israelite camp's reaction to Goliath's taunts. The words *"dismayed"* and *"greatly afraid"* indicate that the Israelite soldiers were not only fearful but also demoralized and shaken by Goliath's challenge. His imposing stature, combined with his audacious words, had struck fear into the hearts of the entire army, including King Saul himself.

Saul, as the leader of the Israelite forces, should have been the one to step forward and face Goliath, but he too was overcome by fear. This verse underscores the desperate and discouraging situation that the Israelites found themselves in. They were faced with a seemingly invincible foe, and their own leader was paralyzed by fear.

The stage is now set for the introduction of David, the young shepherd boy who will rise to the occasion and take on the giant Goliath. This pivotal moment in the narrative highlights the stark contrast between the faith and courage of David and the fear and doubt that had gripped the Israelite army.

In the verses that follow, we will witness the unfolding of the remarkable David and Goliath story, where faith, courage, and trust in God will triumph over seemingly insurmountable odds.

David's Arrival and Concern for the Battle (1 Samuel 17:12-24)

David Introduced To The Story (vv. 12-15)

Verse 12 delves into David's family background, shedding light on the setting in which the young shepherd grew up. Let's dissect this verse to gain a deeper understanding:

In this context, *"Ephrathite"* designates someone hailing from the region of Ephrathah, closely associated with Bethlehem. It's important to recognize that Ephrath and Bethlehem are often used interchangeably in biblical texts. Bethlehem was situated within the territory of Ephrathah. Consequently, David is identified as originating from Bethlehemjudah (Bethlehem in the land of Judah) and being an Ephrathite due to his birthplace and upbringing.

Jesse, introduced as David's father, holds significant prominence in David's early life. His name resounds throughout the biblical narrative.

This text notes that Jesse was a man that *"went among men* for *an old man in the days of Saul."* The phrase signifies that he commanded respect as an elderly or esteemed individual during King Saul's reign. It suggests that he was likely recognized and held in high regard by the inhabitants of Bethlehem and the neighboring areas. This particular detail paints a portrait of Jesse as an elder figure, a characteristic that will prove significant as the narrative unfolds.

In essence, verse 12 furnishes vital background information about David's familial heritage, his father Jesse, and the heritage in which David was nurtured.

Verse 13 introduces us to Jesse's three oldest sons who

50

joined Saul's army to participate in the impending battle against the Philistines. This decision by Jesse to send his sons to the frontlines reflects the gravity of the situation and the sense of duty that compelled many Israelite families to send their sons to the military. The names of Jesse's three sons who went to battle are Eliab, the firstborn, followed by Abinadab, and then Shammah.

Verse 14 further emphasizes David's role and highlights the sequence of events. David, as the youngest son, is not mentioned among those who followed Saul into the army. Instead, he is portrayed as distinct from his older brothers, who are actively engaged in the military campaign.

Verse 15 now elaborates on David's actions. It states that David went and returned from Saul to feed his father's sheep at Bethlehem. This verse clarifies that David had indeed been serving Saul in some capacity (see 1 Sam. 16) but has now temporarily left his role to attend to his family's sheep in Bethlehem.

The chronological sequence indicates that David's return to shepherding occurs after his older brothers have already joined Saul in the battle.

David's Arrival (vv. 16-19)

Verse 16 provides us with important context regarding David's new arrangement and the duration of the impending conflict with the Philistines:

The number four holds significance in biblical numerology. It is often associated with creation, completeness, and the earth. In the case of 40, it can be seen as an intensified or multiplied representation of these themes, signifying a more profound and transformative process. The 40 days of waiting and preparation in this narrative set the stage for the extraordinary events that will follow, culminating in David's confrontation with Goliath and the fulfillment of God's purpose.

In biblical numerology, the number 40 often represents a period of testing, trial, or preparation. It appears frequently in the Bible, signifying a time of transition, purification, or divine intervention. For example:

1. **The Flood:** It rained for 40 days and 40 nights during the Great Flood, cleansing the earth and bringing about a new beginning (Genesis 7:12, 7:17).

2. **Moses' Leadership:** Moses spent 40 days on Mount Sinai receiving the Ten Commandments, a period of divine revelation and preparation (Exodus 24:18, 34:28).

3. **Israel's Wanderings:** The Israelites wandered in the wilderness for 40 years as a form of discipline and preparation before entering the Promised Land (Numbers 14:33-34).

4. **Elijah's Journey:** Elijah journeyed for 40 days and 40 nights to Mount Horeb, where he encountered God in a powerful way (1 Kings 19:8).

In the context of David and Goliath, the mention of 40 days underscores the extended duration of the standoff between the Israelites and the Philistines. During this time, the two armies were positioned for battle but had not yet engaged in combat. The 40-day period serves as a test of faith and resolve for both sides, with each day adding to the tension and anticipation.

This period of waiting and preparation sets the stage for the extraordinary events that will follow, culminating in David's confrontation with Goliath. The number 40, with its rich biblical symbolism, highlights the depth of the challenges faced by the Israelites and the transformation that is about to take place in this pivotal moment of biblical history.

In verses 17-18 David is instructed to take various supplies and provisions to his brothers. No doubt this was both for sustenance and encouragement. The fact that there was a *captain of thousand* indicates the large number of soldiers.

In verse 19, the phrase "fighting with the Philistines" can be understood as "at war with the Philistines." Actual combat had not yet begun.

David's Inquiry - (vv. 20-24)

In 1 Samuel 17:20, the text suggests a pivotal moment in the narrative, underscoring the timing of David's arrival at the scene. The phrase *"he came to the trench, as the host was going forth to the fight"* conveys a sense of urgency and anticipation. It implies that David arrived just as the situation was intensifying and the Israelite army was actively preparing for battle.

The mention of *"the trench"* likely refers to a defensive fortification or barrier that marked the front lines of the Israelite camp, separating them from the Philistine forces. David's presence at this location at that precise moment highlights the significance of his role in the events that are about to unfold.

As the Israelite and Philistine armies were getting ready for what promised to be a decisive and high-stakes confrontation, David's arrival foreshadows the extraordinary turn of events that will follow. His youthful courage and unwavering faith will soon lead him to confront the towering Goliath and challenge the *status quo*, setting in motion one of the most iconic and

53

inspiring stories of faith, bravery, and divine intervention in the Bible. David's timing in arriving at the scene, just as tensions were escalating and the battle seemed imminent, adds to the dramatic intensity of the narrative and sets the stage for the remarkable events to come.

Verse 21 of 1 Samuel 17 is a pivotal moment in the narrative, providing crucial context for the events about to unfold. It states: *"For Israel and the Philistines had put the battle in array, army against army."*

This verse reveals that the initial challenge of "champion warfare" had not been accepted at this point. Instead, both the Israelite and Philistine armies had organized themselves for a more traditional battle. They had arranged their forces in battle formation, preparing for a collective engagement between their respective armies.

The phrase *"army against army"* underscores the gravity of the situation and the looming clash between these two longstanding adversaries. It signifies that a significant conflict is on the horizon, one that has the potential to shape the course of their ongoing struggle. The Israelites faced the daunting prospect of confronting the Philistine army, and the tension on the battlefield was palpable.

It's important to note that this shift from a proposed champion duel to a full-scale army-to-army confrontation heightens the dramatic tension in the narrative. It sets the stage for David's unexpected and courageous intervention, which will soon unfold in the following verses.

David's arrival at this critical juncture, when the two armies are poised for battle, adds an element of surprise and uncertainty to the story. His actions will challenge the norms of conventional warfare and demonstrate his unwavering faith in God. The stage is now set for one of the most iconic and inspiring episodes in the Bible, where a young shepherd will face a giant warrior in the name of the Lord.

In 1 Samuel 17:22, we observe the complex dynamics at play as David arrives at the battlefield.

In this verse, the term *"carriage"* refers to a type of baggage or supplies that David had brought with him to the battlefield. It often included provisions, food, and equipment needed for an extended stay or campaign. In a military context, a carriage would typically be a part of the logistical support for an army.

The word *"saluted"* in this context is not a military term but rather signifies a customary greeting or exchange of pleasantries.

While there may have been a degree of familial affection in his desire to see his brothers and deliver provisions to them, the reception he receives from his brothers is far from warm. The text suggests tension and perhaps even a level of resentment between David and his elder brothers.

David, described as a *"man of war,"* (1 Sam. 16:18) was eager to be part of the action on the battlefield. His character was marked by courage and a desire to prove himself in combat. It's plausible that his haste to join the battle array was driven by this eagerness to demonstrate his prowess as a capable warrior.

As David approached the troops and engaged with his brothers, the atmosphere was charged with anticipation. The Israelite and Philistine armies were on the brink of a major confrontation, with both sides preparing for battle. The mention of David's arrival at this crucial juncture underscores the significance of the impending conflict and sets the stage for the extraordinary events that will follow in this iconic biblical narrative.

In verses 23-24 the focus remains on the tense standoff between the Israelite and Philistine armies, with neither side taking definitive action. Goliath's daily challenge hangs in the air, and the anticipation of the impending conflict intensifies. David's presence adds an element of intrigue, as he is now a participant in this high-stakes confrontation, whether he wants to be or not.

Conclusion

The opening act of this iconic narrative establishes the high stakes confrontation between the Israelites and Philistines. The battlefield is set and the armies prepare to clash in the valley of Elah. Towering over the scene is the imposing figure of Goliath, whose taunts inject fear into the hearts of the Israelites. Even their king, Saul, seems paralyzed and powerless against this giant foe.

Yet the arrival of the shepherd boy David signals a turning point. In contrast to the cowering Israelites, David burns with faith and courage. His eager readiness to fight this uncircumcised Philistine rings of confidence in the power of his God. The stage is now set for a radical clash - not army against army, but a divinely appointed boy against a formidable giant. What unfolds next will demonstrate that the battle truly belongs to the Lord, as humble courage topples arrogance and faith defeats fear. David's encounter with Goliath will become a timeless testament to trusting in God's strength, not man's. As this account continues, a definitive victory will be won through seeming foolishness and weakness.

Chapter 6

DAVID AND GOLIATH: A TALE OF FAITH *(Part 2)*

David's Bold Challenge
(1 Samuel 17:25-37)

David's Reaction:

Upon hearing the Israelite soldiers discussing the rewards King Saul promised for defeating Goliath, David's reaction is marked not by fear but by curiosity and determination. His inquiries about the reward are less about personal gain and more about understanding the stakes and the Israelites' hesitance. David's questions reveal his disbelief at the army's reluctance to face Goliath, exposing a stark contrast between his faith-driven perspective and the soldiers' fear.

Eliab's Disapproval:

Eliab's disapproval of David's presence and questions at the battlefield is deeply rooted in their family dynamics. Having grown up in the shadow of societal scorn and familial estrangement, as suggested by the Talmudic narrative and David's own psalms, David's assertiveness at the battlefront might have struck Eliab as presumptuous. Eliab, perhaps, saw David's boldness as an overstep from someone traditionally seen as illegitimate and unworthy. David's response, however, is marked not just by respect but also by a newfound assertiveness, reflecting his anointing and God's favor upon him.

David, undeterred by Eliab's criticism, remains focused on the task at hand. His response to Eliab is both respectful and firm, indicating his unwavering commitment to face the challenge that others fear.

David's Confidence in God:

David's confidence is rooted in his past experiences of God's deliverance. He recounts to King Saul his encounters with lions and bears while shepherding, emphasizing how God empowered him to protect his flock. David's argument is that the same God who delivered him from these dangers will also deliver him from Goliath. His assurance in God's help is not mere optimism but a faith forged in the trials of life. David sees the battle against Goliath not as a test of his own strength but as an opportunity to demonstrate God's power.

In this narrative, David emerges as a figure of deep faith, contrasting sharply with the fear that grips the Israelite army. His boldness and trust in God's protection mark a turning point in the story, paving the way for what will become a legendary encounter. David's approach to the Goliath challenge encapsulates a profound theological insight: that God's strength is made perfect in human weakness, a theme that resonates throughout the biblical narrative and is vividly illustrated in this iconic episode.

David's Unconventional Battle Plan (1 Samuel 17:38-40)

Saul's Armor:

When King Saul offers his armor to David, it's a practical gesture meant to protect the young shepherd in battle. However, Saul was known for his towering stature, as indicated in 1 Samuel 9:2, where he is described as standing taller than any of the people. This height difference would likely have made his armor ill-fitting for David, contributing to its cumbersome nature. David, unaccustomed to the weight and restrictiveness of

58

such armor, chooses to reject it. His decision is rooted in practicality; he understands the importance of mobility and familiarity in combat.

David's Attire as a Shepherd:

As a shepherd, David's attire would have been vastly different from a soldier's armor. Ancient shepherds typically wore garments that were light and allowed for ease of movement, essential for tending flocks and navigating rough terrain. This would have included a simple tunic, a cloak, and possibly a hat or head covering for protection against the elements. His clothing would have been designed for practicality and endurance, quite the opposite of the heavy and restrictive nature of Saul's armor.

David's Weapon of Choice:

Choosing to forego Saul's armor, David opts for a sling and five smooth stones from a brook. This choice is not only a testament to his skill and experience as a shepherd but also to his understanding of his own strengths and limitations. The sling, a weapon he was adept at using, and the smooth stones, perfectly suited for it, represent David's strategic approach to the battle. His selection highlights the importance of utilizing one's unique skills and experiences, even in the most daunting of challenges.

The Confrontation and Victory (1 Samuel 17:41-51)

Goliath's Mockery:

As the confrontation begins, Goliath, towering and armored, approaches David with disdain. He mocks David's youthful appearance and his simple armament, perceiving it as an insult that a boy armed only with a shepherd's sling would dare face him. He sees before him

59

a youth, ruddy and with a fair countenance, an image seemingly unfit for the brutal realities of battle. Goliath's disdain is evident as he ridicules David for his boyish looks, questioning if this is the best Israel can offer. His contemptuous words, aimed at belittling David, highlight the stark contrast between the seasoned warrior and the inexperienced shepherd, underscoring the absurdity of the matchup in Goliath's eyes.Goliath's taunts are laced with contempt, as he curses David by his gods and promises to feed his flesh to the birds and beasts.

David's Declaration of Faith:

Undeterred, David responds with a fearless declaration of faith. He asserts that while Goliath comes with a sword, spear, and shield, he comes in the name of the Lord of hosts, the God of the armies of Israel. David's words resonate with unshakeable confidence in God's power, declaring that the battle belongs to the Lord, and He will deliver Goliath into David's hands, showcasing His supremacy to all.

The Battle:

The battle that ensues is swift and decisive. As Goliath advances, David runs toward him and quickly slings a stone, striking the Philistine on the forehead. The stone, guided by David's skill, sinks into Goliath's skull, and he falls face down to the ground. David, without a sword of his own, takes Goliath's sword and beheads him, sealing his extraordinary victory. This momentous event demonstrates that true strength and victory come from faith in God and divine providence, not merely from physical might or weaponry. David's triumph stands as a testament to the power of faith over seemingly insurmountable odds.

60

While the primary focus of the narrative is on David's faith, it is worth recognizing his military acumen. Described as a *"man of war,"* David's intuitive grasp of strategy is evident. His selection of a sling, a weapon he had mastered, exemplifies his strategic alignment of his skills with the demands of the situation. Additionally, his proactive charge towards Goliath, rather than passively waiting, showcases his tactical initiative. Such actions underscore a calculated approach, combining his faith with a warrior's understanding of the battlefield, exemplifying a harmony of spiritual trust and strategic warfare.

The Aftermath and Lessons (1 Samuel 17:52-58)

Philistine Retreat:

Upon witnessing the defeat of Goliath, the Philistine army is overcome with panic and retreats in disarray. The Israelites, energized by David's victory, seize the moment to press their advantage. They surge forward, pursuing the fleeing Philistines with renewed vigor, turning the tide of the battle decisively in their favor. This pursuit underscores the impact of a single act of faith on the broader conflict.

David's Return:

In the aftermath of the battle, David returns to Saul, carrying the head of Goliath as a testament to his victory. This act marks his transition from a shepherd boy to a recognized hero and warrior. Saul's inquiry into David's lineage reflects the king's realization of David's significance and potential, further integrating David into the royal court and Israelite society.

Some scholars believe that in terms of chronology, 1 Samuel 17 (the story of David and Goliath) actually fits after

61

1 Samuel 16:13. Furthermore, they propose that 1 Samuel 16:14-23, which depicts David entering Saul's service, comes after the David and Goliath narrative.

Theological Conclusion

1 Samuel 17:4 and 23 refer to Goliath as a *"champion,"* using the words סינבה־שׁיא [*ish habenim*], which means *"a man of the space between."* It is a Hebraism used only of Goliath. In Psalm 9 we see the word "וּבֵּל תוּמ [*muth labben*], which can be translated as *"the death of the man between."*

In concluding the story of David and Goliath, it's important to acknowledge the deep theological and symbolic links this story shares with Psalms 8 and 144. This becomes particularly clear when considering the subscript *"Mūth-labbēn"* in Psalm 9. Bullinger's interpretation suggests that the headings in the Psalms are actually subscripts belonging to the previous Psalm, which makes Psalm 8 to be about *"the death of the man between."*

David's victory over Goliath, a seemingly insurmountable foe, aligns with the themes of Psalm 8, which marvels at God's attention to and care for humanity despite our apparent insignificance in the grand cosmic scale. This Psalm reflects on human frailty juxtaposed with divine majesty, a theme mirrored in David's triumph, where his success is attributed not to his own strength but to God's empowerment.

Linking this with *"Mūth-labbēn,"* interpreted as *"the death of the man between"* or the death of the champion (Goliath), as suggested by Bullinger, we see a deeper narrative thread. This postscript connects David's victory directly to Psalm 8, framing it as a celebration of God's providence and dominion over creation, exercised through David.

Moreover, the connection to Psalm 144, especially noted in the Septuagint's title *"A Psalm of David concerning Goliath,"* reinforces this interpretation. Psalm 144's themes of God's protection and empowerment in battle resonate with the story of David and Goliath. David, in this light, is not just a historical figure but a symbol of divine intervention and the embodiment of God's promise to empower humanity despite our inherent weaknesses.

Therefore, David's celebration following his victory over Goliath is not merely a personal or national triumph but a testament to God's overarching plan and power, beautifully encapsulated in the Psalms. It exemplifies the human experience of overcoming insurmountable odds through divine assistance, a theme that resonates through the ages. One can almost hear David and the armies of Israel shouting, *"O LORD our Lord, how excellent is thy name in all the earth!"* (Ps. 8:9).

Chapter 7:

COVENANT, KINSHIP, AND KINGDOM:

The Ascendance of David
  and Decline of Saul
1 Samuel 18:1-30

At the heart of 1 Samuel 18 lies a rich tapestry of narratives that explore the complex interplay of divine providence, human relationships, and the shifting sands of royal power in ancient Israel. This chapter presents a pivotal moment in the history of Israel, marked by the emergence of David as a central figure and the corresponding decline of King Saul. Here, the themes of covenant, loyalty, and divine anointing intertwine with the politics of jealousy and fear, offering a profound reflection on leadership, friendship, and the sovereignty of God.

The chapter opens with a focus on the extraordinary bond between David and Jonathan, a relationship that transcends conventional friendship and ventures into the realm of a covenantal kinship. This bond, forged in the aftermath of David's triumph over Goliath, is a testament to Jonathan's recognition of David's divine anointing and his own submission to God's unfolding plan for Israel. In contrast, we observe King Saul, whose initial admiration for David gradually morphs into deep-seated jealousy and fear, setting the stage for a tragic conflict.

As we journey through this chapter, we witness David's escalating successes and popularity, which, while celebrated by the people of Israel, fuel Saul's growing insecurity and paranoia. The narrative artfully depicts the dichotomy between David's faith-driven ascent and Saul's fear-driven decline. This contrast is not merely a personal rivalry but a profound exploration of the human response to divine orchestration.

Moreover, the chapter delves into the political and personal dimensions of David's life, from his celebrated military achievements to the complexities of his marriage to Michal, Saul's daughter. These events are not just historical footnotes but are integral to understanding the divine hand in the establishment of David's future kingship and the eventual demise of Saul's reign.

In this chapter, we are invited to reflect on the timeless truths about leadership, faith, and the sovereignty of God in the midst of human affairs. The unfolding drama in 1 Samuel 18 provides not only historical insight but also spiritual lessons relevant for all generations, revealing the enduring power of godly character and the perils of allowing fear and envy to cloud judgment.

David and Jonathan's Covenant (1 Samuel 18:1-4)

Jonathan's Soul Knit to David:

The narrative of 1 Samuel 18 opens with a profound and immediate bond forming between Jonathan, the son of King Saul, and David, the newly emerged hero of Israel. This bond is described as a knitting of the soul, a Hebrew idiom suggesting an unbreakable and deep emotional connection. Such a description is rare in biblical texts, indicating the extraordinary nature of their relationship. It's a bond that transcends mere friendship, entering the realm of a covenantal kinship. This knitting of souls occurs immediately after David's victory over Goliath, suggesting that Jonathan saw in David not just a valiant warrior but a kindred spirit, one whose heart was aligned with God's purposes for Israel.

66

Jonathan's Covenant with David:

Jonathan's initiation of a covenant with David signifies a commitment that goes beyond personal friendship and enters into the realm of solemn vows. In the ancient Near Eastern context, covenants were not entered into lightly; they were binding, sacred agreements, often sealed with rituals and accompanied by blessings and curses. Jonathan's act of making a covenant with David, therefore, speaks volumes about his recognition of David's divine anointing and his own submission to God's plan. Unlike his father Saul, who increasingly becomes hostile towards David, Jonathan accepts and embraces David's future role in leading Israel.

Jonathan's Gifts to David:

The gifts that Jonathan bestows upon David – his robe, armor, sword, bow, and belt – are laden with symbolic significance. These are not mere tokens of friendship but are deeply meaningful in the context of ancient royal customs. The robe, in particular, represents Jonathan's princely status, suggesting a transfer or sharing of royal honor. The giving of weapons, meanwhile, symbolizes trust and mutual defense; it's as though Jonathan is saying, *"Your battles are my battles."* This act of giving is profound, coming from the heir apparent to the throne. It demonstrates Jonathan's humility and recognition of God's hand upon David, a recognition that seems to elude Saul.

In these early verses of 1 Samuel 18, we witness the foundation of what will become one of the most celebrated friendships in biblical history. This covenant between David and Jonathan transcends personal affection and enters into the realm of divine purpose, setting the stage for the unfolding drama of David's ascent to the throne and the challenges he will face along the way. Jonathan emerges as a figure of noble character, his actions contrasting with Saul's growing envy and hostility towards David. In Jonathan, we see a man who, despite his royal lineage and potential claim to the throne, recognizes and submits to God's sovereign choice in David. This covenant, marked by selfless love and mutual respect, stands as a testament to the power of godly friendship and loyalty amidst the often tumultuous landscape of political intrigue and personal ambition.

David's Military Successes and Growing Popularity (1 Samuel 18:5-7)

David's Success in Saul's Service:

Following his victory over Goliath, David's role in Saul's service rapidly ascends. The text portrays David as excelling in every mission assigned to him, earning not only King Saul's trust but also the admiration and respect of the people of Israel. This phase of David's life marks a critical transition from shepherd boy to respected military leader. His success in military campaigns is notable for its consistent excellence. David's ability to lead effectively, coupled with his charismatic and godly character, resonates strongly with Saul's men, who follow him willingly and loyally.

This period in David's life is a fulfillment of Samuel's anointing, showcasing that David's capabilities extend beyond his initial encounter with Goliath. His skills as a leader and warrior are affirmed repeatedly, reflecting the divine favor and empowerment upon him. David's rise is not just a testament to his military prowess but also to his ability to inspire and lead people, a quality essential for his future role as king.

The Women's Song of Praise:

David's increasing popularity comes to a focal point in the spontaneous praises sung by the women of Israel. These songs, while celebrating Israel's victories, specifically attribute greater triumphs to David than to Saul (*"Saul hath slain his thousands, and David his ten thousands"*). This song, while meant as a tribute to David's heroism, unwittingly sows seeds of jealousy and fear in Saul's heart.

The women's song highlights a cultural practice of the time, where victories in battle were celebrated with music and dance, often led by women. This form of communal celebration reflects the collective joy and relief of a people delivered from their enemies. However, the comparison made between Saul and David, though perhaps unintended, highlights a shift in public perception. David is seen not just as a warrior but as a hero whose achievements eclipse those of the king.

The impact of this song on Saul is profound. The king, who should be rejoicing in the victory of his nation, is instead filled with envy and insecurity. Saul's reaction to this song marks a turning point in his relationship with David. From this point on, Saul views David not just as a servant or a military asset, but as a rival, a threat to his throne. The seeds of conflict sown here will grow into a tragic and complex struggle between Saul and David, profoundly affecting both their lives and the future of Israel.

In these verses of 1 Samuel 18, we witness the paradox of David's rise: as his popularity and success grow among the people, so too does Saul's fear and jealousy. This dual development sets the stage for the ensuing chapters, where David's journey will be marked not only by triumphs but also by trials and tribulations.

69

Saul's Jealousy and Fear of David (1 Samuel 18:8-9)

The narrative in 1 Samuel 18 shifts to explore the emotional turmoil within King Saul's heart. Verses 8 and 9 vividly illustrate Saul's growing jealousy and fear, sparked by David's rising popularity and success. This jealousy doesn't emerge suddenly but results from a series of events that gradually position David as not only a hero of Israel but also a potential threat to Saul's reign.

The catalyst for Saul's envy is the women's song of praise for David, which lauds him for slaying *"ten thousands"* compared to Saul's *"thousands."* This comparison strikes a chord of insecurity in Saul. It challenges his self-perception and authority as king, igniting a fear that his reign might be overshadowed or even supplanted by David's rising prominence.

Saul's reaction to this development is profound. His anger and envy are not merely personal feelings; they represent a deep-seated fear for his throne and legacy. As king, Saul had been anointed by Samuel and had led Israel through various battles. Yet, his leadership had been marred by disobedience and a troubled spirit. David, on the other hand, emerges as a figure blessed with God's favor, succeeding in areas where Saul had faltered.

Saul's perception of David as a rival is a significant shift in their relationship. Until this point, David had been a loyal servant to Saul, a valiant warrior fighting for the king's cause. But Saul's inability to see beyond his own insecurities transforms this loyalty into a perceived threat. This change marks the beginning of a tragic trajectory in Saul's reign, where his decisions and actions are increasingly driven by fear and jealousy rather than wisdom and faith.

The text highlights a crucial lesson about leadership and the dangers of letting insecurity and envy dictate one's actions. Saul's response to David's success reveals a lack of trust in God's plan and an inability to rejoice in the achievements of others. Instead of seeing David as a valuable asset to the kingdom and a fulfillment of God's blessings upon Israel, Saul views him through the lens of personal rivalry and threat.

In these verses, we see the unfolding of a significant theme in the narrative of Israel's monarchy: the contrast between Saul's fear-driven leadership and David's faith-driven journey. This contrast sets the stage for the ensuing struggle between the two figures, a struggle that goes beyond personal conflict and delves into the heart of what it means to lead and serve in accordance with God's will.

Saul's Hostile Actions Against David (1 Samuel 18:10-11)

The narrative of Saul and David takes a more ominous turn in 1 Samuel 18:10-11, where Saul's simmering jealousy and fear manifest into overt hostility. The passage describes how Saul, influenced by an evil spirit from God, makes two attempts on David's life using a spear.

This section is critical in understanding the deteriorating mental and spiritual state of Saul. The text notes that an evil spirit from God came upon Saul, an expression denoting a troubled or distressed state, often interpreted as a divine judgment for Saul's disobedience and moral decline. It's in this agitated and spiritually tormented state that Saul confronts David, who was playing the harp for him, as was his custom to soothe Saul's troubled spirit.

The Davidic Chronicles

The first attempt to harm David is described almost casually, yet it marks a profound shift in Saul's behavior—from harboring internal jealousy to taking active steps to eliminate David. Saul hurls the spear, intending to pin David to the wall. David's escape from this attack is a testament to his alertness and possibly divine protection. The incident, however, does not deter Saul, as he makes a second attempt on David's life in a similar manner.

These attempts by Saul to harm David are significant for several reasons. First, they demonstrate the extent to which Saul has succumbed to jealousy and fear, allowing these emotions to override his judgment and kingly duties. Saul's actions are not only unjust but deeply tragic, as he turns against someone who had been nothing but loyal and beneficial to him and the kingdom.

Second, David's escapes from these attempts are crucial moments in the narrative. They not only showcase David's physical agility and alertness but also signify a deeper theme of divine protection and guidance. Despite the king's efforts to harm him, David remains unscathed, suggesting that God's hand is upon him, guiding and protecting him from harm.

Finally, these events mark a turning point in the relationship between Saul and David. What was once a relationship of mutual benefit and respect now becomes a struggle for survival. David's position in Saul's court becomes untenable, setting the stage for his eventual departure and transition from a revered hero to a fugitive.

In these verses, the narrative of 1 Samuel 18 paints a picture of a king losing his grip on reality and righteousness, driven by unchecked emotions and a departure from God's favor.

At the same time, it portrays the rise of David, not just as a warrior and musician, but as a figure of resilience and divine favor, navigating the complexities of royal court life and the dangers posed by a king who sees him as a threat.

David's Marriage to Michal (1 Samuel 18:17-30)

Saul's Offer of Merab:

The story of David's marriage starts with King Saul offering his older daughter, Merab, to David. At first, this offer appears to be an honor, a suitable reward for the hero who defeated Goliath. However, Saul's intentions quickly prove to be less than honorable. When the time for the marriage arrives, Saul deceitfully gives Merab in marriage to another man, Adriel the Meholathite. This act of deception is not only a personal betrayal of David but also a political move, showing Saul's increasing mistrust and fear of David's influence and popularity.

Michal's Love for David:

In the midst of these turbulent events, the narrative introduces Michal, Saul's younger daughter, who loves David. This detail is significant, adding a personal element to the political and military drama in the royal court. Michal's affection for David adds depth to the story, intertwining personal relationships with the overarching theme of Saul's declining kingship and David's ascent.

Saul's Scheme with Michal:

Saul, recognizing Michal's love for David, sees an opportunity to ensnare David in a dangerous situation. He offers Michal to David in marriage, but with a perilous condition: David must bring one hundred Philistine foreskins as a bride price. This demand, under the guise of a royal dowry, is a thinly veiled attempt to put David's life in danger. Saul hopes that in trying to fulfill this gruesome and hazardous task, David would fall at the hands of the Philistines.

David's Response and Fulfillment of the Condition:

David's response to Saul's challenge is marked by humility and courage. Aware of his humble background and the gravity of Saul's condition, David nevertheless accepts the challenge. In a remarkable display of bravery and skill, David not only meets Saul's demand but exceeds it, bringing back two hundred Philistine foreskins. This act secures his marriage to Michal and significantly enhances David's reputation among the people, further solidifying his position in Israel.

Saul's Fear of David Deepens:

Saul's reaction to David's successful fulfillment of the condition is one of increased fear. He realizes that the Lord is with David and has departed from him, a recognition that deepens his paranoia and sense of vulnerability. Saul's fear of David is no longer just political; it is rooted in the acknowledgment of David's divine favor, which he himself has lost.

David's Continued Success:

The chapter concludes with an emphasis on David's ongoing military success and his growing fame throughout the kingdom. Each victory, each act of bravery and leadership, further cements David's place as a beloved and respected figure in Israel. However, these successes are a double-edged sword; they continue to trouble Saul, setting the stage for greater conflict between the king and the future king.

In this portion of 1 Samuel 18, the intertwining of personal, political, and spiritual themes creates a complex and compelling narrative. David's marriage to Michal, while a personal triumph, is also a political and spiritual milestone, reflecting his growing stature and the divine favor upon him. Saul's actions, driven by fear and envy, foreshadow the tragic trajectory of his reign, highlighting the consequences of a leadership that

Conclusion

As we reach the conclusion of this chapter, we find ourselves amid a profound narrative shift. The ascent of David, marked by divine favor and burgeoning leadership, stands in stark contrast to the descent of Saul, whose rule is increasingly marred by jealousy, fear, and spiritual estrangement. The chapter's events, from the covenant between David and Jonathan to the tension-laden court of Saul, underscore a pivotal transition in Israel's history: the emergence of a king after God's own heart and the decline of a monarchy clouded by disobedience and insecurity.

The story of David and Jonathan's covenant, characterized by mutual respect and divine acknowledgment, offers a shining example of godly kinship, while Saul's actions, driven by envy and fear, serve as cautionary tales about the perils of leadership divorced from faith. David's military successes and his marriage to Michal further emphasize his divinely ordained path to kingship, even as they amplify Saul's apprehensions, setting the stage for deeper conflict.

As we look ahead to 1 Samuel 19, the tension between Saul and David escalates, unveiling new challenges and divine interventions. The narrative continues to weave the themes of faith, providence, and human frailty, inviting readers to explore the complexities of divine plans in the face of human resistance. The unfolding saga in the next chapter promises not only further insights into the characters of David and Saul but also deeper reflections on the nature of God's workings in history and the lives of His chosen.

Thus, as we turn the page to 1 Samuel 19, we anticipate a continuation of this rich biblical narrative, where the trials and triumphs of David's journey serve as a testament to the unyielding faithfulness and sovereignty of God amidst the tumult of human affairs and the vicissitudes of ancient Israelite monarchy.

Chapter 8:

FROM ROYAL COURTS TO FUGITIVE NIGHTS
1 Samuel 19: 1-17

1 Samuel 19:1-17 charts a period of fragile peace, a time of uncertainty and transition. This chapter delves into the escalating tensions in the royal court of King Saul, marked by jealousy, betrayal, and the poignant shift of David from a celebrated hero to a fugitive on the run. It paints a vivid picture of the personal and political drama unfolding against the backdrop of providence and destiny. As we journey through this narrative, we witness the complexities of human relationships, the depths of loyalty, the destructive power of envy, and the steadfastness of God's purpose.

Saul's Renewed Plot against David (1 Samuel 19:1)

In 1 Samuel 19:1, we find ourselves immediately drawn into a scene of high tension. King Saul openly declares his intention to kill David, a stark shift from private resentment to an open, political campaign against David. This royal decree is not just aimed at the court, but is also directed towards his son Jonathan. Jonathan, caught in a web of divided loyalties – between his father and his close friend, David – is expected to side with family.

The atmosphere in the court changes dramatically as Saul commands 'all his servants' to take part in this pursuit of David. What was once a somewhat covert operation against David has now become institutionalized, a matter of state. It's not just a manhunt but a test of loyalty for everyone in the court.

Beneath this surface tension, deeper forces are at play. Saul is driven by a fear of losing his throne, a fear amplified by David's growing popularity and God's favor upon him. David's loyalty goes unseen, and Saul's descent into paranoia becomes a tragic part of his character.

Yet, there's a glimmer of hope, a whisper of divine providence. Through Saul's actions, the narrative takes a significant turn, setting events into motion that will lead to David's miraculous preservation. It's a moment that invites reflection on how even flawed human actions can serve divine purposes.

This verse serves as a critical pivot in the larger narrative of 1 Samuel. It signals the final break between Saul and David, setting the stage for a series of events that will see David rise and Saul tragically fall.

In essence, 1 Samuel 19:1 is a verse that vibrates with political, personal, and theological undertones. It exposes the complex character of Saul and sets the stage for the unfolding drama between Saul, David, and Jonathan.

Jonathan's Intervention for David (1 Samuel 19:2-6)

In the royal courts of Israel, under the shadow of a looming threat, Jonathan, son of King Saul, emerged as a beacon of loyalty and friendship. Aware of his father's dark intentions towards David, Jonathan acted swiftly, a testament to the strength of his bond with David, transcending blood and duty. In secrecy, he warned David, advising him to hide in the fields while he navigated the treacherous waters of Saul's wrath.

The fields, away from the prying eyes of the court, became their sanctuary, a place for plotting and planning. Jonathan, taking on the role of an intercessor, devised

78

a strategy. He would confront his father, gauge his intentions, and then bring word back to David. It was a role fraught with risk, yet Jonathan embraced it, driven by a sense of righteousness.

Jonathan stood before Saul, his father, not just as a son but as an advocate for justice. With courage that belied his youth, he spoke of David's deeds, his loyalty, and his innocence. He reminded Saul of the joy that David's victories had brought to Israel, urging him to see David not as an adversary but as a loyal servant and a blessing to the kingdom. Jonathan's words were a blend of strategic wisdom and heartfelt sincerity, painting David as a hero, anointed by the Lord's favor.

He reminded Saul of that fateful day when David, facing Goliath, risked everything for Israel. It was a victory that God had delivered through David, a victory that brought joy and relief to the people of Israel, including Saul himself. Jonathan's appeal was not just to Saul's reason but to his emotions and sense of morality. How could one justify harming someone who had risked so much for the nation?

Saul, the king, listened. In that moment, swayed by Jonathan's passionate plea, he took an oath. *"As the Lord liveth, he shall not be slain,"* he declared, a vow that seemed to echo through the halls of the palace. It was a promise that brought temporary relief, a brief pause in the storm of jealousy and fear that had gripped Saul.

Yet, this oath, as solemn as it seemed, hung precariously in the balance of Saul's turbulent spirit. The king's inner turmoil and spiritual decline cast a shadow over his commitment. The resolution was but a momentary calm, a fleeting reprieve in the ongoing saga of Saul's jealousy

79

and David's divine destiny. Jonathan's intervention had averted immediate danger, but the seeds of conflict were far from being uprooted.

In these moments, the royal court of Israel became a stage where loyalty, friendship, and moral dilemmas intertwined, setting the scene for the unfolding drama of kingship, destiny, and divine providence.

Saul's Temporary Reconciliation with David (1 Samuel 19:7)

In the unfolding drama of Israel's royal court, a moment of reconciliation emerged as fleeting as it was fragile. Jonathan, having swayed his father King Saul with passionate pleas for David, now embarked on a mission of restoration. He sought out David, who had been forced into the shadows by Saul's murderous intent.

Jonathan's message to David was one of cautious hope. He relayed Saul's oath: *"As the Lord liveth, he shall not be slain."* These words, spoken by the troubled king, echoed with a promise of safety, a reprieve from the looming threat of death. With this assurance, Jonathan beckoned David back from the fringes of exile, back to the presence of the king.

David, whose life had become a tapestry of triumph and peril, heeded Jonathan's call. He returned to Saul, stepping back into the court, a place where his heroic deeds had once been celebrated but had recently become a stage for his near demise. The reunion was a complex tapestry of emotions – relief, suspicion, and a tenuous hope that perhaps reconciliation was possible.

In the court, David stood once again before Saul. This was not the triumphant return of a warrior; it was the cautious re-entry of a man who had been marked for death by his sovereign. The dynamics of power and mistrust hung heavily in the air, a silent witness to the fragile peace that now reigned.

Saul's eyes met David's, and for a fleeting moment, the shadows of jealousy and paranoia seemed to recede. The king who had hurled a spear with lethal intent now faced the very target of his ire, bound by his own oath made before God and man. It was a scene laden with irony – the anointed king, Saul, momentarily subdued by his own words, and David, the anointed successor, standing in the precarious mercy of his ruler.

Yet, beneath this veneer of reconciliation, the undercurrents of tension and unresolved conflict persisted. The court, with its intrigues and power plays, remained a precarious place for David. His return was a testament to his faith and courage, a decision to face potential danger head-on, trusting in God's protection and the fidelity of Jonathan's word.

In this moment, the narrative of 1 Samuel 19:7 captures a brief interlude in the saga of David and Saul – a pause in the relentless pursuit, a momentary bridge over the chasm of distrust. It was a scene that held within it the complexities of human relationships, the fickleness of power, and the ever-present hand of God in David's life.

David's Continued Success and Saul's Jealousy (1 Samuel 19:8-10)

The fragile peace brokered in the courts of King Saul was not destined to last. As the wheel of time turned, the land of Israel found itself once again under the shadow of war. David, reinstated in Saul's service, took up arms to defend his people. His courage and skill in battle shone bright, a beacon of hope against the encroaching darkness of the enemy. Each victory added to his legend, each triumph a testament to his divine anointment as a warrior of Israel.

However, back in the royal chambers, a different battle was brewing, one not against foreign enemies but against the inner demons of jealousy and fear. King Saul, tormented by the spirit that had departed from him and the knowledge of David's divine favor, found his heart darkened once more. The temporary reprieve, the oath sworn in a moment of clarity, crumbled under the weight of his festering envy.

The stage was set once again in the palace, with David playing the lyre to soothe the troubled king. Music, which once was a balm for Saul's tormented soul, now played the prelude to treachery. As David's fingers danced over the strings, drawing out melodies of peace and tranquility, Saul's hand gripped a spear – a harrowing echo of past attempts on David's life.

The spear hurled by Saul was not just a weapon of iron and wood; it was the manifestation of a king's wrath, a symbol of a fractured spirit. David, quick in body and spirit, evaded the deadly intent, the spear finding its home in the wall instead. This act of aggression severed the last threads of trust and safety in the palace for David. It was a glaring declaration that not even the king's chambers were a sanctuary from Saul's rage.

In the wake of this near-fatal encounter, David faced a harrowing choice. The palace, once a place of honor and triumph, had turned into a den of danger. His position as a favored servant and son-in-law to the king offered no protection against the madness that consumed Saul. With a heart heavy with the realization of his perilous position, David knew that the time had come to flee. The night's shadow became his cloak as he stepped into the uncertainty and danger of the life of a fugitive.

These verses, 1 Samuel 19:8-10, paint a vivid picture of the tragic deterioration of Saul's character and his relationship with David. They depict the turning point where David's journey shifts from the royal courts to the life of an outlaw, marked by Saul's irreversible act of aggression. The narrative here is a poignant reminder of the destructive power of jealousy and the impermanence of human favor, contrasted with the steadfastness of divine purpose.

David's Escape to His Home (1 Samuel 19:11-17)

In the darkened hours of the night, the royal residence of King Saul became a stage for a desperate and cunning escape. David, now marked for death by the king, found himself in peril within his own home. Michal, Saul's daughter and David's wife, stood at the center of this nocturnal drama. Aware of her father's intent to kill her husband, her loyalty to David spurred her into action.

With the urgency of imminent danger pressing upon them, Michal devised a plan. She lowered David from a window, a symbolic descent from the heights of royal favor to the uncertain depths of fugitive life. As David vanished into the night, a mix of fear and hope must have gripped his heart – fear for the unknown path ahead and hope for divine protection.

The empty bed left behind by David became a canvas for Michal's deception. She placed an image in the bed,

83

disguising it to resemble David, complete with goat's hair for effect. This ruse was not merely a wife's attempt to buy time for her husband; it was a bold statement of defiance against Saul's unjust decree.

Morning light revealed the deception. Saul's messengers, sent to seize David, were met with Michal's cunningly crafted illusion. Confused and thwarted, they returned to Saul with the news of David's apparent illness. This twist in the tale brought Saul himself to Michal's door, demanding David be brought to him, sick or not, for execution.

Confronted by her father, Michal chose to protect herself with a lie. She claimed David threatened her life, forcing her to aid his escape. This lie, while saving her from immediate reprisal, cast David as the aggressor, further complicating the web of family, loyalty, and royal intrigue.

In these moments, captured in 1 Samuel 19:11-17, the narrative unfolds a story of escape, loyalty, and deception. Michal emerges as a key figure, her actions driven by a mix of love and pragmatism. David's flight marks a significant turn in his journey – from a celebrated hero in the royal court to a fugitive on the run, a transition fraught with danger but illuminated by the hope of divine guidance.

This passage is rich in its portrayal of the personal and political dynamics of Saul's household. It underscores the tragic breakdown of relationships within the royal family and highlights the complexities of Michal's position as both Saul's daughter and David's wife. The narrative here is a poignant reflection on the consequences of Saul's jealousy, not only affecting David but also tearing apart his own family.

84

Conclusion

In the compelling narrative of 1 Samuel 19:1-17, we observe the widening rift between King Saul and David. The story, marked by jealousy, loyalty, divine intervention, and survival struggle, brilliantly merges personal affairs with politics, mirroring complex human relationships amid royal schemes and divine fate.

The transformation of Saul's private jealousy into a public vendetta is evident from his open intention to kill David. This triggers a chain of events that expose the characters' depth and motivations. Jonathan's loyalty to David, despite his father's wishes, underscores friendship and integrity themes. His intercession for David momentarily persuades Saul, hinting at a potential reconciliation.

However, the peace is fleeting. Saul's internal conflict and jealousy reemerge, culminating in another assassination attempt on David. The scene of Saul throwing a spear at David, playing the lyre, symbolizes the king's irreparable detachment from reality and righteousness. David's evasion of this attack signals the end of his royal court tenure and the start of his fugitive life.

Michal's assistance in David's escape adds complexity to the narrative, displaying her bravery and quick wit. Her actions, while saving David, also expose Saul's family's tragic divisions, ripped apart by the king's obsession.

As David flees into the night, abandoning his known life, the narrative prepares for his transformation from a court hero to an outlaw. This shift is not merely physical but a spiritual and character-enhancing journey, shaped by adversity, faith, and relentless pursuit by a God-abandoned king.

85

The Davidic Chronicles

Looking forward, David's story evolves. As a fugitive, David will face tests of his character, faith, and leadership skills. His journey will take him to unexpected places and alliances, molding him into the foretold leader and king. In contrast, Saul's plunge into paranoia and desperation highlights the perils of unchecked jealousy and divine guidance rejection.

In summary, 1 Samuel 19:1-17 encapsulates the broader Davidic narrative - a tale of ascent and descent, divine favor and human weakness, and the intricate destiny dance that interweaves the lives of those standing at the intersection of history and prophecy.

Chapter 9

THE FLIGHT AND COVENANT:

David and Jonathan's Bond
1 Samuel 19:18-20:42

Having narrowly escaped Saul's murderous rage, David now finds himself cast out of the royal court and into the precarious life of a fugitive. Chapter 9 chronicles this difficult transition as David seeks refuge and divine protection while Saul's obsession drives the kingdom towards conflict.

Picking up from Michal's daring assistance of David's flight in chapter 8, we now follow David as he flees for his life to the prophet Samuel. There, in the company of the prophets, David experiences God's supernatural preservation from Saul's grasp. However, it becomes clear David cannot return to the court or his home. A heartbreaking separation from Jonathan follows, along with a covenant that binds their friendship amidst divided loyalties.

With nowhere left to hide in Saul's kingdom, David takes his first steps across the threshold into exile. His path will lead him towards the wilderness, where he will learn to evade Saul's relentless pursuit. No longer a celebrated hero, David becomes an outlaw relying on his wits, faith, and a few loyal allies. His anointing as the future king now seems impossibly distant.

Yet through it all, divine providence continues to shape David's journey. As Saul descends further into jealousy and tyranny, David is refined by hardship, gaining the experience and character to one day lead Israel. The contrasts between the two anointed yet fatally flawed leaders deepens. A nation and a throne hang in the balance.

Divine Protection at Naioth
(1 Samuel 19:18-24)

At this critical juncture, David has no safe place left within the palace or Saul's kingdom. With nowhere else to turn, he makes the decisive choice to flee to Samuel, the spiritual leader of the nation. This choice reflects David's unshakeable belief in God's providential hand upon his life. He entrusts his fate to the divine guidance he expects to receive through Samuel.

Upon arriving in Ramah, he unburdens himself to Samuel, recounting all that Saul has done. His disclosure is an act of faith and a testament to his confidence in Samuel as a confidante and wise counselor. This occurs in a general area under the name Ramah, which means *'heights,'* and the more specific but unknown location of Naioth.

Upon hearing of David's location, Saul gathers his men to pursue David, but Saul himself stays behind. They arrive in Naioth, where they see *"the company of the prophets prophesying"* (v. 20) under Samuel's leadership. This suggests that Naioth may have been the home of a *"school of the prophets."* Interestingly, Saul's men also become overcome by the Spirit of God and begin to prophesy. The content of their prophecies is not disclosed.

Saul sends a second wave of messengers, who also came under this prophetic influence, and then a third (v. 21). After the third, Saul himself went in pursuit, and, lo and behold, *"the Spirit of God was upon him also, and he went on, and prophesied"* (v. 23).

The situation becomes even more intriguing in verse 24. It states that upon reaching Naioth, King Saul *"stripped off his clothes also, and prophesied before Samuel in like manner, and lay down naked all that day and all that night."* The words *"also"* and *"in like manner"* suggest that Samuel, and probably the entire group of prophets, were prophesying in the nude.

So, what's the reason behind this?

The specific Hebrew term translated as *"naked"* appears 16 times in the Hebrew scriptures. Though it's used figuratively on a few occasions, it's most commonly and clearly used in its literal sense. This is the second instance of its usage; the first is in Genesis 2:25, which describes Adam and Eve as being naked and unashamed.

Some have tried to say that Saul only removed his royal armour or outer garment (as we have seen in 1 Sam. 18:4), but support for this is thin, if non-existent.

Others have attempted to interpret this as indicative of a common spiritual practice of the time. However, such interpretations are purely speculative and lack substantial evidence.

It is also important to consider that our modern, Western interpretations and cultural understandings may not fully grasp the nuances and cultural practices of the ancient Near East. Even if these practices were explained to us, it is likely that we would still struggle to truly understand their significance and implications in their historical and cultural context.

Jonathan and David's Plan (1 Samuel 20:1-23)

David's Fear and Jonathan's Assurance (1 Samuel 20:1-4)

Upon his departure from Naioth, David seeks out his

89

dearest friend, Jonathan. In a poignant scene, David expresses his fear and confusion, asking Jonathan, *"What have I done? What is mine iniquity? ...that he seeketh my life?"* (v. 1). The depth of David's fear and despair is evident, and it is a testament to his trust in Jonathan that he turns to him in this critical moment.

Jonathan, however, seems unaware of his father's renewed intent to kill David, responding, *"it is not so"* (v.2). Whether Jonathan is genuinely uninformed or in denial about his father's intentions is unclear. Nonetheless, he reassures David and promises to do whatever David requests of him.

The Covenant Renewed (1 Samuel 20:5-9)

In response to Jonathan's promise, David reveals his plan. He suggests that he should go into hiding, and if Saul notices his absence and reacts negatively, it will confirm his murderous intent. As part of this plan, David asks Jonathan to send him away in peace, should it prove that his life is indeed in danger.

Jonathan agrees, and they renew their covenant with each other. Jonathan asks that when David becomes king, he shows kindness to his family, a request that David will honor in the future (2 Samuel 9:1-13).

The Three Arrows (1 Samuel 20:10-23)

David and Jonathan further refine their plan, agreeing on a signal to communicate Saul's reaction. Jonathan will shoot three arrows as if aiming at a target, and his words to his servant will carry the hidden message for David. If Jonathan indicates that the arrows are near him, then it is safe for David to return. But if he says that the arrows are beyond his servant, then David must flee.

This moment underscores the perilous situation David and Jonathan find themselves in, and the lengths they must go to protect themselves and their friendship. Their mutual trust and commitment to each other are evident, and their covenant is renewed with a solemn oath before the Lord.

Saul's Anger and Jonathan's Intercession (1 Samuel 20:24-34)

In the following days, David's absence at the royal table is noted. Initially, Saul says nothing, thinking that David is ceremonially unclean (v. 26). However, when David's place remains empty the second day, Saul questions Jonathan.

Jonathan sticks to the cover story he and David had agreed upon: that David urgently needed to attend a family sacrifice in his hometown of Bethlehem (v. 29). This explanation, however, does not assuage Saul's suspicions. Instead, he accuses Jonathan of choosing David over his own family and potential royal inheritance. *"As long as the son of Jesse liveth upon the ground, thou shalt not be established, nor thy kingdom"* (v.31), Saul warns.

In a fit of rage, Saul even attempts to kill his own son with a javelin (v. 33). This violent reaction confirms Saul's murderous intentions towards David, revealing the depth of his jealousy and paranoia.

Jonathan leaves the table in fierce anger, grief-stricken at his father's unjust treatment of David (v. 34). This incident marks a turning point in Jonathan's relationship with his father and solidifies his allegiance to David. The die is cast, and the course of the future is set. Jonathan must now send the agreed signal to David, launching him into a life of exile.

The Covenant between David and Jonathan (1 Samuel 20:35-42)

The next morning, Jonathan goes out to the field to send the agreed-upon signal to David. Accompanied by a young servant, Jonathan shoots three arrows, deliberately shooting them beyond the servant as the signal for David to flee (v. 36-38).

After sending his servant back to town with the arrows, Jonathan is left alone in the field. It is here that David emerges from his hiding place, and the two friends share a heartbreaking farewell (v. 40-41). Their grief is evident, with the text noting that *"David arose out of a place toward the south, and fell on his face to the ground, and bowed himself three times: and they kissed one another, and wept one with another, until David exceeded"* (v. 41).

This poignant scene underscores the deep love and respect between David and Jonathan. Their parting is marked by sorrow, but also by the renewal of their covenant. Jonathan reassures David of his steadfast loyalty and love, saying, *"Go in peace, forasmuch as we have sworn both of us in the name of the LORD, saying, The LORD be between me and thee, and between my seed and thy seed for ever"* (v. 42).

This solemn oath not only reinforces their personal bond, but also has future implications for their descendants. The enduring nature of their covenant will later be honored by David in his kindness to Jonathan's son Mephibosheth (2 Samuel 9:1-13).

With this, David leaves, and Jonathan returns to the city. Thus begins a new chapter in David's life as he steps fully into his role as a fugitive. Meanwhile, Jonathan is left to navigate the dangerous waters of his father's increasingly volatile court.

This section of scripture highlights the power of their friendship, the cost of loyalty, and the tragic consequences of Saul's jealousy. It paints a vivid picture of the human drama at the heart of these historical events, reminding us of the deeply personal toll that political and familial conflict can take.

While this parting is significant, it's important to note that David and Jonathan will have one more encounter in 1 Samuel 23:16-18, further illuminating the depth of their bond.

Chapter 10:

DAVID AT NOB - A FUGITIVE'S STRUGGLE

1 Samuel 21:1-9

In the unfolding account of David's life, 1 Samuel 21 marks a critical juncture, offering a vivid portrayal of David as a fugitive, a man both cunning and devout, navigating the treacherous terrain of political and spiritual survival. This chapter, standing at the crossroads of David's transition from revered hero to a beleaguered outcast, presents a multifaceted character study steeped in tension, faith, and moral ambiguity.

In this chapter, we are not merely tracing David's physical journey but are also invited to ponder the deeper implications of his actions and decisions. The text challenges us to consider the complexities of faith when confronted with dire circumstances. How does David, an anointed yet beleaguered future king, navigate the tension between religious observance and practical survival? What do these events reveal about the nature of God's provision and protection in times of crisis?

As we explore 1 Samuel 21, we continue to piece together the mosaic of David's life, a life marked by divine favor, human frailty, and a relentless pursuit of God's will amidst life's uncertainties. This chapter, therefore, stands as a pivotal narrative in understanding David's journey from anointed shepherd boy to the king of Israel, offering profound insights into his character and his era.

David's Arrival and Inquiry at Nob (Verses 1-3)

On the run, David came to Nob, an unknown location speculated to be near modern day Jerusalem. We are

95

introduced to Ahimelech the priest. There is some confusion with the name, likely due to double names. Ahimelech, we believe, is the same person as Ahiah in 1 Samuel 14:3 and Abiathar in Mark 2:26. The priest expresses fear upon David's arrival, which turns out to be well-founded in the next chapter. Ahimelech asks what seems a natural question, *"Why* art *thou alone, and no man with thee?"* (v. 1). A man of such important position as David would rarely travel alone.

David's response is simple: *he lied.* He made up a story about being on a secret mission for the King, and therefore leaving his men at "such and such a place" (v. 2). The text uses the word יְנוֹמְלִא: [*almoni*]. The word *"is derived from 'almon' (a widower), bereft of a name, (as a widower is bereft of his spouse), for I do not wish to mention it, since it is a secret matter."*[1]

David proceeds to ask Ahimelech for whatever he has available. In this case, it happens to be the five loaves of shewbread from the Tabernacle. The text does not specify if David knows the type of bread, but it is likely that he does.

In this portion of the narrative, David appears desperate. His actions, including his lack of honesty and outright deception, can be interpreted in two ways. On one hand, we may judge him harshly for his actions. On the other hand, we can empathize with his situation, understanding that the pressure of hunger and fear can drive a person to extreme measures. This serves as a reminder of the human element in these biblical narratives, as even figures like

---

1   The Complete Jewish Bible with Rashi Commentary." Chabad.org, https://www.chabad.org/library/bible_cdo/aid/15850/showrashi/true. Accessed January 6, 2024.

David, anointed by God, struggle with their circumstances and make morally ambiguous decisions.

Ahimelech's Response and the Holy Bread (Verses 4-6):

Ahimelech explains that he only has the holy bread (showbread), which is usually reserved for priests. In the narrative, Ahimelech does not immediately agree to give David the holy bread. Instead, he appears to internally debate the decision, asking David if he and his men have kept themselves ceremonially clean. By focusing on the issue of ceremonial cleanliness, Ahimelech is essentially trying to find a justification for his inclination to help David. This reveals the complexity of his decision-making process and the moral dilemmas faced by those who found themselves caught in the political and religious crosswinds of the period.

In verse 5, David responds to the situation with another falsehood. He attests to the purity of the young men—the fictitious young men, as there are no such young men! This is a classic example of how one lie can lead to another, even in the life of King David.

David argues that the bread is, in a sense, common. He suggests that it's time to remove the bread and give it to the priests, a suggestion confirmed in verse 6, implying it's not technically the shewbread anymore. However, he continues to argue, even if it were freshly dedicated to the Table of Shewbread. While the text doesn't explicitly state it, as it appears to end mid-thought, it seems that David implies such desperate hunger would necessitate the priest's compassion in giving him the bread.

97

Once again, we observe the creativity of the mind when it fervently desires something. This holds true whether it's hunger, lust, or even some imagined need. The human mind struggles to perceive reality accurately when it is fixated on a desire.

Ultimately, Ahimelech gives David the holy bread, violating the letter of the law. It's unclear if there were other bread or provisions nearby, or why Ahimelech didn't propose an alternative. The situation was likely so seemingly critical and perilous that Ahimelech couldn't formulate another plan quickly enough.

This account is referenced by Jesus in Mark 2:25-26. He uses it to challenge the credibility of the Pharisees, who revered David but sought to destroy Jesus. Jesus neither condemns David nor Ahimelech (also known as Abiathar), but uses the event as an illustration of the Pharisees' inconsistency. They held Jesus to a different standard than they did David.

The Presence of Doeg the Edomite (Verse 7)

In verse 7, we encounter an *"uh oh"* moment. It appears there is a witness, and an important one at that. God introduces us to Doeg the Edomite, Saul's chief shepherd. He was *"detained before the LORD,"* possibly for some kind of ceremonial duty, but the circumstances are unclear. One rabbinical interpretation suggests that he was standing there, giving the impression of being religious by studying Torah, but was actually strategically eavesdropping.

While no further information is provided, the reader senses the foreshadowing of a plot twist.

It's important to note that Doeg is identified as *"an Edomite."* This refers to his ethnic group rather than his location. The land of Edom, located to the east of Jerusalem and across the Jordan, is home to the descendants of Esau. As such, they are considered *"cousins"* to the Jewish people.

David's Request for a Weapon (Verses 8-9):

In verse 8, David not only requests a sword but also adds the request to the list of lies, stating that he did not have a sword because *"the king's business required haste."* Ahimelech notes that there is only one sword, but it is an important and significant one, the one belonging to Goliath. The priest states that *"it is here wrapped in a cloth behind the ephod."*

Almost all translations and commentaries suggest that the sword was hidden behind the ephod. I want to provide support for another idea, held by ancient sages of Judaism like Rashi and Jonathan. This idea is that *"behind the ephod"* should be translated as *"following the ephod,"* with the suggestion that the ephod (including its Urim and Thummin) gave divine guidance for Ahimelech to give Goliath's sword (wherever it was kept) to David.

The text allows for such an interpretation, but is there additional evidence? Let's explore. Initially, Ahimelech was the high priest conducting his priestly duties. It's probable that he would be wearing ceremonial attire, including the ephod. So, if the sword was *"behind the ephod,"* this implies Ahimelech was carrying a concealed weapon during his priestly duties. Given the emphasis on ceremonially clean and ritually dedicated attire for the

99

high priest, the idea that Ahimelech was carrying Goliath's sword, hidden behind the ephod, seems unlikely.

Furthermore, 1 Samuel 17:51 tells us that David used that very sword to cut off Goliath's head. Therefore, the sword was not just a weapon of war, but one that had been used to kill Goliath. It seems unlikely that this could be considered ritually clean under any circumstances. Being a deadly weapon, it also seems highly unlikely that Ahimelech would hide it in a cloth behind the ephod. But it makes perfect sense that, upon David's request for a sword, and knowing of Doeg's presence, Ahimelech feels the need for divine guidance. Going to God through the Urim and Thummim, God instructs him to give David the sword of Goliath.

If this is true, then it could be God's protective act for David's life, hidden in plain sight within the text. God, despite David being a deceitful man on the run, protects him to fulfill His ultimate plan for Israel.

Chapter 11:

DAVID IN GATH:
A Study of Irony and Divine Providence

1 Samuel 21:10-15

David's Arrival in Gath (v. 10)

After departing from Nob, David carries with him the hallowed bread given by Ahimelech, the priest, and the sword of Goliath, a previous spoil of victory (vv. 1-9). David now has sustenance and sword, yet, he has no place to go.

Unexpectedly, he departs for Gath, Goliath's very city, and seeks refuge from Achish. Achish may not be the actual name of the King, as it could be a title. Outside of the Biblical text, we know nothing about him. Though Gath has been excavated (Tell es-Safi), no archeological clues as to his reign have been unearthed.

It's ironic that David would go to the very location of the Jewish Kingdom's arch-enemy. Was it due to panic or lack of options? Or was it a case of *"the enemy of my enemy is my friend?"* Was David thinking that he could take Goliath's sword and cut a deal? Or was he thinking he could slay his enemies in Gath with the sword and gain a foothold? It's unclear why David goes to Gath, but there is an interesting outcome in verse 11.

Recognition by the Servants of Achish (v. 11)

The King's servants make an unusual statement: *"Is not this David the king of the land?"* However, David was not the king of any land. He had been anointed by Samuel as the next king of Judea, but the extent to which this event was publicized is unknown. He definitely wasn't the king yet.

What if the servants were *recognizing David as the King of Gath?* It seems like a preposterous idea at first, but let's not forget 1 Samuel 17:9 in which Goliath proposed, *"If he be able to fight with me, and to kill me, then will we be your servants."* Could it be that the servants of Achish were telling the king that *David has a legitimate claim to the throne?* Further, in bringing up the fantastic songs about David, are they saying, *"we have a* huge *problem on our hands?"*

David's Realization and Response (vv. 12-13)

Regardless of David's intention in going to Gath, the king's servants' fear that David had arrived to claim the throne instilled fear in David himself. He quickly became *"sore afraid of Achish the king of Gath"* (v. 12). This fear suggests that this situation was not part of David's original plan. Instead, he appears to have been taken by surprise by their reaction.

And so, as we have seen before, David makes a quick and seemingly rash decision. Knowing he needs to act, he acts crazy...literally. David *"feigned himself mad"* (v. 13), along with all the requisite behaviors of a madman.

This brings up so many questions about David and his leadership. Is David an impetuous young man who doesn't think through a situation before he gets himself into it? Or is David a brilliant young man who knows how to get out of a dangerous situation? Is David showing a habit of lies in order to protect himself, and is this a characteristic we want in a king?

As in the previous situation at Nob, I suspect that none of us can fully imagine what we would do in a sudden life-threatening situation. Especially considering David is a very young man, possibly not even 20, it seems we should be gracious in judgement. This grace is even more appropriate since we are at such a disadvantage of knowing the facts of the situation at hand.

Sometimes Christians engage in debates about the morality of behavior in certain biblical passages, like this one. In this case, the Bible itself does not debate, but merely states the facts. It might be best to leave it at that.

Achish's Dismissal of David (vv. 14-15)

It seems as if the King did not know that it was David in his midst. With other things on the agenda, he chastised his servants for bringing this madman, and sent David on his way. Whether divine providence or quick thinking, David was spared what would have at least been a battle, if not arrest and death.

Psalm 34: A Commentary On The Gath Experience

The Psalm Itself

Psalm 34 is inscribed as "A Psalm of David, when he changed his behavior before Abimelech; who drove him away, and he departed" (v. 1). Note that **Abimelech** is the same as Achish.

In verses 1-4, David gives praise to God for delivering him. This makes it rather difficult to call this deception an immoral act. Perhaps it was God's mean of getting David out of danger? David certainly sought it that way.

In verses 5-10, celebrate the salvation that the Lord gave in this tense situation. David's view is certainly that the Lord, "saved him out of all his troubles" (v. 6).

103

In verses 11-16 almost seem to be a *"lessons learned"* segment of the Gath experience. David seems to commit himself to trusting in the Lord and refraining from deceptive behavior.

Verses 17-18 give a general lesson, and a great encouragement: "The righteous *cry, and the LORD heareth*" (v. 17).

In verses 19-22 David closes his *alphabetic acrostic* of praise. In verse 20 he celebrates, *"He keepeth all his bones: not one of them is broken."* This was shown to be a prophetic word of the coming Messiah, mentioned shortly after the death of the Lord when the Roman soldiers did not break the bones of the Savior.

David As A Type

I am convinced that each Psalm is prophetic of Israel's future. Since Psalm 34 and so many others reflect on something in Israel's past, this creates a level of interpretation in which events of the past foreshadow truths of the future, or *typology*. The Jewish teachers call this *"Remez"* (hint or allusion).

There are three kinds of prophetic Psalms: revelation (which provides information not known in other passages), remnant (which speaks of the tribulation), and reign (which speaks of the millennial kingdom). Since Psalm 34 is a victorious afterthought, it is a Psalm of *"reign."* This implies that during the tribulation Israel will either be considered to have gone mad, or even feign madness, in order to escape an almost sure death.

Such an interpretation is, of course, implicit, not explicit, and thus must be approached with caution. However, there is no doubt that Psalm 34 is explicitly tied to the Achish event. It is also explicitly broader than the event, celebrating the salvation of the nation, not just the man.

Conclusion

What an encouragement that an account that seems so suspicious has become not only celebrated in the Psalm but even Messianic and Millennial in outlook. Ultimately, the Psalm celebrates the rescue that God will give to Israel at the Second Coming, when Messiah begins to reign. It is a reminder that *all is not what it seems*. In this case, what appears to be a bad decision and a moral failure turns out to be the grounds of the celebration of deliverance.

Chapter 12

From Fugitive to Leader:

David's Ascent at Adullam

1 Samuel 22:1-5

In the unfolding drama of David's life, a significant turn of events led him to the cave of Adullam, a refuge in the wilderness. This escape was not merely a flight from danger, but a pivotal transition in his journey from a favored servant of King Saul to a fugitive, and eventually, a leader of men.

David's departure from Saul's court was marked by a series of harrowing escapes. With Saul's jealousy turning into deadly intent, David found himself increasingly in peril. His first escape was a dramatic evasion, as his wife Michal, Saul's daughter, helped him flee through a window, using an image and goat's hair to deceive the pursuers. From there, David's path was one of constant movement and uncertainty.

Seeking refuge, David first went to Samuel at Ramah, sharing his plight with the prophet who had anointed him. However, even here, Saul's reach extended as messengers sent to capture David were divinely hindered, repeatedly falling into prophetic ecstasy.

Realizing the gravity of his situation, David made a pivotal decision to leave Israel's heartland. He journeyed to Nob, where he encountered Ahimelech the priest. In a moment of desperation, David deceived Ahimelech, claiming to be on a secret mission for Saul. This stop was crucial as David obtained Goliath's sword here, a symbol of his past victory and perhaps, a reminder of God's deliverance.

The next phase of his escape took him to the Philistine city of Gath, where he sought refuge with King Achish. However, the danger of seeking shelter with Israel's enemies soon became apparent. Recognized by the Philistines, David feigned madness to save his life, an act of desperation that underlined his precarious situation.

But as we enter into 1 Samuel 22, though David is still on the run, we will encounter the first glimpses of David as King.

David's Escape to Adullam (Verse 1)

David's escape led him to *"the cave of Adullam."* The exact location of this cave is not definitively known, but it is generally believed to be situated in the Shephelah area, just outside of Philistine territory and Gaza. Today, in that region, there are quarry-made caves known as the *"Bell Caves."* These were formed much later, during the Byzantine era, but they provide a sense of the kind of environment David might have encountered.

To gain a deeper understanding of David's emotions during this period, one can look to Psalm 142. This psalm was written by David *"when he was in the cave."* It is not specified whether this refers to his time in the cave of Adullam or another instance, but the psalm gives us a glimpse into the despair, loneliness, and ultimately, the hope and reassurance David experienced during this period of his life.

While at the cave, **"his brethren hear, and all the house of his father."** It's unclear whether this was intentional or accidental. However, the text does not indicate that his whereabouts being somewhat public information is cause for concern. Given David's somewhat tumultuous past relationship with his family, it's unclear whether he rejoiced at or regretted their arrival.

Gathering of the Discontented (Verse 2)

As David settles into the cave of Adullam, a remarkable transformation begins. No longer a solitary fugitive, David becomes a magnet for others who are also struggling under Saul's reign. The text in 1 Samuel 22:2 paints a vivid picture of those who are drawn to David:

The people who come to David are described in three distinct groups:

1. **Those in Distress:** This group likely includes individuals who are suffering under Saul's increasingly unstable and oppressive rule. Their distress could be political, social, or personal. In ancient Israel, being in distress often meant living under unjust treatment or persecution. These individuals saw in David not just a fugitive but a potential deliverer, someone who had also known great suffering and could empathize with their plight.

2. **Those in Debt:** Economic hardship was a common plight in the ancient world. Those in debt might have been facing servitude or extreme poverty due to unfair taxation or economic policies under Saul's rule. Their coming to David signifies their hope for a leader who would understand and possibly alleviate their economic burdens.

3. **Those Discontented with the Current State of Affairs:** This group represents a broader dissatisfaction with Saul's kingship. They were likely disillusioned with the direction in which Saul was taking the nation, longing for change and a return to godly leadership. These individuals saw in David the qualities of a true king as anointed by Samuel – a leader who would rule with justice, integrity, and in accordance with God's will.

The Formation of a Loyal Band

Remarkably, about four hundred men gather around David. This significant number indicates that David's appeal and influence extend far beyond his immediate family or personal acquaintances. These men, in their collective diversity of struggles, recognize David's leadership and anointing.

David Assumes Leadership

At this point, David implicitly takes on the role of a leader for these men. We are told that *"he became a captain over them,"* being the first time that David has an army, yet his leadership suggests more than just a military role; it points to moral and spiritual guidance. David subtly emerges as a beacon of hope and a potential agent of change for those who felt they had no other option.

This gathering at Adullam is a microcosm of what David's future kingship will represent: a refuge for the downtrodden, a voice for the voiceless, and a leader who draws his strength not from wealth or power but from his ability to connect with and lead people from all walks of life. It foreshadows the kind of king David will become – one whose reign is marked by a deep understanding of the needs and struggles of his people.

A Repeated Pattern

Indeed, the Bible often presents us with a microcosm of humanity that recurs throughout history. The gathering of those in distress, in debt, and in discontent, and their transformation into a loyal band, is a scenario that has been replayed countless times. From the oppressed Israelites banding together under Moses for their exodus from Egypt, to the early Christian communities forming around the teachings of Jesus, we see over and over again how those under hardship or oppression seek change and find solace in collective action. This pattern not only underscores the enduring human capacity for resilience and hope, but also reminds us of the transformative power of compassionate and visionary leadership, as embodied by figures like David.

David's Provision for His Parents (Verses 3-4)

David's next move takes him into Moab, which is an interesting choice considering the Moabites' tumultuous history with Israel. However, at this particular time, there is no indication that the Moabites were enemies, unlike the Philistines in Gath. Recognizing a potential ally and a safer location, David approaches the King of Moab.

David's primary concern is the safety of his parents. Therefore, he respectfully asks the king if his parents could stay in Moab until he knows what God will do for him. This phrase *"till that I know what God doth for me"* can be interpreted in two ways. It either suggests that David is uncertain about his future, or he is unclear about how God will fulfill His promise. However, given that David has already been anointed as king, it's likely that he has some level of confidence in his future, although the path to it may be unclear.

Consequently, David's parents stayed in Moab while David was in *"the fortress."* This period of time in the fortress possibly refers to the stronghold in the cave of Adullam, or it might refer to a different location in Moab.

Intriguingly, this is the last time we ever see David's parents. We are not fully aware of what happened to them.

Rashi, a medieval Jewish scholar, introduces a narrative, not found in the biblical text, that when David left the stronghold for the forest of Hereth, the king of Moab killed David's parents and siblings. This act of betrayal is not mentioned in the canonical text of the Bible but is a tradition found in some midrashic literature, which are ancient Jewish exegetical texts that provide additional details to biblical stories. One of David's brothers is said to have survived the massacre, preserved by Nahash, the Ammonite king. Rashi connects this story to a later event in 2 Samuel 10:2, where David speaks of kindness that had been shown to him, interpreting it as a reference to the survival of his brother due to the intervention of Nahash.

Divine Direction through the Prophet Gad (Verse 5)

Introducing Gad

Gad the prophet is a biblical figure who appears in several passages in the Hebrew Bible, particularly in the books of Samuel. Here's what we know about him based on the biblical text:

1. **Advisor to David:** Gad is first mentioned in 1 Samuel 22:5, where he advises David to leave the stronghold and go into the land of Judah. This suggests that Gad had a role as a counselor or prophet providing divine guidance to David during his period of fleeing from King Saul.

2. **Historiographer of David:** Gad is also noted to be a historian or recorder of events during David's reign. In 1 Chronicles 29:29, the *"acts of David the king, first and last,"* are recorded in the writings of Samuel the seer, Nathan the prophet, and Gad the seer. This

indicates that Gad was involved in documenting the history of David's reign, contributing to what might have been a larger chronicle of Israel's history during this time.

3. **Gad's Writings:** While Gad's writings are mentioned, they are not part of the biblical canon, and no such writings are known to exist today. They might have been sources used in the compilation of the Books of Samuel or Chronicles.

4. **Other Appearances:** Gad appears later in 2 Samuel 24, during David's census of Israel and Judah. In this story, God is displeased with the census, and Gad, as David's seer, presents David with three options as divine retribution for his actions. David chooses a plague, which Gad is then instructed to announce.

Gad's Directive

Gad, the prophet, instructs David to depart from *"the stronghold"* and move into the land of Judah. David complies with this instruction and relocates to the forest of Hareth. The forest of Hareth is believed to be located in the hill country of Judah, though its exact location is not definitively known.

By advising David to leave the stronghold where he was hiding and move to the land of Judah, Gad may have helped David avoid capture by King Saul, who was pursuing him. This change in location could have been a strategic move that helped ensure David's safety at a critical time. However, the text does not confirm whether or not Saul was in pursuit of David and headed toward the stronghold.

Another interpretation is that Gad, recognizing David's future role as the king of Judah, instructed him to take a more aggressive and public stance. By moving to the land of Judah, David was effectively aligning himself with his future kingdom, positioning himself as a leader, and challenging the status quo of Saul's reign. This bold move could have been a strategic step towards his eventual ascension to the throne.

Conclusion

The narrative of 1 Samuel 22:1-5 is a significant turning point in David's life. From being a fugitive, he transitions to assume a leadership role. The cave of Adullam becomes a gathering point for those in distress, in debt, and dissatisfied with Saul's reign. David's appeal and influence extend to draw about four hundred men, marking the beginning of his leadership. Furthermore, David's move to the forest of Hareth, upon Gad the prophet's advice, aligns him with his future kingdom. This proactive move positions him as a leader and challenges the status quo of Saul's reign, effectively setting the stage for his eventual ascension to the throne.

Chapter 13:

MASSACRE AT NOB

1 Samuel 22:6-23

In the preceding verses of 1 Samuel 22, David's fortunes took a turn. He found refuge in the cave of Adullam, where people in distress, in debt or discontented rallied around him. David, once a solitary fugitive, now found himself the leader of at least 400 men.

As David's star rose among the discontented, Saul's paranoia grew. And this is where our story picks up.

Saul's Paranoia (Verses 6-8)

There are one of two possibilities explaining how Saul became aware of David's whereabouts and his growing group of followers. Firstly, the fame of David and his 400 followers may have simply become too significant to keep hidden, and word naturally spread. Alternatively, the direction given to David by Gad could have implied that he was to boldly confront Saul, which would mean there was no effort to keep their activities secret. Regardless of the exact circumstances, it is clear from the text: *"Saul heard that David was discovered, and the men that were with him"* (v. 6).

Saul was at his hometown, Gibeah, at this time. The text describes him as "abiding in Gibeah under a tree". However, it's important to note that this doesn't literally mean he was living under a tree. Instead, it's a description of where he was when he heard the news about David and his followers. He was situated under a tree in Gibeah when he received this information.

The imagery of a king sitting under a tree is actually quite common in ancient Near Eastern literature. It symbolizes a place of judgment or ruling. For example, in the book of Judges, Deborah, a judge of Israel, held court under a palm tree (Judges 4:5). Similarly, Absalom, King David's son, used to sit under a terebinth tree to offer judgment to those who had any dispute or claim (2 Samuel 15:2-6). So, when we read that Saul was *"abiding in Gibeah under a tree,"* it suggests he was likely performing kingly duties or holding court.

While *"Ramah"* is known as a town within the territory of Benjamin and holds significance as such, the Hebrew word "הָרָמָה" (*Ramah*) can also mean a *"high place"* or *"hill."* I suspect that this is the usage of the word in verse 6.

The term *"paranoia"* originates from the Greek words *"para,"* meaning *"beside, near, along with,"* and *"nous,"* which stands for *"mind, intellect."* Originally, it was used to describe a mental condition where a person loses touch with reality. Over time, it has evolved to refer to an irrational fear or distrust that others are conspiring against them.

In verses 7-8, Saul's paranoia becomes evident. He fears his servants are *"for sale,"* with David being the highest bidder, potentially granting them monetary and leadership benefits if they follow him. If there were any signs that David was actively seeking the throne or planning a coup, Saul's concerns would not be characterized as paranoia. However, with no such indications and knowing that David has demonstrated kindness and honesty towards the king, we can only conclude that Saul is indeed paranoid.

Saul's accusations of conspiracy also suggest that he must have discovered the episode between David and Jonathan (1 Samuel 20:35-42). This was a covert signal agreed upon between David and Jonathan to communicate Saul's intentions towards David. Saul, in his paranoia, likely believed that his men knew of this *"league with the son of Jesse"* and had deliberately kept him in the dark, further fueling his suspicion and mistrust.

All we know about Jonathan is that he was a loyal son, striving to see the best in his father while also attempting to safeguard his friend David's life. Nothing in the biblical record portrays Jonathan negatively regarding his support for his father's reign. Again, the only conclusion we can make is that Saul suffers from paranoia.

Doeg's Report (Verses 9-10)

Do you recall Doeg the Edomite, subtly mentioned in 1 Samuel 21:7, during David's visit to Nob, where he pleaded with Ahimilech the High Priest? Here comes the snake again! Doeg seems eager to share a report he had been holding onto, waiting for the right moment, and now, it has arrived. "I saw the son of Jesse coming to Nob," Doeg reports in v. 9. Regarding Ahimilech, Doeg reports, "he inquired of the LORD for him, gave him provisions, and gave him the sword of Goliath" (v. 10). The glee in Doeg's voice is almost audible.

In this passage, we find an interesting confirmation that Ahimelech *"inquired of the LORD for him."* This may remind you of our commentary on 1 Samuel 21:9, regarding the sword that was *"wrapped in a garment behind the ephod."* I had previously commented on this point, saying;

> I want to provide support for another idea, held by ancient sages of Judaism like Rashi and Jonathan. This idea is that "behind the ephod" should be translated as *"following the ephod,"* with the suggestion that

> the ephod (including its Urim and Thummin) gave divine guidance for Ahimelech to give Goliath's sword (wherever it was kept) to David.

This idea seems confirmed with the report from Doeg that Ahimelech *"inquired of the LORD for him."*

Saul's Cruelty | vv. 11-19

King Saul calls on Ahimelech the priest and his entire family from Nob to question them about their dealings with David. Ahimelech is accused of conspiring against Saul with David. The priest responds with an assertion of ignorance. As he states in verse 14, David had always shown public loyalty to the King. Was Ahimelech expected to treat him any differently that what he had proven himself to be? Furthermore, you might remember that David asserted he was on a special mission for Saul. On what grounds could Ahimelech have dismissed David's testimony?

In 1 Samuel 22:15, Ahimelech's statement, *"Did I then begin to enquire of God for him? be it far from me,"* can be seen as a justification of his actions, not a denial. He's not negating the act of consulting God for David; instead, he emphasizes that these priestly services to David were routine, not unique to this specific instance. Ahimelech is indicating that consulting God on behalf of David (or anyone else) was part of his regular priestly duties, not a special service suggesting a conspiracy against Saul.

His statement can be viewed as a rhetorical question emphasizing the normalcy of his actions. He's pointing out that his conduct was not unusual or conspiratorial; it conformed with his regular priestly responsibilities, which he's performed over time, including during Saul's reign. The phrase *"be it far from me"* strongly rejects the idea that his service to David was a recent or unique act motivated by disloyalty to Saul.

In fact, Ahimelech's response is not a denial or evasion but a declaration of truth about his priestly role. He's not trying to absolve himself through denial but aims to clarify the nature of his priestly duties. His actions towards David were not unusual or suggestive of a conspiracy against Saul. Instead, they were an integral part of his priestly duties, including providing religious services to all who approached him, like consulting the Lord on their behalf. This practice was standard and not specific to David. To sum up, Ahimelech is stating that his actions were in accordance with his priestly role and responsibilities and should not be misinterpreted as an act of disloyalty towards Saul.

Ahimelech's words of truth and reason fall on deaf ears as Saul is consumed by paranoia, disregarding any attempt at rational explanation. Saul, in his blinded state, orders his footmen to execute Ahimelech and the priests of Nob. However, these men, guided by a stronger moral compass, refuse to *"put forth their hand to fall upon the priests of the LORD"* (v. 17). They will not stoop so low as to commit such a heinous act.

Seeing his orders disobeyed, Saul turns to Doeg the Edomite, who harbors no such moral qualms. Whether he acts alone or with the assistance of others, the text does not specify. Doeg engages in a horrific massacre, slaughtering 85 defenseless priests. His bloodlust not yet quenched, Doeg proceeds to the priestly town of Nob for further carnage, leaving devastation in his wake. This chilling act of violence marks a dark moment in the history of Israel, underlining the depths to which Saul's paranoia has sunk him.

Abiathar's Escape (Verses 20-23)

One son, Abiathar, providentially escapes the massacre and flees to David to report the tragic event. David, upon hearing the news, is filled with grief and remorse. He recognizes his own role in the tragedy, as he had suspected Doeg's malicious intentions from their initial encounter in Nob. However, David is also quick to assure Abiathar. He promises to provide him with protection and safety under his care, demonstrating his characteristic empathy and responsibility.

In the upcoming Chapter 23, we will observe the providential significance of this event. The Ephod, being the means of communicating with God, was kept by the high priest. The high priest was selected by lineage, therefore, Abiathar, now being the sole survivor of the priestly line, naturally assumes this role. With the ephod and its blessings in his possession, Abiathar is now the high priest of Israel, and most importantly, he has aligned himself with David.

The Psalm 52 Connection

The story becomes even more dramatic when we link it to Psalm 52, which is believed to have been written by David after he heard about the massacre at Nob. In this psalm, David expresses his horror and shock at the senseless violence carried out by Doeg the Edomite. He also condemns the evil of those who use their tongues to deceive and destroy, a direct reference to Doeg's report to Saul that led to the massacre. This connection provides a powerful emotional context to the events described in 1 Samuel 22, highlighting the deep personal impact they had on David.

But it also gives us prophetic insight. In the prophetic nature of the Psalms, the wicked man is almost always a prophetic reference to the coming Antichrist. This makes Psalm 52 a prophecy of the Antichrist, and Doeg a "type" of the Antichrist. Interestingly, King Herod, who was also an Edomite, is often considered another type of Antichrist.

In his work *"The Numerical Bible,"* F. W. Grant suggests that Doeg the Edomite serves as a relatively weak representative, or typology, of the ultimate enemy of God and humanity in the end times, often referred to as the Antichrist. This interpretation further underscores the biblical narrative's prophetic undertones. Grant calls Doeg, "a feeble representative of the great enemy of God and man at the time of the end."[2]

From this perspective, we might question whether Doeg's action against Ahimelech reflects future events. Could it be possible that the Antichrist will kill the priests of Israel, except for one who manages to escape?

Conclusion

In conclusion, 1 Samuel 22:6-23 exposes the depths of Saul's paranoia and the horrific violence it leads to, resulting in the massacre at Nob. Despite the tragedy, we also witness divine providence at work, as Abiathar escapes to join David, bringing with him the ephod.

---

2   F. W. Grant, *The Numerical Bible; Being a Revised Translation of the Holy Scriptures with Expository Notes: Arranged, Divided, and Briefly Characterized according to the Principles of Their Numerical Structure: The Psalms (Study Text)* (Neptune, NJ: Loizeaux Brothers, 1897), 210.

The Davidic Chronicles

This chapter underscores the destructive consequences of unchecked paranoia and the importance of staying grounded in truth and reason. In the face of adversity, we see David's empathy and sense of responsibility shine through, providing a beacon of hope in these dark times. As we continue our study, we look forward to understanding more about the providential significance of these events and their implications for Israel's future.

Chapter 14

The Trials of David in Keilah and Ziph

1 Samuel 23:1-29

David Saves Keilah (1 Samuel 23:1-5)

As we delve into the narrative of 1 Samuel 23, we find ourselves amid the tumultuous period of King Saul's reign. In this chapter, we encounter the town of Keilah, a fortified city situated in the lowlands of Judah. Keilah is a town known for its agricultural prosperity, with its walls, gates, and threshing floors where grain is processed. Yet, this prosperity has attracted the unwelcome attention of the Philistines, a formidable force and a recurring antagonist in the lives of the Israelites.

The Philistines invade, intent on crippling the economic lifelines of their adversaries. Terrorizing the inhabitants of Keilah, they seize the harvested grain from the threshing floors. Such actions are not just attacks on resources but are also psychological warfare, striking fear and despair into the hearts of the Israelites.

In this climate of fear and uncertainty, the inhabitants of Keilah find themselves in a dire predicament. It is worth noting that their appeal for help is directed not towards King Saul, the reigning monarch, but towards David. At this juncture, David, anointed but not yet crowned, is with his band of over 400 men, forging a life in the wilderness of Judah. Despite his own precarious situation, marked by Saul's relentless pursuit, David stands as a figure of hope and deliverance for those in distress.

Uncertain of what to do, David *"enquired of the LORD"* (v. 2). It's unclear whether this was simply his own prayer, or if he consulted Abiathar the high priest who had the ephod. Regardless, God's command was explicit: *"David, Go!"*

But the men were not so sure. This was a new *"army,"* if it could even be called that. The army was made up of those who were under distress, in debt, and discontent (1 Sam. 22:1), none of which necessarily comes with a healthy dose of bravery. One thing they were not afraid of was expressing their fear, and recognizing that being afraid while hiding in the forest was surely a bad thing for needing bravery in going up against the enemy.

David took the extra measure of caution and assurance, inquiring of the Lord a second time, and a second time hearing God say, *"Go!"* This time there was the added assurance, *"I will deliver the Philistines into thine hand"* (v. 4). God did just as He promised, and gave David a great victory.

This act of military heroism could do nothing else, i suppose, than strengthen David's following and giving him credibility as a brave man of war and warfare. While he had already proven this in his own right, this episode shows David as a leader who, even in dire circumstances, is not going to back away from what needs to be done.

Time, however, will not allow David much time to revel in victory, as we see in verses 6-14.

Saul Pursues David (1 Samuel 23:6-14)

It's unclear whether Abiathar joined David before or after the battle. However, it's evident that he had the ephod, and thus held the unique power to inquire of the Lord. This was before the time when anyone could approach God directly, as Israel was under the priestly system.

When Saul learns that David is in Keilah, he sees it as a great opportunity. Verse 7 reveals two things about Saul in this context. Firstly, he was a strategic thinker with military acumen, aware that David was in a location that could be easily isolated. However, it also shows that Saul, despite believing that *"God hath delivered him into mine hand,"* failed to realize that the Lord had abandoned him and was now with David. This lack of spiritual discernment was the most perilous facet of Saul's leadership.

Saul gathered the troops, *"to go down to Keilah, to besiege David"* (v. 8). One wonders where Saul was when the real enemy was terrorizing his own citizens. Why had Saul not instinctively done what David had done, risking his life to protect his realm? This, again, displays a self-serving and out-of-touch King.

By verse 9, David clearly has access to the ephod, and gives the Lord a two-fold inquiry. Firstly, will Saul, who was known to have "secretly practiced mischief" against David, come to Keilah for David? Clearly David had inclination or indication that Saul would be coming for him. Secondly, David wanted to know, *"Will the men of Keilah deliver me up into his hand?"*

But I have presented this in its natural and expected order, and David presented it to the Lord in reverse order, first asking if the men of Keilah would hand him over, and second if Saul would even come. Why did David do this? The text gives no answer. It could be inconsequential, or it could be David, strategically thinking, *"What if God only answers one of my questions?"* Clearly the question about the men of Keilah was more important.

127

The answer concerning the men of Keilah came back in the affirmative, which was certainly bad news for David and his men. They were not safe even if Saul did not arrive.

But why would the citizens not stand at David's side and rise to his aid if he needed it? Why would they disregard the heroic act of bravery that saved them from their enemy?

It seems to be human nature to sometimes overlook those who do the most for us, particularly when the danger has passed. However, I suspect this wasn't just a typical forgetfulness brought on by worldly worries. Perhaps the citizens of Keilah were simply showing loyalty to the reigning king, as was their obligation. And fear itself could have been their motivator. David wasn't going to harm them...but Saul might.

David and his men, now numbering 600, departed. The move was wise, for Saul had been informed and cancelled his trip to Keilah.

The small army retreated to *"a mountain in the wilderness of Ziph"* (v. 14). This wilderness area is located south of Hebron, within the larger Judean wilderness. While he was in hiding, *"Saul sought him every day, but God delivered him not into his hand."*

Jonathan's Encouragement (1 Samuel 23:15-18)

In the midst of David's exile in the Wilderness of Ziph, an unexpected reunion occurs. Jonathan, David's steadfast friend and ally, manages to locate David. The text does not elaborate on how Jonathan was able to find David in this vast wilderness, a detail that only serves to underscore the extraordinary nature of this feat.

Venturing into this wilderness, Jonathan was undoubtedly putting his own life at risk. He was venturing away from the relative safety of his father's court into a dangerous wilderness, and aligning himself with a fugitive. Yet, Jonathan's courage and loyalty to David are unwavering. He seeks out David not out of a sense of duty, but out of deep friendship and shared faith.

When they met, Jonathan *"strengthened his hand in God"* (v. 16). This phrase, clearly metaphorical, does not appear elsewhere in the Scriptures. *"Hand"* is likely best interpreted as his *"position."* With Jonathan's support, even though secret, both heart and mind are uplifted.

In Verse 17, we find Jonathan providing a tremendous source of encouragement to David, assuring him that *"the hand of Saul my father shall not find thee."* It's important to note that this statement isn't prophetic in nature, but rather a testament to Jonathan's conviction and his commitment to preventing such an occurrence. He goes on to assert, with certainty, that David is destined to be the next king of Israel. Interestingly, he also states, *"I shall be next unto thee."* However, as the narrative unfolds, we find that due to Jonathan's untimely death in battle, this part of his assurance never materializes. The conviction that David would ascend to the throne was not only held by Jonathan but also, as he concludes, by Saul. It's unlikely that this knowledge was communicated directly, but rather, Saul's knowledge is discerned by Jonathan. This fact further highlighting the complex dynamics at play.

As the encounter between David and Jonathan concludes, they renew the covenant they had previously established, reinforcing their fraternal bond. This was more than a mere agreement between friends; it was a sacred pact, made before God. This moment of shared faith and commitment, set against the backdrop of danger and uncertainty, undoubtedly carried profound emotional weight for both David and Jonathan. It stands as a testament to their unwavering friendship, mutual respect, and shared destiny.

Indeed, the friendship between David and Jonathan is one of the most profound and moving relationships in the Bible. Their unyielding loyalty, mutual respect, and shared faith serve as a model of true friendship. This reunion in the Wilderness of Ziph marks their last meeting, adding a layer of poignancy to their parting. Despite the danger and uncertainty of their circumstances, their bond remains unbroken, reflecting the depth of their commitment to each other. The subsequent chapters in 1 Samuel detail the continued pursuit of David by Saul and the eventual tragic end of Saul and Jonathan, who die in battle as recorded in 1 Samuel 31. David's lament over Jonathan's death is found in 2 Samuel 1:17-27.

The Ziphites' Betrayal and Saul's Continued Pursuit (1 Samuel 23:19-29)

In a display of treacherous opportunism, the Ziphites approach Saul, divulging David's location in their territory. They not only reveal his whereabouts but also proffer their assistance in capturing him, promising to deliver David into Saul's hands. This act of betrayal underscores the precariousness of David's situation, as he navigates through a landscape marred by shifting allegiances and the constant threat of being handed over to his relentless pursuer, King Saul.

130

Saul, seizing the opportunity provided by the Ziphites, commands them to meticulously track David's movements. This sparks a tense and perilous game of *"cat and mouse,"* with Saul in relentless pursuit and David ingeniously evading capture. Throughout verses 21-26, David's life hangs by a thread as he masterfully navigates the wilderness, leveraging his wisdom and survival skills. This episode not only showcases David's adeptness in wilderness tactics but also illustrates a fundamental truth: the concealed inherently possess a strategic advantage over the seeker, a principle that David skillfully exploits to stay a step ahead of Saul's advances.

In verses 27-28, the intense pursuit of David by Saul is abruptly halted by an urgent call to confront a Philistine incursion, an intervention that can only be seen as providential. This unexpected development leads to the naming of the place as *"Selahammahlekoth,"* a symbolic designation reflecting the dramatic turn of events. *"Selahammahlekoth,"* meaning *"rock of division"* or *"rock of escape,"* a reminder of the exact location where Saul's pursuit was forcibly divided from David's flight, marking the spot where the king had to abandon his chase and turn back, leaving David to live another day.

From here, David moves to nearby Engedi, an oasis on the Dead Sea, to find a place of sanctuary in the rugged terrain.

Chapter 15:

DAVID'S INTEGRITY:

Navigating Morality, Strategy, and Divine Order

1 Samuel 24, 26

Setting The Stage (Verses 1-3)

You may remember that chapter 23 concluded with a crisis that Saul had to address. This crisis potentially saved David's life by sending Saul far away, allowing David time to escape. However, Saul has now returned and discovered that David is in Engedi.

En-gedi is an oasis region located on the eastern edge of the Judean Desert, near the Dead Sea, in what is now Israel. The area is characterized by rugged hills, rocky cliffs, and deep ravines. Despite the arid desert surroundings, En-gedi is known for its fresh water springs and lush vegetation, making it a place of refuge in the harsh wilderness.

The variations in spelling, Engedi in the King James Version (KJV) of the Bible and En-Gedi in modern references, are due to differences in transliteration methods. Transliteration is the process of converting letters or characters from one alphabet or script to another. Over time, transliteration practices have evolved, leading to differences in the spelling of some biblical place names in newer Bible translations and modern references when compared to the KJV. The modern spelling, *"En-Gedi,"* reflects the current standard transliteration from the original Hebrew.

Saul took a considerable force of 3,000 men with him—a sizeable number for almost any battle, but particularly huge for the task of capturing just one man and his ragtag army of 600. Nevertheless, David had the strategic advantage of having arrived there first. The topography of the area, with its high vantage points and numerous caves, rocky crags, bushes, and other hiding spots, all served to David's advantage.

"Rocks of the wild goats" refers to the rugged, rocky terrain of the area where wild goats could often be found. These goats were well adapted to the harsh conditions and were able to navigate the steep cliffs and rocky crags with ease.

"Sheepcotes" are shelters or enclosures for sheep. In the context of this scripture, they likely refer to natural caves or crevices in the rocks that were used as makeshift shelters for sheep or goats.

We should be reminded that shepherding in the desert is an ancient practice and a vital part of life in many desert societies. The arid and harsh environment of the desert requires specific skills and knowledge for successful shepherding. Shepherds must be familiar with the locations of water sources and grazing areas, which are often scarce and may be distant from each other. Herds typically consist of sheep or goats, both of which are well-adapted to desert conditions. Sheep are grazers, preferring to eat grasses and other ground vegetation, while goats are browsers and will eat a variety of plant life, including shrubs and trees.

Shepherds move their flocks seasonally, following rains and the growth of new plants. This is often a challenging task due to the extreme temperatures, lack of water, and potential threat of predators. Despite these challenges, desert shepherding has sustained communities for thousands of years, providing meat, milk, wool, and hides.

David, being a shepherd himself, had a further strategic advantage. He doubtlessly had spent many months at a time in locations just like this, giving him an intimate knowledge of the terrain and how to navigate it.

The phrase "to cover his feet" is a *"Hebraism,"* a characteristic feature of the Hebrew language. In this case, it serves as a polite way to refer to Saul's need to relieve himself. This phrase is also found in other biblical passages. For example, in Judges 3:24, after Ehud left Eglon, the King's servants waited to the point of embarrassment for their master to finish *"covering his feet"* in the cool chamber.

It is interesting to note that many modern versions of the Bible, which claim to be the *"most literal,"* are in fact, non-literal in many phrases, opting for interpretation rather than direct translation. One such example is the phrase *"to cover his feet,"* which is translated in many versions as *"relieving himself."* This interpretative translation creates a distance between the English reader and the original text, preventing the reader from questioning the translators' decisions. This could potentially be exactly what the translators intended, to shield their interpretations from scrutiny.

Saul was not aware that David and his men were present in the cave, suggesting that perhaps the entire group of 600 were not with David at that time, considering the size limitations of most caves in the area.

David Spares Saul's Life (Verses 4-7)

In verse 4, a quote is attributed to God. However, it's worth noting that there is ambiguity surrounding this quote. It is unclear whether God directly communicated this promise, or if David's men inferred it as God's will or intent.

Both interpretations could hold some merit, but it's challenging to find any fulfillment of the prophecy unless this episode does so. My perspective is that these men presumed these words upon God. They knew God had anointed David and extrapolated this to mean that Saul was being delivered to David to do as he pleased.

An incidental area where this becomes interesting is when New Testament writers are sometimes accused of *"making up"* quotes that do not actually exist. This serves as a reminder that quotes can be provided in the Scripture, even if they were not previously recorded.

Whether God directly promised this to David, or David's men simply inferred it from the situation, David acted nobly and discreetly cut the corner of Saul's robe. It's questionable if David's men viewed this as a noble deed. It was their moment of opportunity - perhaps the only one they would ever have. In giving up this opportunity, with 3,000 men out to get him, the chances of things worsening were substantial.

David's heart was immediately convicted, providing an intimate glimpse into the life of one of history's greatest figures. He deeply trusted the Lord's timing and protection, to the point where he felt remorse for merely cutting Saul's garment. In David's view, Saul was still his *"master"* (אֲדֹנִי - *adoni*) and *"the Lord's anointed."* In David's mind, the fate of Saul was solely the prerogative of God Himself.

136

Verse 7 states that David *"stayed his servants,"* suggesting they were initially prepared to kill him, but were also highly obedient to David's directive. Consequently, Saul lived to see another day.

The fact that Saul was unaware of the men in the cave demonstrates another tactical skill of David and his men: their ability to operate in "stealth" mode. In 1 Samuel 26 this stealth mode will show again, when David and Abishai are able to sneak into Saul's camp at night and take Saul's spear and water jug right from beside his head without being noticed.

David Reveals His Integrity to Saul (Verses 8-15)

David not only wanted to spare Saul's life, but also to clarify misperceptions with Saul. Giving Saul enough distance, David emerged and respectfully addressed the king, immediately stooping with his face to the earth. David's main concern was why Saul listened to those who claimed, *"David seeks your harm."* It's unclear whether people were actually saying that, or if it was solely Saul's perception. However, David tactfully allowed Saul some distance between his stance and reality.

Displaying the cut piece of the robe, David calls out to Saul to plea and demonstrate that he means him no harm. As evidence, he shows Saul the piece of the robe, proof that he was close enough to kill Saul if he had wished, yet chose not to. In a pledge of his intentions, David proclaims, *"mine hand shall not be upon thee"* (v. 12). David's words echo *"the proverb of the ancients,"* (v. 13) a saying that, apart from this citation, has been lost to history. As before, David is not fabricating quotes. Instead, he is quoting something not previously recorded in Scripture; a common practice in oral tradition. This assertion once again underscores David's commitment to righteousness, even in moments of extreme tension and danger.

David then proceeds to compare himself to Saul, using humble metaphors of a *'dead dog'* and a *'flea'* (v. 14). This could be interpreted as David acknowledging the vast power imbalance between them, pointing out that while Saul has a large force of 3,000 men, David is the sole target. David then turns to God, pleading for protection and justice (v. 15). He entrusts his cause to God, illustrating his deep faith and reliance on divine intervention and justice.

Saul's Response and Recognition of David's Righteousness (Verses 16-22)

In verse 11, David had referred to Saul as *"my father,"* signaling a deep respect and familial bond. Now, in verse 16, Saul, his heart softened, reciprocates by calling David *"my son."* This reaffirms the familial connection between them - after all, David was Saul's son-in-law. Saul seems to be coming to his senses about David, acknowledging David's righteousness, which he recognizes as surpassing his own. Remarkably, Saul even prophesies that David will indeed ascend to the throne. Saul's only plea is for David to honor his family and preserve his legacy once he is gone. This exchange reveals a moment of clarity for Saul, recognizing David's inevitable rise to kingship and expressing his hope for mercy and respect towards his lineage.

A Reprisal - 1 Samuel 26

1 Samuel 26 presents a strikingly similar situation to the events of 1 Samuel 24, yet with distinct nuances that further

illuminate the character of David, the patience and strategy underpinning his eventual ascent to the throne, and the continuing decline of Saul's moral and kingly authority.

A Second Test of Integrity (Verses 1-12)

Once again, we find Saul pursuing David, this time in the wilderness of Ziph. Saul, despite his previous recognition of David's righteousness and his own flawed pursuit, falls back into his obsessive quest to eliminate David, illustrating the tragic cycle of Saul's jealousy and paranoia. In contrast, David's actions in this chapter underscore his unwavering commitment to righteousness and his deep respect for the Lord's anointed.

David and Abishai's nighttime infiltration into Saul's camp represents not just a physical stealth operation but a profound ethical examination. They find Saul asleep, surrounded by his army, with his spear stuck in the ground at his head—a symbol of his kingly authority and personal vulnerability. Abishai, David's companion, sees this as an opportune moment to end Saul's life, interpreting their ease of access as divine providence. However, David once again demonstrates his principle of not laying hands on the Lord's anointed. He rebukes Abishai's suggestion, reinforcing the concept that it is not their place to harm Saul; instead, they should leave his fate in God's hands. This moment amplifies David's adherence to divine order and his belief in God's sovereignty over judgment and kingship.

The taking of the spear and the jug of water serves as tangible proof of David's proximity to Saul and his ability to harm him, yet choosing not to. This act is symbolic, echoing the earlier episode where David cut a piece of Saul's robe. Both instances highlight David's integrity and his commitment to ethical conduct, even in the face of personal danger and opportunity for vengeance.

David's Appeal to Saul (Verses 13-20)

After retreating to a safe distance, David's confrontation with Saul through a dialogue across the space between them further reveals David's rhetorical skill and his appeal to reason and morality. David calls out to Saul, presenting the spear as evidence of his presence by Saul's side and his decision not to kill the king. This exchange is critical in showcasing David's unwavering respect for Saul's position as God's anointed and his reliance on God to judge between them.

David's speeches to Saul are laden with appeals to justice, righteousness, and the absurdity of Saul's pursuit. He questions the basis of Saul's enmity and invites divine judgment to discern the righteousness of their causes. This discourse not only highlights David's innocence and moral high ground but also serves as a public testament to the unjust nature of Saul's vendetta against him.

Saul's Momentary Repentance (Verses 21-25)

Saul's response to David's plea is a moment of self-realization and temporary repentance. He acknowledges his wrongdoing and blesses David, recognizing his future as king and his conduct as more righteous than his own. This acknowledgment, however, is fleeting, illustrating the tragic pattern of Saul's moments of clarity followed by relapses into destructive behavior.

Saul's request for his life to be spared and his lineage to be remembered echoes his earlier plea in chapter 24, revealing a consistent concern for his legacy amidst his moral and spiritual decline. David's assurance, through returning the spear and refraining from further violence, reinforces his commitment to justice and mercy, principles that would define his reign as king.

A Typology?

An interesting typology emerges if we consider David as a type of Christ. With this twofold opportunity to kill Saul, which David passed on, we can see a parallel in Christ's life. First, during His crucifixion, He said, *"Father, forgive them."* At that moment, He could have called for legions of angels to strike down those around Him, but He chose not to. Then, during the stoning of Stephen, Christ was standing in Heaven, ready to come down in judgment once again. Yet, at Stephen's plea, He chose not to initiate judgment. In both instances, Jesus turned down what could have been His, choosing to wait for the Father's timing instead. This aligns with David's actions in chapters 24 and 26, underscoring the typology of David as a precursor to Christ in terms of their shared commitment to righteousness and divine timing.

Conclusion

1 Samuel 24 and 26 offer crucial insights into David's character and his life journey. From the very start, we see David's strategic advantage in understanding the terrain due to his experience as a shepherd. He uses this knowledge to evade Saul's forces, highlighting his skill as a tactician.

However, what truly stands out is David's moral integrity. Despite having the opportunity to kill Saul, who was hunting him down, David chooses not to lay a hand on him. He believed that he should not harm the Lord's anointed, displaying an unwavering commitment to righteousness and respect for divine order. David's actions show a deep trust in God's timing and protection, even when facing extreme danger.

David's interaction with Saul further demonstrates his rhetorical skill and his ability to reason and appeal to morality. He openly communicates with Saul, attempting to clarify misperceptions and assert his innocence. David's plea for divine judgement to discern the righteousness of their causes paints a picture of a man deeply reliant on divine intervention and justice.

Lastly, David's interactions with his own men show his leadership and the respect he commanded. Despite their readiness to kill Saul, David's men obeyed his directive, showing their respect for him as their leader.

In conclusion, this chapter offers a detailed portrait of David's character - a tactician, a leader, a man of integrity, and a deeply faithful servant of God.

Chapter 16:

LESSONS FROM THE FOOLISH AND THE WISE

1 Samuel 25

The Death of Samuel (1 Samuel 25:1)

Samuel was a key figure in Israel's history, acting as a prophet, judge, and leader during an important transitional period. His story begins with his miraculous birth to Hannah, who was previously unable to have children. In gratitude, Hannah dedicated Samuel to the Lord's service and entrusted him to Eli, the high priest at Shiloh. Under Eli's tutelage, Samuel grew up in the tabernacle.

His prophetic calling came at a young age when God revealed a forthcoming judgment on Eli's house due to Eli's sons' wickedness. This marked Samuel as a significant prophet who consistently communicated God's word to the people. As he grew older, Samuel became recognized as a judge over Israel. He traveled between Bethel, Gilgal, Mizpah, and his home in Ramah to administer justice.

Under Samuel's leadership, Israel experienced a religious revival and a return to worshipping God alone. His role as judge was not only judicial, but also military, as he led the Israelites to victory against the Philistines at Mizpah.

In his later years, Samuel appointed his sons as judges, but they did not follow his ways. This led to the elders of Israel demanding a king, marking a turning point in Israel's history. Despite this request being a rejection of Samuel's leadership, God instructed him to comply, laying the groundwork for the monarchy.

Despite some loss of respect among the people in his later years, Samuel's significance as a prophet is highlighted in the words of the Lord in Jeremiah 15:1, *"Then said the LORD unto me, Though Moses and Samuel stood before me, yet my mind could not be toward this people: cast them out of my sight, and let them go forth."* Here, God refers to Samuel, alongside Moses, as a powerful intercessor for Israel. This could be considered the best *"epitaph"* for Samuel, indicating his stature and importance in Israel's history.

Interestingly, it is mentioned that Samuel was buried *"in his house."* This is an unusual detail that is only otherwise noted in the cases of Joab (1 Kings 2:34) and King Manasseh (2 Kings 21:18). This could suggest a unique burial practice in the Near East during this period. Archaeologists have discovered ancient "basement tombs" occasionally, indicating that there may have been a precedent for burying people literally in their own homes. Because such a practice was not common, it was specifically noted in the scripture.

After Samuel's death, David and his 600 companions, journeyed to the wilderness of Paran, located in the northern Sinai Peninsula.

Nabal and Abigail Introduced (1 Samuel 25:2-3)

The narrative now shifts to a man who lived near Maon, whose possessions were in Carmel. It's important to note that this Carmel is distinct from the famous Mount Carmel where the prophet Elijah called down fire from heaven in a contest against the prophets of Baal. In 1 Samuel 15:12, a victory of King Saul over the Amalekites is noted to have taken place at this Carmel, which may provide some background to the animosity we will encounter towards David in the following interactions. It is possible that the local residents were strong supporters of Saul, and David's falling out with Saul had become common knowledge, contributing to the hostility he faced.

The man's wealth is evident in his possession of three thousand sheep and a thousand goats. This also explains why the text differentiates between Maon, which is arid, and the nearby Carmel, a location that provides ample grazing ground for such a large number of livestock.

We meet a man named Nabal, whose name appears 18 times in this chapter. He is described as *"churlish and evil in his doings"* (v. 3). In Hebrew, *"churlish"* originates from "קָשֶׁה" (*Qasheh*), which can be interpreted as harsh, severe, or difficult. In English, *"churlish"* describes someone who is rude, mean-spirited, or ungracious in their manner or behavior.

Abigail, his wife, however, is a "a woman of good understanding, and of a beautiful countenance" (v. 3). In Jewish Rabbinical literature, Abigail is celebrated as a woman of great wisdom, beauty, and prophetic insight, who played a significant role in the history of Israel.

David's Interaction with Nabal (1 Samuel 25:4-13)

David's Introduction (vv. 4-9)

David sends some of his men to Nabal, seeking peace and provisions. He carefully instructs them on what to say, suggesting that he may be worried about how Nabal will receive them. This worry could be based on previous interactions, Nabal's reputation, or simply an understanding of the situation. Notably, in verse 6, a three-fold *"peace"* greeting is used, which could be seen as a strong diplomatic protocol or perhaps a sign of fear that peace might not be offered. In verse 9, it's carefully pointed out that the men only say what David instructed them to and then remain silent. This careful approach to communication, taken by both David and his men, likely suggests an expectation of hostility.

An Unfortunate Response (vv. 10-13)

Nabal responds with a dismissive and disrespectful reply, *"Who is David?"* (v. 10). He also mentions the number of rebels, showing disdain for those who defy their masters. This suggests that Nabal was indeed in favor of Saul and was antagonistic towards David, who he had undoubtedly heard of before.

Both David's request (v. 8) and Nabal's response (v. 11) highlight the custom of the time, where landowners provided for military expeditions passing through their areas. This provision was akin to a "tax" intended to cover the expenses of those who offered protection. Nabal's answer clearly aligned him with Saul, not David, who he considered to be unfaithful to the kingdom.

In response to Nabal's refusal, David's reaction was swift and decisive. He immediately prepared for battle against Nabal. If "the fool" would not help him, then he would help himself. Displaying his military mind, David mustered 400 men to gird for battle and left 200 to protect their supplies.

This response presents a stark contrast to the preceding Chapter 24 and the following Chapter 26, which show David in deference to Saul. Was David having a bad day and making a poor decision? Or had he determined to forget about "God's anointed" and begin conquering Saul's territory? It is hard to know exactly what is going on in David's mind. While a conquering leader might find justification for his actions, David's approach was different. He preferred to let God's hand guide him to leadership, instead of forcefully seizing power. This raises the question: what is going through David's mind? Why is he taking this uncharacteristic action?

Abigail's Intervention (1 Samuel 25:14-35)

A *"young man"* (v. 14) appears to inform Abigail about recent events. From the pronouns used, we infer this individual is one of Nabal's servants. As the conversation progresses, it's evident that this young man, who is notably courageous, is aware of his master's shortcomings and appreciates his master's wife's virtues. His report that Nabal *"railed on them"* suggests he did not see his master's response as suitable.

The unnamed young man speaks highly of David's men, reporting, *"They were a wall unto us both by night and day"* (v. 16). This comment implies that there may have been hostilities in the area, and David's men provided them with protection. Furthermore, he emphasizes that David's men never took anything from Nabal or his servants, demonstrating their respect and integrity.

The young man pleads with Abigail for a solution, warning her that *"evil is determined against our master"* (v. 17). In the King James Version of the Bible, the term *"evil"* is used in its broad sense to refer to calamity, without any reference to moral right or wrong. However, the phrase *"a son of Belial,"* used by the young man to describe Nabal, does refer to moral evil. The phrase suggests that Nabal is so controlled by the devil that nobody can reason with him.

147

Abigail then demonstrates both her resourcefulness and wealth by quickly gathering a significant amount of provisions. These include two hundred loaves, two skins of wine, five sheep already prepared, five measures of parched grain, a hundred clusters of raisins, and two hundred cakes of figs (v. 18). This readily available variety and volume of provisions serve to underline the extent of the family's wealth. Given the large scale of their operations, it is likely that such provisions were typically used to support their many servants. However, in this instance, Abigail likely intends them both as payment for the protection David's men have provided and as a peace offering. In a strategic decision, she chooses to keep her actions secret from Nabal (v. 19).

As Abigail is making her way to David (v. 20), David is sulking about the extensive efforts he made to safeguard Nabal, despite receiving nothing in return (v. 21). David's reaction makes it clear that he had expectations that Nabal did not meet. Despite Nabal's evil character, he provided strategic advantages to David. Could this episode be a lesson to David about the dangers of deviating from trusting in the Lord and forming alliances with a *"son of Belial"*? While this interpretation is not explicitly stated in the text, it certainly could be a valid conclusion.

David's proclamation in verse 22 includes a phrase that may seem undignified or crude to modern readers. When he refers to *"any that pisseth against the wall,"* he is not simply referring to any male. The phrase is a Hebrew idiom that describes arrogant, uncouth, and boisterous males. In this context, it refers to the kind of men that Nabal would likely turn to in a moment of trouble. This

148

curse of God that David invokes is an expression of his extreme anger and frustration with Nabal and his men.

Upon seeing David, Abigail quickly dismounted her donkey and fell before David in a posture of submission and respect (v. 23). Then, she fell at his feet, a common Near Eastern gesture of reverence and supplication. She took the blame for Nabal's iniquity upon herself, pleading with David to listen to her despite her husband's foolishness (v. 24).

In verse 25, Abigail acknowledged the truth about her husband, saying, *"For Nabal is his name, and folly is with him."* The Hebrew word for folly, *"nebalah,"* sounds like Nabal's name and carries a connotation of moral and ethical foolishness. Abigail was not merely calling her husband a fool; she recognized his moral failing and appealed to David's better judgment, asking him to disregard Nabal's foolishness and let her rectify the situation.

Abigail proceeds to plead with David, initially pronouncing a curse on David's enemies (v. 26). Subsequently, she presents her offering as compensation for the protection his men have provided (v. 27). Notably, in verse 28, she delivers a statement many interpret as prophecy: *"The LORD will certainly make my lord a sure house."* This has led to Abigail being considered one of the female prophets in the Hebrew scriptures by many rabbinical teachers. Whether this was truly prophecy or simply astute foresight, Abigail clearly aligns herself with David. She explains that this *"sure house"* will transpire *"because my lord fighteth the battles of the LORD."* It is intriguing to consider whether this is a subtle persuasion—implying that the impending battle is not one of the Lord's battles, thus suggesting a change of course—or simply an observation of some other nature.

149

Abigail's words in verse 29 are intriguing. She says to David, *"the soul of my lord shall be bound in the bundle of life with the LORD thy God."* The Hebrew phrase used here (סְיָּחָה רוֹרְצָב וְהָרִוּרְצָ) can be translated as *"bound in the bundle of life"* or *"tucked away in the pouch of life."* This phrase is reminiscent of the *"book of life"* mentioned elsewhere in the Bible.

One theory about this phrase draws from the practices of ancient shepherds. Shepherds would often put a small pebble in a pouch for each of his sheep. As he brought the sheep into the fold, he would toss out a stone each time a sheep entered. This was a way for the shepherd to keep track of his sheep and ensure their safety.

This interpretation fits with the second part of the verse, where Abigail refers to David's enemies, saying, *"the souls of thine enemies, them shall he sling out."* If this interpretation is correct, then Abigail's statement can be understood as a prayer or blessing for David's safety and the downfall of his enemies.

It's important to note that the Hebrew concept of the *"book of life"* or *"book of the living"* did not distinguish between heaven and hell as the New Testament concept does, but rather between *"alive"* and *"dead."* So, Abigail's words may be interpreted as *"May God keep you alive and bring your enemies to death."*

While this verse and phrase are almost unknown in Christian groups, they are very familiar to Jews. The Hebrew letters "הבצנת" (T.N.Tz.B.H), often seen on Jewish tombstones, form an acronym. The letters represent "התמשנ/ותמשנ היהת םייחה רורצב הרורצ" (*Tehi Nishmato/Nishmata Tzrurah Bitzror Hachaim*), translating to *"May his/her soul be bound up in the bundle of life."* This acronym serves as a written wish and is not typically pronounced. It is a traditional Jewish epitaph derived from 1 Samuel 25:29, conveying a wish for the deceased's soul to be protected in the afterlife.

Abigail's subtlety continues in verses 30 and 31, where she presents a moral argument to David. She predicts that the Lord will establish David's kingdom and expresses her hope that David will not be burdened with needless guilt or needless bloodshed. Her argument is an appeal to David's future conscience: *"And it shall come to pass, when the Lord shall have done to my lord according to all the good that he hath spoken concerning thee, and shall have appointed thee ruler over Israel; That this shall be no grief unto thee, nor offence of heart unto my lord, either that thou hast shed blood causeless, or that my lord hath avenged himself."* In essence, she's saying, *"I hope that when you are king, you don't have to look back and regret this day."*

This is a subtle but powerful way of saying, *"Let the Lord deal with Nabal. You have better things to do."* Abigail is strategically appealing to David's future self, knowing that his actions today will impact his conscience when he becomes king. She's essentially asking him to consider the legacy he wants to leave and the kind of king he wants to become.

Finally, she concludes her plea by saying, *"And when the Lord shall have dealt well with my lord, then remember thine handmaid."* This request shows her wisdom and foresight, understanding that her actions today might significantly impact her future. It is a humble request, but also a strategic one, as she aligns herself with David and his future success.

David's reaction to Abigail's plea (vv. 32-35) displays his humility and wisdom. He praises God for sending Abigail to him and recognizes the disaster he was about to bring upon himself. He acknowledges that her wise counsel has prevented him from shedding blood needlessly and taking revenge with his own hands (v. 33).

David's response here shows his deep respect towards Abigail and his gratitude for her intervention. It is clear that he values her insight and wisdom, and he credits her with saving him from making a grave mistake that could have marred his future reputation and legacy.

David accepts Abigail's gift and sends her home in peace, assuring her that he has heard her and respected her plea (v. 35). This exchange marks a turning point in the narrative, as it not only displays the wisdom of Abigail but also reveals David's ability to listen to wise counsel and correct his course of action.

Nabal's Demise and David's Marriage to Abigail (1 Samuel 25:36-42)

Upon her return home, Abigail found Nabal in a state of drunkenness, apparently participating in some form of revelry with his friends (v. 36). Given his inebriated condition, Abigail wisely opted to wait until the following morning, when he had sobered up, to inform him of her actions in aiding David. When Nabal was informed of the events, *"his heart died within him, and he became as a stone"* (v. 37). This could suggest that he suffered a stroke, or it could be a form of hyperbole used to express his shock and subsequent incapacitation. Regardless, the consequences of this event were severe, as it is noted that *"the LORD smote Nabal, that he died"* just ten days later (v. 38).

Verses 39-42 describe a practice that might seem foreign to our modern sensibilities but was common in the royal families up until relatively recent history. David's proposal to Abigail can be seen as a strategic move, as marriages during this time, particularly among royalty, were often politically motivated. These arrangements were typically brokered by courtiers and involved careful negotiations over dowries, positions, and other related matters.

The primary goal of these marriages was often to strengthen political alliances and ensure the continuity of the dynasty through the procurement of a male heir. While these marriages were not always based on love, there were instances where genuine affection developed between the spouses. For example, the union of Ferdinand and Isabella is often seen as a successful and loving partnership.

However, there were also instances where these arrangements led to miserable conditions for the bride, particularly if the marriage displeased the king. The plight of Catherine of Aragon, who was cast aside by King Henry VIII, serves as a stark example of this.

In this context, David's marriage to Abigail can be seen as a strategic move to strengthen his position and possibly to protect her in the wake of Nabal's death. Yet, the text also displays a mutual respect and perhaps even affection between them, indicating that their relationship might have been more than just a political alliance.

David's marriage to Abigail not only brought him a wise and discerning wife but also potentially facilitated strategic social and political connections in the southern regions of Israel. They resided in the vicinity of Carmel, near Maon, an area significant for its wilderness where David found refuge and support before ascending to kingship. Though references to Abigail in the biblical narrative are sparse following her marriage to David, each mention identifies her as a 'Carmelitess,' highlighting her origin from Carmel and possibly her influence or standing in that region.

Additional Wives (1 Samuel 25:43-44)

In addition to Abigail, David also took Ahinoam of Jezreel as his wife. The timeline of this marriage is not explicitly detailed in the scripture, but it presumably occurred after the events of chapter 25. Throughout his time in Hebron, these two women, Abigail and Ahinoam, would be his wives. Later, when he moved to Jerusalem, David would take on more wives, one of which was the infamous Bathsheba. In total, we know of eight wives who were named in the scriptures, but there were likely more who were not named.

David's first wife, Michal, was also a result of a political arrangement with Saul. However, Saul altered this arrangement, taking back Michal to give to Phalti, the son of Laish, in a political arrangement that he deemed would serve him better.

The practice of polygamy, as seen in David's life, serves as a historical record rather than a doctrinal endorsement. Throughout the scriptures, God's progressive revelation and His ultimate purpose for marriage—one man and one woman in a covenant relationship—are revealed more fully. The practice of polygamy, although recorded in the Bible, often led to problematic outcomes, further underscoring the wisdom of God's design for monogamous marriages. Regardless, we should always remember not to make a doctrine out of an historical account.

Chapter 17:

STRATEGIC ALLIANCES:

*A Tale of Survival, Deception, and
   Moral Compromise*

1 Samuel 27

David's Decision for Safety (1 Samuel 27:1-4)

Between Chapter 26, where David boldly infiltrates
Saul's camp and takes his sword and bottle, and Chapter
27, David loses confidence. He becomes convinced that
he won't survive Saul's pursuits and will eventually die by
his hand. David decides to flee to the enemy, embodying
the old saying, *"the enemy of my enemy is my friend."*
Likely exhausted, David chooses to seek protection from
the Philistines.

We must note an inconsistency in David's thinking at this
point. In 1 Samuel 21, he had fled to the Philistine king for
refuge but soon realized the disaster of his decision and
feigned madness to escape. Now, he returns to the same
situation. David appears desperate, illustrating the duality
of his character - at times bold, at other times driven by fear.
Despite proclaiming, *"It is better to trust in the LORD than
to put confidence in man"* (Psalm 118:8), he now places his
confidence in man. This serves as a reminder that all men,
even the greatest among us, have their *"feet of clay."*

King Achish of the Philistines was the same king before
whom David feigned madness. Likely, David formed a
political alliance this time, benefiting both Achish and
himself. Remember that David previously had no army,
followers, or strength. Now that David has something to
offer, maybe Achish decides that David is not a threat. Or

perhaps Achish is simply adhering to the adage, *"keep your friends close and your enemies closer."*

Regardless of the circumstances, David does find refuge in the land of the Philistines. This move results in Saul ceasing his relentless pursuit of David, bringing what is no doubt a welcome respite for him. It's a significant turning point in David's life, offering him a chance to regroup and strategize for his future.

David's Alliance with Achish, King of Gath (1 Samuel 27:5-7)

David also demonstrates his strategic acumen by requesting a city in which to dwell, thereby not becoming a burden on King Achish. This move of providing a city within a king's reign was not uncommon and was practiced at least until the 1500s. It was an indirect method of taking care of family, friends, or alliances. The tax revenue from the city would become the property of the one given the *"keys"* to the city. This arrangement ensured that David had a source of income and was self-sufficient, further solidifying his strategic alliance with Achish.

Ziklag, the city granted to David, became more than just a place of residence; it was a strategic base for his operations. From Ziklag, David was able to gather strength and plan his moves. Notably, he conducted raids against the Geshurites, Girzites, and Amalekites. However, he cleverly portrayed these actions to Achish as raids on territories of Judah. This *"half-truth"* allowed him to maintain the support of his fellow Jews, who appreciated his efforts against their enemies, while also earning the praise of Achish, who believed David was weakening his own people. Thus, Ziklag became a pivotal location that enabled David to navigate his complex political and social landscape. Later, Ziklag became part of David's Kingdom, and was mentioned as part of Judah in the return of Nehemiah (Neh. 11:28).

The scripture states that David resided in Philistine territory for *"a full year and four months"* (v. 7). In Hebrew, the words literally say *"days and four months."* Some scholars argue that a span of 16 months seems lengthier than what aligns with known chronological markers. However, the timeline of King Saul's reign is notoriously challenging to determine. Regardless of David's stay's precise duration, which we'll assume as 16 months for our discussion, this period led to David losing favor with his men and people. In retrospect, David's decision to reside in Philistine for such an extended period seems to have been ill-advised.

David's Brutal Campaign (1 Samuel 27:8-12)

David embarks on a brutal campaign against the historic enemies of Israel, who were also *"of old the inhabitants of the land"* as per verse 8. This aggressive move is open to interpretation. Some may view this as an indication of God's favor upon David, allowing him to exert his strength and protect his people. Others may interpret this as David relying on his own strength instead of trusting in God's providence. This period of David's life presents a complex picture of a man caught between survival, strategic alliances, and his personal faith.

One could argue that Joshua should have removed all these citizens during the conquest, and that David is now stepping in to do what Joshua failed to do. In another perspective, one could also argue that David is simply hellbent on establishing strength for his own cause.

157

I tend to take a more negative view because of David's conduct in verses 10-12.

When Achish asked David for a report on his military activities, David claimed that his campaigns were focusing on "the south of Judah," specifically against the Jerahmeelites and the Kenites (v. 10). This was a blend of truth and fabrication. While David's raids were indeed carried out in *"the south of Judah,"* they were not directed against the Jerahmeelites, a Jewish clan (see 1 Chron. 2:9), or the Kenites, the tribe of Jethro, which had long been allies with the Jews. By spinning this tale, David was attempting to ingratiate himself with Achish, who would be led to believe that David was attacking his own people.

Verse 11 presents the stark truth: David *"left neither man nor woman alive"* (v. 9) to ensure no one could report the truth to Gath. This allowed David to maintain his deception, risking either his standing in Philistia or an attack from Achish.

There is no good spin on this. David had turned brutal, likely to save his own skin.

The *Treasury of Scripture Knowledge,* in its cross reference segment for 1 Samuel 27:11, has a good comment on the Bible's presentation of such *"black eyes"* of Biblical heroes.

> David's answer, therefore, though not an absolute falsehood, was certainly an equivocation intended to deceive, and therefore incompatible with that sense of truth and honour which became him as a prince, and a professor of true religion. From these, and similar passages, we may observe the strict impartiality of the Sacred Scriptures. They present us with the most faithful delineation of human nature; they exhibit the frailties

158

of kings, priests, and prophets, with equal truth; and examples of vice and frailty, as well as of piety and virtue, are held up, that we may guard against the errors to which the best men are exposed.[3]

Achish makes the only conclusion one could make upon accepting the report as true: David will now forever be hated by Israel, and therefore he will be forced to be *"my servant for ever"* (v. 12).

Conclusion

1 Samuel 27 presents a complex and conflicted David, a man who is strategically brilliant yet morally compromised. He has dug a hole for himself by aligning with the Philistines and deceiving King Achish. His actions, driven by fear and a need for survival, have far-reaching consequences that will become apparent as we progress further into his story. David's story serves as a reminder that even the best of men can falter when faced with fear and desperation. As we move forward, we will see David continue to navigate his complicated circumstances and the repercussions of his decisions.

---

3   B. Blayney, Thomas Scott, and R.A. Torrey with John Canne, Browne, *The Treasury of Scripture Knowledge*, vol. 1 (London: Samuel Bagster and Sons, n.d.), 209.

Chapter 18:

DAVID AND THE PHILISTINES

1 Samuel 29

In the last chapter of this book, we found ourselves in 1 Samuel 27, where David entered into an alliance with Achish. As we concluded that chapter, Achish believed that David had become a stench to Israel and a loyal ally to the king of Gath. As we move forward, we will skip over chapter 28, save a short mention of verses 1-2, as it is solely dedicated to Saul, and it details his notorious visit to the witch of Endor. Now, we pick up with chapter 29, where the story of David in Gath continues.

In 1 Samuel 28:1-2, we see David and his men being appointed as Achish's personal bodyguards. This sets the stage for the ensuing conflict as David is thrust into the center of Philistine military operations.

The Setting (1 Samuel 29:1-2)

As the narrative continues, the Philistines, under the leadership of Achish, prepare to wage war against the Israelites and King Saul. The Philistine army manages to set up camp by a fountain located in Jezreel, deep within Israeli territory. This location suggests that the Philistines must have embarked on an extensive journey from Gath. The probable route would have taken them southwards through the wilderness, crossing the Red Sea, moving through Edom and Moab, and finally passing over the Jordan to reach Jezreel, which is situated just south of the Sea of Galilee. The exact location of the fountain is not specified, but it is conceivable that it could be Ein Herod, the same fountain where Gideon encamped in his victorious battle against the Midianites. This strategic positioning of the Philistine forces sets the stage for the impending conflict.

The Philistine army was massive, with the soldiers marching *"by hundreds, and by thousands"* (1 Samuel 29:2). David and his men, having been appointed as Achish's personal bodyguards in 1 Samuel 28:1-2, were positioned at the rear with the king. This strategic placement signifies their importance and the trust that Achish put in David and his men.

In ancient warfare, it was not uncommon for the king or the commanding officer to position themselves at the rear of the army. This strategic location provided them with a comprehensive view of the battlefield, enabling them to direct the troops and make tactical decisions based on the unfolding battle. However, being at the rear also shielded them from the front-line dangers, ensuring their safety and the continuity of leadership should the battle turn in the enemy's favor.

The word *"rereward"* appears in the King James Version (KJV) of the Bible and is an archaic term that means *"rear guard."* It is derived from the Middle English term *"rere-ward,"* where *"rere"* is an alternative form of *"rear,"* meaning behind, and *"ward"* means guard or protection. In a military context, the *"rereward"* refers to the troops stationed at the rear of an army to protect it from a potential attack from behind. In its ontology, the term *"rereward"* is largely obsolete in modern English and is mostly encountered in historical or literary contexts, particularly in older translations of the Bible.

162

The Philistine Commanders' Objection
(1 Samuel 29:3-5)

When the Philistine commanders question David's presence among their ranks, asking, *"What do these Hebrews here?"* (v. 3), they are expressing a natural suspicion stemming from David's known history as an Israelite hero. Their query is justified given the impending conflict with the Israelites. Achish, however, quickly comes to David's defense, asserting, *"I have found no fault in him."* Though Achish's loyalty to David appears commendable, it's crucial to remember that this allegiance is founded on a false pretense. David has not been entirely truthful about his intentions, thereby misleading Achish. Achish's choice of words, *"since he fell,"* alludes to an apparent belief that David was cast out from Israel, and that Achish, in turn, came to David's rescue. This misconception further complicates the dynamics between David, Achish, and the Philistine commanders, underscoring the precarious nature of alliances formed under deceptive circumstances.

The Philistine leaders are not swayed by Achish's trust in David. They boldly demand that David be sent back to Ziklag, recognizing the potential risks of his presence in their ranks. They understand the possibility of deception or, more likely, they fear that in the heat of battle, David might seize an opportunity to *"reconcile himself unto his master"* by sacrificing Philistine lives. This skepticism shows their pragmatic approach and the inherent tension in David's precarious position among the Philistines.

The Philistine commanders express their suspicion of David, even recalling and repeating the song sung about him in their own lands. This song, which glorifies

163

David's military victories — *"Saul has slain his thousands, and David his ten thousands"* (1 Samuel 29:5) — reveals that David's fame as a warrior has spread far beyond the borders of Israel. His reputation, while a point of pride for the Israelites, stokes fear and distrust among the Philistines, further complicating his position within the Philistine ranks.

Achish's Defense of David (1 Samuel 29:6-7)

Caught in a difficult position, Achish assures David that he harbors no ill-will towards him and completely trusts him. Interestingly, he swears by *"the LORD,"* using the sacred name of the God of Israel. He may have done this to show respect to David by acknowledging his God. However, it is highly unlikely that this is an indication of Achish worshipping YHWH. Evidence from the ancient Near East suggests that polytheists were quite liberal in their usage of the names of different gods, as is almost inherent in the definition of polytheism.

This phenomenon, where a foreign king uses the name of the God of Israel, is not exclusive to this 1 Samuel 29:6 passage. This also happens in Jonah 1:14 and Daniel 4:37.

In Jonah 1:14, the sailors, who are non-Israelites, cried out to the LORD, *"O LORD, let us not perish for this man's life, and lay not on us innocent blood, for you, O LORD, have done as it pleased you."* Here, the sailors acknowledge the God of Israel and His sovereignty, much like Achish did when he was speaking to David.

Similarly, in Daniel 4:37, King Nebuchadnezzar, the Babylonian king, praises, extols, and honors the King of heaven, a reference to the God of Israel. All of these examples show that non-Israelite figures in the Bible sometimes acknowledged the God of Israel, often as a sign of respect to Israelites they were dealing with.

Ultimately, Achish, in efforts to appease the Philistine military leaders, requests David to depart from the battle. The subsequent response from David is yet to be seen, and his true intentions remain a mystery. One can't help but question whether David, who had previously refrained from harming Saul out of respect for his anointed status, would now rise against Saul in battle. This seems highly unlikely given David's past display of loyalty and respect for God's anointed. It is plausible that David might have even been relieved to be released from a situation that could potentially force him into conflict with his own people.

David's Response (1 Samuel 29:8)

David, taken aback by Achish's request, pleads his innocence and questions the reason behind his dismissal from the battle. His words reflect either feigned shock and regret or a genuine turn against Saul and his own people. Considering David's track record of deception throughout his interactions with Achish, it seems more plausible that his surprise is a pretense. It's likely that David is relieved to have found a way out of the precarious situation of potentially having to fight against his own people.

Regardless of the circumstances leading to David's dismissal from the battle, it is important to note that this event likely saved his future reign. As it transpires, Saul loses his life in this very battle. Had David been present and participated, his involvement could have drastically altered the course of his destiny and the future of the Israelite monarchy.

Achish's Final Verdict (1 Samuel 29:9-11)

Achish, having faced the opposition of his commanders, finally yields to their counsel and insists that David and his men depart. He makes it clear that his decision is final and there is no room for negotiation. Despite his personal trust in David, Achish acknowledges the potential risks that his advisors have pointed out and chooses not to go against their collective wisdom. With the break of dawn on the following morning, David and his soldiers obediently leave the Philistine camp, marking the end of an unusual and precarious alliance. Meanwhile, the Philistine army advances to Jezreel, ready to engage in a crucial battle that will ultimately reshape the course of history.

Conclusion

In this chapter, we have seen David caught in a web of deception, forming an uneasy and precarious alliance with Achish, the king of Gath. His situation highlights the potential pitfalls of straying from reliance on God and instead trusting in our own understanding. The Philistine commanders' suspicions and their subsequent demand for David's dismissal expose the inherent risks in such alliances, especially those built on untruths. Despite his seeming loyalty to Achish, David's true allegiance lies with his people, the Israelites.

However, David's dilemma of misplaced trust is not yet over. As we venture into the next chapter, we will find that David's decisions have far-reaching consequences. His wives, the wives of his men, their children, and all their possessions will soon find themselves in grave danger. This further emphasizes the need for wisdom and discernment, and the importance of placing trust in the Lord rather than in human alliances.

Chapter 19:

REAPING THE WHIRLWIND:
The Amalekite Retribution

1 Samuel 30

In this chapter, we continue our exploration of King David's life, specifically focusing on the consequences of his recent actions. The previous two chapters illuminated David's dangerous and deceptive alliance with Acish. Now, we delve into the repercussions of this alliance. As the saying goes, *"when you sow the wind, you reap the whirlwind."* Let's uncover what this whirlwind entails for David.

The Calamity at Ziklag (1 Samuel 30:1-6)

The Amalekites were a nomadic group of people who lived in the desert region of the Arabian Peninsula, including parts of modern-day Saudi Arabia, Jordan, and Israel. Their territory was known as Amalek, and the people are often associated with the descendants of Esau. While David and his men were away at battle, the Amalekites took advantage of their absence. They attacked Ziklag, the city that had been given to David and his men. This act of aggression set the stage for the events that follow in the story.

It's important to note that in 1 Samuel 27:8-9, we are told that David attacked the Amalekites and killed every man and woman. However, we now see the Amalekites attacking. This is due to the fact that the Amalekites were a nomadic people, not residing in one particular region. Now another band of Amalekites comes and gives a payment-in-kind for David's actions, whether purposefully or coincidentally.

However, it's worth noting a notable difference in the approach of David and the Amalekites towards their adversaries. While David had slain every Amalekite man and woman in his attack, the Amalekites, when they raided Ziklag, chose to take the women hostage instead of killing them.

Imagine the scene: you've returned home from what was supposed to be a battle. You haven't fought, and there's a sense of humiliation lingering. But as you approach your town, you see smoke billowing in the distance. Your heart sinks as you draw nearer and the reality sets in - your town has been burned to the ground. Your home, your possessions, all reduced to ashes. And then the most devastating realization of all: your wives and children are gone. You don't know where they are or what has happened to them. The uncertainty and fear grip you like a vice. This is the harsh reality faced by David and his men.

David, too, was not left unscathed. Both of his wives, Ahinoam of Jezreel and Abigail, the widow of Nabal of Carmel, were taken captive during the Amalekite raid (v. 5). The disaster at Ziklag not only caused personal loss for David but also provoked the anger of his men, to the point that they talked about stoning him (v. 6). David, their leader, had led them into this alliance with Achish, and it was while they were away, drawn from their homes by his decisions, that the calamity had fallen. In their eyes, there was no one else to blame but David himself. He had chosen to align with human forces, placing his trust in man rather than God, and this catastrophic event was a direct consequence of his actions.

In the midst of this tumultuous situation, there is a crucial line that stands out - *"David encouraged himself in the LORD his God"* (v. 6). This statement may seem out of place, almost uncaring, as David withdraws from the sad reality he has created to find solace in the Lord. Yet, there's a part of us that thinks, *"It's about time."* David, who had long strayed from his spiritual path, was finally returning to his faith. Was this calamity the *"wake up call"* that David needed to remind him of his need for God? It certainly appears so.

David Seeks God's Direction (1 Samuel 30:7-8)

The return to the Lord in verse 6 appears to have been a true wake-up call for David. Recognizing his need for divine guidance, David calls for Abiathar the priest to inquire of the Lord through the Ephod. He seeks to know if he should pursue the men who brought this calamity upon him and his men. In response, he receives a positive answer and is assured of victory.

This is a stark contrast to the events of 1 Samuel 28, a chapter we have skipped in this study. In that chapter, Saul, having massacred the priests at Nob and thus without the benefit of the priests or the Ephod, resorts to the witch at Endor to summon Samuel. Samuel gives him a message of defeat.

Abiathar, the lone escapee from Nob, had rescued the Ephod and brought it to David. Now, with the benefit of the Ephod, David could inquire of the Lord directly. Unlike Saul, who had turned to a witch in his desperation, David turns to the Lord in his time of need. This marks a significant turning point in David's spiritual journey and sets the stage for the events that follow.

We are left to ponder how differently things might have unfolded had David sought the Lord's guidance before aligning with Acish. Could this tragic episode at Ziklag, precipitated by David's deception, have been avoided and replaced with a scenario more beneficial to all involved? Unfortunately, until we reach heaven, we can only speculate about the alternative outcome.

The Pursuit (1 Samuel 30:9-10)

After receiving assurance from the Lord, David and his 600 men began their pursuit of the Amalekites. Their journey led them as far as the Brook Besor, which is believed to be Wadi Ghazzeh today. However, upon reaching this point, 200 of the men were too exhausted from their travels to continue. To understand their exhaustion, it's important to note the journey they had taken. If the locations are correct, the 600 men had traveled approximately 50 miles from Ziklag to Aphek (as mentioned in 1 Samuel 29:1) and then returned, making a round trip of about 100 miles. Upon their return, they discovered the destruction of Ziklag and the loss of their wives and children, which led them to travel approximately 15 miles farther to Besor. At this point, 200 men were so exhausted that they simply couldn't proceed any further. Undeterred, David continued the pursuit with the remaining 400 men.

An Egyptian Slave Provides Crucial Information (1 Samuel 30:11-15)

David, being a seasoned military leader, understood the vital importance of good intelligence. When his men stumbled upon a young man in the throes of death in the isolated expanse of the Negev desert, their suspicions were aroused. This was an area where any passerby would likely have knowledge of an army, however big or small, moving through the region. With this in mind, they made the wise choice to rescue the young man with the hope of extracting potentially useful information from him. Their gamble paid off; the young man revealed himself to be an Egyptian-born slave of the Amalekites, the very people David and his men were pursuing.

The boy's revelation came as a vital piece of information for David. He informed David that they had invaded the *"south of the Cherethites."* The term *"south"* is translated from the Hebrew word בֶּנֶּ [*negev*], which today signifies both a direction (south) and a location, the Negev Desert. The northern Negev in David's era was home to both Israelites and others, some friends and some foes to Israel. The *"Cherethites"* are believed to be a tribe that migrated from Crete, based on the etymology of the word, branding *"Cherethites"* an early equivalent term to *"Cretans."* Later, Cherethites would form a valuable group of mercenary soldiers in David's Kingdom. The slave also mentioned that they ventured into Judah, just north of the *"Negev of the Cherethites,"* as well as to the *"Negev of Caleb,"* to the east of the Cherethites. But the most crucial piece of information he provided was that *"we burned Ziklag with fire"* (v. 14). This was a windfall of information for David in his pursuit of the hitherto unknown culprits.

After the young man reveals his identity, David asks for his assistance. The wise young man, understanding his precarious situation, negotiates terms for his cooperation. He seeks assurance from David that he will neither kill him nor return him to his Amalekite master. This negotiation reveals that the young man is likely well versed in the differences in the legal treatment of slaves among Israel and the surrounding nations.

171

Various known legal codes of the pagan nations, such as the Hittite Law and the Code of Hammurabi, required that anyone found harboring a fugitive slave be put to death. In stark contrast, Hebrew law explicitly stated, *"Thou shalt not deliver unto his master the servant which is escaped from his master unto thee"* (Deut. 23:15). Furthermore, it mandated that the escaped slave be treated with dignity and respect (Deut. 23:16).

This incident underscores the stark differences in the laws of Israel and its neighboring nations, reflecting the unique humanitarian ethos embedded in the Israelite legal system, a rare virtue in the ancient Near East.

David's Victory Over the Amalekites (1 Samuel 30:16-20)

Guided by the intelligence provided by the Egyptian slave, David and his men were able to locate the Amalekite encampment. They found their adversaries in a state of revelry, celebrating their ill-gotten spoils, oblivious to the impending attack.

David and his men launched a surprise attack, catching the Amalekites off guard. The ensuing battle was fierce and lasted the entire day, from twilight until the evening of the next day. Despite their exhaustion, David and his men fought valiantly, and their efforts paid off. They routed the enemy, with only 400 young Amalekite men escaping on camels.

Most importantly, David was able to recover all that they had lost. Every woman and child who had been taken captive, including his own wives, Ahinoam and Abigail, were rescued without harm. They also recovered their possessions in their entirety, leaving nothing behind.

In addition to recovering their own possessions, David and his men also took possession of the flocks and herds of the Amalekites. These spoils of war were a significant gain for David and his men, who had recently faced the devastating loss of their own possessions. The victory, thus, was twofold - a recovery of what was lost and an acquisition of an unexpected bounty.

The Dispute Over Dividing the Spoils (1 Samuel 30:21-25)

Upon returning to the Besor Valley, where the 200 men had been left behind, an interesting conflict arose. Some of the warriors, derogatorily referred to as *"the wicked men and men of Belial,"* did not want to share any of the spoils with the men who had stayed behind. However, David, as the leader, stepped in to resolve the dispute. He insisted that the spoils be divided equally among all 600 men, not just the 400 who participated in the battle. In fact, he *"made it a statute and an ordinance"* (v. 25) in his kingdom that this would be the policy moving forward.

While at first glance, this may seem like a socialist policy, it's important to note that David's kingdom was not socialist. The key to understanding David's decision lies in verse 23, where he attributes the victory and the resulting spoils to the Lord. He states, *"That which the LORD hath given us, who hath preserved us, and delivered the company that came against us into our hand,"* should be shared equally. David viewed the victory not as a result of their strength or prowess, but as a gift from God to all of his followers. This episode underscores David's understanding and acknowledgment of God's providence and his commitment to ensuring that all his followers, regardless of their strength or contributions, partook in God's blessings. In David's view, that which God gives graciously cannot be appropriated to just a few.

David Sends Gifts to the Elders of Judah (1 Samuel 30:26-31)

In these verses, we see a significant turn of events. David begins to express his loyalty to the citizens of Judah, especially those in the southern portions from Hebron and further south. By sending gifts to the elders of these areas, he is not only sharing the spoils of his victory over the Amalekites, but he is also making a strategic move to re-establish relations with these communities. This gesture of goodwill serves to remind them of his leadership and his concern for their welfare. It is these very people who will soon consider David to be their king. His actions in this chapter, therefore, serve as an important precursor to his eventual ascension to the throne.

Conclusion

In conclusion, this chapter in David's life represents a poignant example of the consequences of fear and deception, as well as the redemptive power of repentance and reliance on God. David's time in Gath, living among enemies and resorting to deceit, was born out of fear and resulted in immense pain and loss. Yet, it was in this crucible of hardship that David finally learned his lesson. He repented of his ways and renewed his trust in God, which led to his deliverance and a restoration of his fortunes.

This narrative is a timeless tale that holds valuable lessons for all of us. Like David, we too often forget God's promises and provisions. We rely on our own wisdom and, in the process, create unnecessary complications and pain in our lives. However, no matter how far we stray, the path to redemption is always open. If we can learn from our mistakes and turn back to God, relying on His wisdom and guidance, we will be blessed.

While we do not experience the direct anointing and protection in the same manner as David, we can certainly benefit from the general blessing that comes from making wise and godly decisions based on His Word. This not only helps us avoid potential pitfalls but also fosters a life that is in harmony with God's will. In the end, the story of David serves as a powerful reminder of the enduring truth found in Proverbs 3:5-6: *"Trust in the LORD with all thine heart; and lean not unto thine own understanding. In all thy ways acknowledge him, and he shall direct thy paths."*

Chapter 20:

THE DAWN OF DAVID'S REIGN

2 Samuel 1:1-16

In the previous chapter, we learned about how David was spared from the battle against Saul and returned to Ziklag, only to encounter disaster. As we enter into the narrative of 2 Samuel 1, we find David learning about the tragic outcome of the battle between Saul and the Philistines.

David Learns of Saul's Death

David had just returned to Ziklag, a city that had been given to him by the King of Gath, after his victorious battle against the Amalekites. On the third day of his return, a man unknown to David arrived from Saul's camp. This man's appearance, with torn clothes and dust on his head as signs of mourning, made it clear that a significant disaster had occurred. Furthermore, the man's actions of obeisance towards David suggested that he now regarded David as a figure of authority, perhaps even as a king. Despite not knowing this man, David was interested in hearing the news he brought, anticipating its importance.

In verse 4, we see that David is clearly concerned with the battle against the Philistines. He is eager to know the outcome, a sign of his deep concern for his people and their leadership, despite his strained relationship with Saul. The man delivers the tragic news of the deaths of Saul and Jonathan, an event detailed in 1 Samuel 30. This information, though not included in our current study, represents a significant turning point in the narrative, marking the end of Saul's reign and the beginning of a new era under David's leadership.

The young man who presents himself to David is a figure of uncertain identity. He identifies himself as an Amalekite (v. 8) and also as coming "out of the camp of Israel" (v. 3). Yet, as the narrative unfolds, we learn that he is not a reliable source, as he is willing to lie about his actions. This casts doubt on his true identity and motivations. Is he a friend or foe to David and Israel? One plausible interpretation is that he is, indeed, an Amalekite and the reference to being in Israel's camp could be taken in a more general sense, indicating that he had been present in the region or involved in the battle in some way. He might be seeking to align himself with David, who he perceives will be the next king of Israel. However, these are speculations, and the text does not provide a definitive answer to the question of his true identity and alignment.

The young man's approach to ingratiate himself with David is ill-conceived. Despite identifying himself as an Amalekite, a group David has just defeated, he believes that delivering the news of Saul's death will gain him favor. However, he fails to understand that David respects Saul as God's anointed king, and that any perceived participation in Saul's demise would not be viewed positively.

The young man's story is a fabrication with elements of truth, designed to put him in a favorable light. His account, while it contains enough elements of truth to be superficially confirmed by anyone investigating, does not align with the actual account as recorded in 1 Samuel 30. His attempt to manipulate the narrative for his own gain demonstrates a lack of understanding of David's character and the values he holds.

The young man presents to David what he claims to be Saul's crown and bracelet, a significant gesture symbolizing the transfer of power. However, the text does not provide any additional evidence to support these claims, and it remains uncertain whether the items presented were truly Saul's. Furthermore, the narrative does not mention these items again, leaving their authenticity and their fate ambiguous.

In verses 11-12, we see that David and all his men mourn and weep for Saul. This may appear strange given the past relationship between Saul and David, where David was on the run from Saul, fearful for his life, and had even come very close to going into battle against Saul. The depth of this grief, which seems very genuine, is hard to fully comprehend. It could potentially stem from a deep love for their country, or perhaps guilt, considering that they had fled and were not present to potentially alter the outcome of the battle. However, the exact reason behind this intense mourning remains uncertain and open to interpretation.

In verses 13-16, we see David's interrogation and subsequent execution of the Amalekite man. At first glance, this may seem like a brutal act fueled by David's grief and anger over Saul's death. However, when viewed in its broader context, David's actions likely reflect both his commitment to enact justice against the Amalekites and his duty to protect Israel.

David's decision to execute the man aligns with his responsibility as the future king of Israel. If the man truly had the audacity to kill Saul, as he claimed, he posed a significant threat to any future king, including David himself. By executing him, David was acting not out of personal vengeance but to safeguard the Israelite monarchy and its people.

David's Lament (2 Samuel 1:17-27)

The Lamentation of the Bow (vv. 17-18)

Verse 18 introduces the term *"The Bow,"* which has been subject to various interpretations. While some suggest that this could point to David instructing his people in the art of warfare (the use of the bow) following the death of Saul, it seems more likely, given the context, that *"The Bow"* refers to the lamentation David composed. Thus, a more fitting interpretation would be that David taught [the lamentation of] *"The Bow."* This aligns better with the narrative flow, connecting verse 18 with the surrounding verses more effectively. Notably, the term *"bow"* is mentioned again in verse 22, further supporting this interpretation. Compare also 1 Chronicles 8:40, where the children of Benjamin (from whom Saul and Jonathan come) are noted archers.

It is noted that this is written in the Book of Jasher. If translated, this means *"the book of the upright."* Most likely, this is a book of records no longer available to us.

The Lament (vv. 19-27)

David begins his lamentation by mourning the loss of *"the beauty of Israel,"* (v. 19), referring to Saul and Jonathan who were slain on the battlefield. He begs that the news of their deaths not be proclaimed in Ashkelon or Gath, Philistine cities, for fear that the enemies of Israel might rejoice in their downfall (v. 20).

In his deep sorrow, David proclaims a curse upon Mount Gilboa, the very place where Saul and Jonathan met their tragic ends, wishing that no dew or rain would fall upon it (v. 21).

In verses 22-23, David remembers Saul and Jonathan, celebrating their prowess in battle and their inseparable bond in life, which continued even into their death. They are metaphorically described as being *"swifter than eagles"* and *"stronger than lions,"* highlighting their heroic qualities.

David then calls upon the women of Israel to weep over Saul, who had enriched them with spoils taken in battle (v. 24).

Finally, David laments the loss of his dear friend Jonathan (v. 25-27). Their friendship, which began the moment they met, was a special bond. David states, *"your love to me was more wonderful than the love of women"* (v. 26). This is not to be interpreted in a modern homosexual context, but rather as a deep, platonic love between two friends. It speaks to the unique and treasured bonds that can form between men who have bonded into brotherhood, transcending all other forms of love.

The refrain of the lament, *"How are the mighty fallen"* (vv. 19, 25, 27), has transcended its biblical origins and become a culturally iconic phrase. Often used in literature, speeches, and popular media, it has come to symbolize the tragic downfall of great individuals or entities. Its applicability to many situations and its poignant commentary on the nature of power and fallibility has ensured its lasting resonance through the centuries.

From Fugitive to King

2 Samuel 1 marks the transition from Saul's reign to David's rise. It begins with David mourning Saul and Jonathan's deaths, showing his respect for Saul as God's anointed king and his loss at Israel's defeat. The Amalekite

messenger, expecting a reward, is instead executed, demonstrating David's commitment to justice and respect for God's anointed.

David's lament for his friend Jonathan reveals his deep love and emotional expression, qualities that would endear him to his people as a king. Despite being God's anointed king, David is still transitioning from fugitive to ruler. Saul's death ends his fugitive status, but he must carefully navigate his path to kingship, showing respect for God's timing and authority.

In the upcoming chapter, 2 Samuel 2, the narrative continues to unfold as David steps into his kingly calling. After mourning Saul and Jonathan's deaths, David seeks God's guidance on his next steps. He moves to Hebron, where he is anointed king over the house of Judah, marking the beginning of his reign. However, strife is on the horizon as Abner, Saul's former army commander, instigates conflict by making Ish-bosheth, Saul's son, king over the rest of Israel. This sets the stage for a long war between the house of Saul and the house of David. Stay tuned for a dive into this era-defining conflict.

Chapter 21:

DAVID THE KING

2 Samuel 2:1-3

In this chapter, we explore a significant milestone in David's journey from a humble shepherd boy to a king. Anointed by Samuel, David has walked a long and challenging path. Now, in 2 Samuel 2, we delve into his first experiences of kingship.

David's Seeks And Obeys God's Will

Now that David has learned of the tragic loss of Saul and Jonathan and has taken the time to grieve, he begins to consider his own anointing. He is left to contemplate what the correct path would be in light of these recent events and the significant shift in Israel's leadership. He directs his request to the Lord.

David's inquiry to the Lord was likely conducted through the priest using the Urim and Thummim. These sacred objects were part of the priestly garments and used for divine communication. This method was the standard way of seeking God's will during that time period.

David comes to the Lord with a specific question: *"Shall I go up into any of the cities of Judah?"* The Lord's initial response is affirmative, a simple *"yes."* However, undeterred, David further inquires about which city he should venture into. The Lord's response is definitive and directed, *"Hebron."*

Hebron, the city to which David was directed by God, holds significant historical and geographical importance. It is one of the oldest established cities in the world. It was near Hebron that Abraham dwelt and where he chose to bury Sarah, his wife. In addition, Hebron was designated as a Levitical city, a place set aside for the priests of the Levite tribe.

Hebron's location, in the central part of the land given by Joshua to the tribe of Judah, added to its strategic significance. Not only was it well-fortified, but its central location made it a politically and militarily strategic choice. This combination of historical significance and strategic location likely contributed to why God directed David to Hebron. Later, Abasalom will use Hebron as the starting place for the coup against his father, recognizing its strategic location.

Upon receiving these divine instructions, David does not hesitate to obey. He gathers his two wives, Ahinoam of Jezreel and Abigail, the widow of Nabal of Carmel. Along with his men and their families, they leave Ziklag, the Philistine city where they had been staying, to dwell in Hebron and its vicinity.

David Crowned King (2 Samuel 2:4)

The men of Judah were the first to anoint David as their king, a crucial event given that Judah was just one of the twelve tribes of Israel. Excluding the priestly tribe of Levi, which had no political stance but seemed to align with David, this anointing initially appeared to be a foregone conclusion, at least to the tribe of Judah, David's own tribe. However, as we will explore in subsequent verses, the rest of the nation didn't necessarily share this sentiment. This initial anointing was merely the start of David's path to becoming the recognized king of all Israel.

According to biblical chronology, it is believed that David was 30 years old at the time of his anointing by the men of Judah. This event marked the second of three anointings

David would receive during his lifetime. His first anointing was conducted by the prophet Samuel (1 Samuel 16:13), marking God's chosen future king. The second, as we have just discussed, was by the men of Judah, signifying his acceptance as king by his own tribe. The third and final anointing would be by the elders of Israel, representing all the tribes, and establishing David as the undisputed king of all Israel (2 Samuel 5:3).

At the end of this verse, it is announced that *"the men of Jabesh-Gilead"* had buried Saul. This is a significant detail that will be expanded upon in the following verses, shedding more light on the circumstances surrounding Saul's burial and the role of the men of Jabesh-Gilead.

David's Message to the Men of Jabesh-gilead (2 Samuel 2:5-7)

Jabesh-gilead was an ancient city located east of the Jordan River. It was inhabited by the tribe of Gad, one of the twelve tribes of Israel. This city holds significant historical value due to its recurring presence in the biblical narrative. Most notably, its inhabitants are remembered for their bravery and loyalty, demonstrated when they risked their lives to recover the bodies of Saul and his sons from the walls of Beit Shean.

After their tragic defeat at Mount Gilboa, the bodies of Saul and his sons were taken by the Philistines. They were then desecrated - a common practice of the time to dishonor the defeated - and hung on the walls of Beit Shean, a Philistine city (1 Samuel 31:8-10). Upon hearing this, the brave men of Jabesh-Gilead embarked on a dangerous mission to retrieve the bodies. They succeeded, returned to their land, and gave Saul and his sons a proper burial (1 Samuel 31:11-13).

185

David, in his newly anointed role as king of the tribe of Judah, immediately acknowledges this act of bravery and respect shown by the men of Jabesh-Gilead towards Saul and his sons. His first official act as a king is to send a message of gratitude and commendation to these men, praising their courage and loyalty. This highlights David's character as a leader who values courage, loyalty, and respect for the fallen.

Moreover, this act also reflects a deeply ingrained belief in Jewish culture where respect for the deceased, including the body, is considered a sacred duty. This principle, known as *"Kavod HaMet,"* emphasizes the inherent dignity of every human being, in life and in death. It is this sacred duty that the men of Jabesh-Gilead fulfilled and David, in turn, acknowledged and praised.

The Competing Kingdoms (2 Samuel 2:8-11)

Following David's anointing as king of Judah, the nation of Israel enters a period of divided rule that lasts seven years, as stated in verse 11. This is the start of a dual monarchy, with David ruling over the tribe of Judah and Ishbosheth, Saul's son, ruling over the rest of Israel.

Abner is introduced in this narrative as the commander of Saul's army. After Saul's death, Abner took on the role of a kingmaker. He was the one who made Ishbosheth, Saul's son, the king over Israel and Judah (excluding Hebron). Abner was a powerful figure during this time, and his support was crucial for Ishbosheth's reign.

Ishbosheth was Saul's youngest son. He is a somewhat obscure figure, with little information available about his life or personality. What we do know, however, is that he was 40 years old when he began his reign, and he ruled over Israel for two years. Although he was king over Israel, his reign was largely under the influence of Abner. His rule ended abruptly when he was assassinated by his own captains, who hoped to curry favor with David.

In Genesis 35:11, the Lord tells Jacob, *"Kings shall come out of thy loins."* At this point, all of Jacob's children, except for Benjamin, had already been born, which makes this statement puzzling. However, when examined closely and considered within the larger context of the biblical narrative, this phrase appears to be a prophecy. It suggests the emergence of two future kings from Benjamin, who was yet to be born at the time of this prophecy. One of these kings was Saul, and another, as revealed in the narrative in 2 Samuel, was Saul's son, Ishbosheth. This subtle but significant detail highlights the intricate weave of prophecies, events, and individuals that make up the biblical narrative.

Interestingly, the sons of Saul are listed in 1 Chronicles 8:33 and 9:39, and do not include an *"Ishbosheth"* but rather an *"Eshbaal."* The name Eshbaal means *"man of Baal."* One may wonder why Saul, the king of Israel, would give his son this name. However, it's crucial to understand that he didn't give him that name as we interpret it now.

Baal was the name of a Canaanite god, but it also served as a generic term for *"god"* (much like *"Allah"*), and occasionally, it was used in reference to the God of Abraham (as seen in 2 Samuel 5:20 in the naming of Baalperazim). It's plausible that Saul originally named his son *"man of God."*

However, by the time the book of Samuel was written, the context had changed. Baal was increasingly associated with Canaanite deities, and the name would have carried a negative connotation for the Israelites. The substitution of 'bosheth' for 'baal' in biblical names was an editorial strategy to distance Israel from Baal worship, aimed at reinforcing monotheistic devotion among contemporary readers. This change, which took place in almost all Israelite names containing the word Baal (for example, Mephibosheth), should be viewed as a symbolic rejection of idolatry rather than a commentary on the moral or historical legacy of the individuals bearing these names.

As the narrative unfolds, it becomes clear that Abner, Saul's army captain, wields the true power. Although Ishbosheth is anointed king, he essentially acts as a puppet, with Abner manipulating the situation behind the scenes.

The Battle of Gibeon (2 Samuel 2:12-17)

As we continue, two prominent figures come to the forefront - Abner and Joab. Abner, the commander of Saul's army, assumes a significant role in the power dynamics of Israel after Saul's death. His influence is so substantial that he essentially controls the reign of Ishbosheth, Saul's son, who he installs as king.

On the other hand, we have Joab, David's nephew, and the commander of his army. Joab is a fierce warrior and a loyal supporter of David. As we progress in the biblical narrative, we will see that Joab plays an integral role in David's reign and has a profound impact on the future of Israel.

The scene we are about to explore in verses 12-17 takes place in Gibeon. Gibeon is a city located approximately six miles northwest of Jerusalem, in the tribal territory of Benjamin.

Abner proposes a challenge in verse 14: *"Let the young men now arise, and play before us."* This phrase suggests a form of athletic or military competition, designed to symbolize a larger battle. It's akin to a jousting match, where victory is determined by the performance of a select few, rather than a full-scale battle involving entire armies.

David's men accept the challenge and, in a swift and decisive victory, they overpower Abner's men. This event is so significant that the location is named *"Helkathhazzurim,"* which translates to *"the field of strong men."*

Following this defeat, Abner's men depart in humiliation, their pride wounded. This episode demonstrates the strength and skill of David's men, further solidifying David's position as the rightful King.

It's Not Over Until... (2 Samuel 2:18-32)

In 2 Samuel 2:18-32, we see the introduction of three sons of Zeruiah who are with David - Joab, Abishai, and Asahel. Asahel, noted for his swiftness and speed, pursues Abner, the commander of Saul's army. Despite Abner's warnings, Asahel continues his pursuit, resulting in Abner fatally striking him in self defense. This event incites a bitter feud between Joab and Abner, which plays out in later chapters.

Following Asahel's death, an intense battle ensues between David's men and Abner's forces, resulting in a heavy loss for Abner's side. Abner and his men are forced to retreat. Joab ceases pursuit of Abner out of respect for the setting sun, a traditional signal to end hostilities for the day. Asahel's body is retrieved and buried, and the men with David return to Hebron.

The events of this section demonstrate the escalating tensions between David's and Saul's factions, and the conflicts that arise as they vie for control over Israel.

Conclusion

This chapter marks the beginning of the intense drama between Abner and Joab, two formidable figures in the saga of Israel's history. Both men, in time, will become part of David's kingdom. However, their paths take dramatic and violent turns. Abner will be murdered, and in a surprising twist, David will honor him posthumously. Joab, on the other hand, will face a grim fate as David, on his death bed, gives specific and horrific instructions regarding him. These developments lay the groundwork for a complex narrative of power, betrayal, and conflict in the chapters to follow.

Chapter 22:

SHIFTING ALLEGIANCES AND THE TRAGEDY OF REVENGE

2 Samuel 3

In the previous chapter, we saw David's journey to kingship begin to unfold in earnest. After learning of Saul and Jonathan's tragic deaths and taking time to grieve, David sought God's guidance on his next steps. Acting on divine instruction, David, his wives, and his men moved to the city of Hebron. Here, in the land given to the tribe of Judah, David was anointed king by the men of Judah, marking the second time he was anointed, the first being by the prophet Samuel. This anointment, however, only recognized him as king within his own tribe. The chapter concluded with the revelation that the men of Jabesh-Gilead had buried Saul, and David makes his first royal act an act of appreciation for those who blessed Saul.

As we progress, we dive into the third chapter of 2 Samuel, where David faces new challenges and experiences as the anointed king. He will continue to seek and obey God's will, and we will witness the unfolding events as he is recognized as king by the rest of Israel.

David's Growing Family (2 Samuel 3:1-5)

Before we delve into the details of David's growing family, it's important to remember that the "house of Saul" referred to in verse 1 is led by the puppet king Ishbosheth, with the real power behind the throne being the captain of his guard, Abner. What we are witnessing in this chapter is an ongoing war between the renegade kingdom of Judah, under David, and the previously established kingdom of Israel, under Ishbosheth. It's a battle of attrition, with the house of Saul growing weaker and weaker.

First among David's sons mentioned here is Amnon. It's important to pay attention to him, as he will play a prominent role in later events. Specifically, in 2 Samuel 13, Amnon's actions will lead to significant conflict within David's family. His story serves as a warning of the heartache and turmoil that can result from unchecked sin and the complex dynamics within a royal household.

In verse 3, we are introduced to Chileab, the son of David and Abigail, whom we've encountered previously. Abigail was the wise and discerning woman who was initially married to Nabal, a wealthy but foolish man. Following Nabal's death, David married Abigail. Chileab (also known as Daniel in 1 Chronicles 3:1) is their first son. Not much is known about Chileab compared to David's other sons. He is mentioned only briefly in the scriptures, and there is no record of him causing trouble or rebelling against his father like some of David's other sons. Some speculate that he may have died young, but the scriptures do not provide us with specifics.

The third wife of David, introduced in verse 3, is Maacah, the daughter of Talmai, king of Geshur. Geshur was a small Aramean kingdom located in the region of modern-day Syria and Jordan. This marriage was likely a political alliance, a common practice among ancient kingdoms.

Maacah gave birth to Absalom, a name that means *"Father of Peace,"* but his life was anything but peaceful. Absalom is a key figure in the narrative of 2 Samuel. His rebellious nature and eventual revolt against David will generate major turmoil within the royal family and the kingdom. His story, filled with intrigue, rebellion, and tragic end, will significantly impact the life and times of King David. Stay tuned as we continue to delve deeper into these fascinating biblical narratives.

The fourth son of David, as mentioned in the scripture, is Adonijah, the son of Haggith (2 Samuel 3:4). Adonijah's story is notable as he declares himself king in his father's old age, leading to a power struggle that is eventually resolved by Solomon's ascension to the throne.

David's fourth wife is Haggith, mother to Adonijah. Like the other wives of David, Haggith was likely part of a marriage of alliance or political convenience.

The fifth son of David is Shephatiah, born to his wife Abital (2 Samuel 3:4). Little is known about Shephatiah, as he plays no significant role in the subsequent narratives in the book of Samuel. We know nothing of his mother, Abital, other than what is mentioned here.

The sixth and final son mentioned in this passage is Ithream, born to David's wife Eglah (2 Samuel 3:5). Not much is known about Ithream from the biblical text, as he does not play a significant role in later accounts.

Eglah, the mother of Ithream, is also a somewhat obscure figure in the Bible. Some Jewish tradition, including the interpretation of Rashi, a famous medieval rabbi and scholar, suggests that Eglah is another name for Michal, David's first wife. Michal was the daughter of Saul, the first king of Israel, and she had a complex and often difficult relationship with David. If Eglah is indeed Michal, it would add another layer of complexity to the already intricate dynamics of David's family.

Shifting Allegiances (2 Samuel 3:6-21)

) The Fateful Accusation (2 Samuel 3:6-11)

As the extended war continues, Ishbosheth, Saul's son and the puppet king of Israel, accuses Abner, his chief military commander, of having an illicit relationship with one of Saul's concubines, a serious violation of royal rights (v. 7). This accusation greatly angers Abner, who had been loyal to Saul's house despite the ongoing conflict with David.

Abner's anger leads him to declare that he will switch his allegiance from Saul's house to David (v. 9-10). He promises to assist in fulfilling God's covenant with David, to make him ruler over all of Israel, from Dan to Beersheba. This is a significant turning point in the narrative, indicating a shift in power away from Saul's house and towards David.

Upon hearing Abner's declaration, Ishbosheth is left speechless and fearful (v. 11). He is unable to respond or challenge Abner, demonstrating his weak position and lack of authority. This moment marks the beginning of the end for Ishbosheth's rule over Israel.

) The Abner Negotiations (2 Samuel 3:12-21)

Continuing the narrative, Abner initiates negotiations with David (v. 12-13). He sends messengers to David on his behalf, proposing a covenant and stating his intention to bring all Israel under David's rule. David agrees to meet with Abner, but stipulates that his first wife, Michal, must be returned to him. Michal had been given to another man by Saul, and David's demand for her return is a symbolic assertion of his royal rights.

David sends messengers to Ishbosheth, demanding Michal's return. Ishbosheth, weak and fearful, complies with David's demand and sends Michal to David, further demonstrating his loss of power and control (v. 14-16).

With Michal returned, Abner is free to meet with David. He gathers the elders of Israel and Benjamin and shares his plans to transfer their allegiance to David (v. 17-19). He then meets with David, who welcomes him and throws a feast in his honor (v. 20). Abner leaves the feast with David's blessing, ready to fulfill his promise to deliver all Israel to him (v. 21).

Remember, Abner, who had previously been self-serving and made Ishbosheth the puppet king, is now turning to David in anger and pledging the rest of the tribes to him, mostly out of spite. However, in times of war, motivations are rarely of concern.

Joab's Revenge (2 Samuel 3:22-30)

) Joab's Return and Confrontation (2 Samuel 3:22-25)

While these negotiations were taking place, Joab, David's nephew and the commander of his army, had been away on a military raid. Upon his return, Joab was informed about Abner's visit and the agreement he had made with David. This news did not sit well with Joab.

Joab had a personal vendetta against Abner for killing his brother Asahel during a previous battle (2 Samuel 2:23). So, he met with David and expressed his concerns about Abner's sudden change of allegiance. Joab suspected that Abner had visited David under the guise of peace, but with the real intention of spying on David and gathering information that could be used against him in the ongoing war (vv. 24-25).

In fact, Joab's suspicion could have been valid. Abner might have had ulterior motives, leveraging his newfound alliance with David to gain strategic information and advantage for his own purposes. However, it's equally possible that Abner genuinely wanted to support David. Given his disappointment with Ishbosheth and his recognition of David's growing strength, Abner might have seen aligning with David as the most logical and advantageous course of action. Unfortunately, the text does not provide a definitive answer to Abner's motivations, leaving us in the realm of speculation.

) Murder At The Gate (vv. 26-27)

Joab, driven by his suspicion and a need for personal vengeance, called for Abner to return from his journey. Notably, Joab did this without David's knowledge, acting entirely on his own.

Abner was met by Joab at the gate of Hebron. It's important to understand the structure of city gates during this time period. City gates in the ancient Near East were complex structures, often consisting of a series of chambers that provided space for various activities, including commerce, legal proceedings, and social gatherings. These chambers could also provide a certain level of privacy, allowing actions to occur out of the public eye.

Under the guise of a private conversation in a secluded chamber, Joab lured Abner away. Unseen by the city's residents, Joab struck Abner *"under the fifth rib,"* echoing the manner in which Abner had killed Joab's brother Asahel.

However, Abner's act occurred somewhat in self-defense during the height of battle. In contrast, Joab's action was deliberate and premeditated, motivated by personal revenge rather than self-defense.

196

☞ In the biblical context, the phrase *"under the fifth rib"* is used to describe fatal wounds, and it appears a few times, particularly in the books of 2 Samuel and 1 Kings. These references often describe the death of a character by stabbing, implying a targeted and effective method of assassination or combat killing.

Here are a few specific examples:

1. **2 Samuel 2:23:** – Abner kills Asahel by striking him *"under the fifth rib."*

2. **2 Samuel 3:27:** – Joab kills Abner with a stab *"under the fifth rib."*

3. **2 Samuel 4:6:** – Rechab and Baanah kill Ish-bosheth, hitting him *"under the fifth rib."*

4. **2 Samuel 20:10:** – Joab kills Amasa, striking him *"under the fifth rib."*

5. **1 Kings 2:25:** – Solomon has Adonijah killed by Benaiah, who strikes him *"under the fifth rib."*

Medically speaking, referring to a wound *"under the fifth rib"* would imply a stab wound to the torso, potentially reaching vital organs. The heart itself lies slightly left of the center of the chest and under the ribs, so a stab wound *"under the fifth rib"* could indeed reach the heart, particularly if the weapon were directed slightly towards the left side of the chest.

However, the area under the fifth rib could also encompass other critical structures such as parts of the lungs and major blood vessels like the aorta.

) David's Response (vv. 28-30)

Upon learning of Abner's death, David immediately distanced himself and his kingdom from Joab's actions. He declared his innocence and the innocence of his kingdom before God, marking Joab and his family as the guilty party (v. 28). David understood the political and social implications of Abner's murder. It was not only an act of personal vengeance but also a significant political assassination that could disrupt the fragile relationship between David's and Saul's houses.

In response to Joab's actions, David pronounced a curse on Joab and his descendants (v. 29). The curse was comprehensive, affecting Joab's family line with various afflictions, including physical ailments, economic hardship, and social disgrace. David called for there to always be someone in Joab's family who is a leper, a man who leans on a crutch (possibly due to disability or injury), a man who falls by the sword, or a man who lacks bread. The curse reflected the severity of Joab's crime and David's strong condemnation of it.

The passage concludes by naming Joab and his brother Abishai as the murderers of Abner, reiterating that they killed him to avenge the death of their brother Asahel (v. 30). While Abner had killed Asahel in self-defense during a battle, Joab's murder of Abner was a premeditated act of vengeance, carried out in a time of peace.

As for the fulfillment of David's curse, the biblical narrative does not provide explicit instances of Joab's family suffering from the specific afflictions mentioned in the curse. However, Joab himself met a violent end. In 1 Kings 2:28-34, Joab was killed by Benaiah, under the orders of Solomon, for his past murders and for supporting Adonijah's claim to the throne. Joab's death, and the subsequent transfer of his military position to Benaiah, can be seen as a form of divine retribution for his actions and a partial fulfillment of David's curse.

) Lamenting Abner (vv. 31-39)

In verse 31, David orders Joab and all the people with him to tear their clothes, put on sackcloth, and mourn for Abner. This is a significant gesture, as the tearing of clothes and wearing of sackcloth were traditional signs of deep grief and mourning in ancient Israel. By ordering his people to mourn for Abner, David is publicly expressing his sorrow and respect for Abner, despite their past conflicts.

David further honors Abner by fasting until the evening, a sign of deep personal grief. His lament over Abner is heartfelt and profound, as he calls Abner *"a prince and a great man"* who has fallen in Israel (v. 38). Despite their past adversities, David acknowledges Abner's status and contributions, and he mourns his death sincerely. This public display of grief also serves to distance David from Joab's act of vengeance, showing the people that he had no part in Abner's murder.

"The sons of Zeruiah" referred to in verse 39 are Joab and his brothers Abishai and Asahel. Zeruiah was their mother and the sister of David, making the brothers David's nephews. David's lament that these men are *"too hard"* for him could be an expression of his frustration and inability to control their violent and vengeful actions, which have complicated his political and personal relationships and threatened the unity of his kingdom.

199

The fact that the people of Judah did not blame David for Abner's death (v. 37) is significant. It shows that they recognized David's integrity and sincere grief over Abner's death, and they did not associate him with Joab's act of vengeance. This likely strengthened their trust and loyalty towards David.

Finally, in verse 36, the people's agreement with David's lament for Abner is an affirmation of their support for David. Their approval of his words and actions shows that they were not just blindly following their king, but they were genuinely proud of his leadership and his commitment to justice and peace.

Conclusion

In this chapter, we've seen the complexities of political alliances and personal grudges in the early days of David's reign. We've witnessed the turning of allegiances, the tragic aftermath of unquenched revenge, and the deep mourning of a king. David's integrity and commitment to justice shine through, as he distances himself from Joab's act of vengeance and mourns sincerely for his adversary, Abner.

As we look forward to Chapter 4, be prepared for further political intrigue, personal conflicts, and shifts in power. The narrative will continue to unfold with surprising twists and turns, revealing more about the lives, motivations, and fates of the key players in this remarkable period of biblical history.

Chapter 23:

RISE OF A KING: POWER, CONFLICT, AND FAITH

2 Samuel 4:1-5:5

In the previous chapter of 2 Samuel, David, as the anointed king, faces new challenges and experiences. Amidst an ongoing war between the kingdom of Judah, under David, and the kingdom of Israel, under Ishbosheth, we witness the weakening of Saul's house. The narrative brings us closer to David's family life, introducing his six sons, Amnon, Chileab, Absalom, Adonijah, Shephatiah, and Ithream, from his different wives. The tales of David's sons foreshadow the heartache, intrigue, rebellion, and political struggles that lay ahead in their lives and the kingdom. As we move on to 2 Samuel 4, brace yourselves for further twisting tales of power, loyalty, and conflict.

Ishbosheth's Weakness and Murder (2 Samuel 4:1-8)

Upon learning of Abner's death, Ishbosheth, the figurehead king, felt his strength dissipate. He was described as a king with feeble hands (v. 1). Abner was the real power behind his reign, and without him, Ishbosheth knew there was no one left to guide him. His fear wasn't only personal, it permeated the entire nation. The gap left by Abner's death destabilized the country, leading to all the Israelites being troubled. The future of the kingdom was uncertain, causing widespread distress among the people.

Verses 2-3 introduce us to Baanah and Rechab. These brothers, like Saul, were Benjamites. They are pivotal figures as we progress through this chapter. After the death of Abner, they are presented as the new men in charge. Their actions and decisions will significantly influence the unfolding events in the kingdom.

In a somewhat abrupt transition in verse 5, we are introduced to Mephibosheth, the son of Jonathan. He was only five when his father and grandfather, Saul, died in battle. In the chaotic rush to flee from the impending danger, Mephibosheth was involved in an accident that left him lame. Although Mephibosheth's introduction here seems random, he will play a significant role later in the narrative. At this point, his mention serves to highlight the precarious state of the kingdom's leadership. With a fearful king, two ambitious generals, a nation gripped by fear, and a crippled child as the only heir apparent, the kingdom was indeed in dire straits.

As we continue with the narrative, we find Baanah and Rechab visiting Ishbosheth in the middle of the day, only to find him in bed - at noon! While there might be a multitude of reasons why Ishbosheth was in bed at such an hour, it paints a rather unflattering picture of the state of his kingship. Ishbosheth, being the youngest son of Saul, was never groomed for kingship and was likely used to the comforts provided by his father's wealth. It seems probable that sleeping until noon wasn't an unusual luxury for him, but rather a normal part of his daily routine. This depiction underlines the weakness of his rule and further highlights the instability of the kingdom.

The two individuals enter and end up assassinating him, but it is unclear whether this was premeditated or a spur-of-the-moment act. His death is described using the familiar phrase, *"they smote him under the fifth rib"* (v. 6). They entered *"as though they would have fetched wheat."* In the King James Version, this phrase is interpreted as a ruse or a cover, likely indicating a premeditated assassination. However, if we remove the interpretive

202

phrase *"as though,"* it could mean that they actually came with the intention of fetching wheat. Already anxious about the kingdom's state, they might have found the king asleep, become enraged, and taken matters into their own hands.

The phrase *"they smote him under the fifth rib"* (v. 6) is clarified further in verse 7, where we see that *"they smote him, and slew him, and beheaded him."* This helps us understand that the phrase to be smote *"under the fifth rib"* can be understood somewhat idiomatically. It likely refers to a fatal wound to the torso, possibly the heart or other vital organs located in the chest area. The phrase is repeated in several instances in the Old Testament, generally referring to a lethal stab wound. It's not necessary to take the phrase strictly literally, but rather as an idiomatic expression denoting a fatal injury.

In fact, this assassination appears to be something akin to a *"crime of passion."* Here, the *"passion"* is not romantic or sexual in nature, but rather born out of fear and concern for the future. Seeing their king, Ishbosheth, in such a state of weakness and incompetence, and faced with the prospect of a continued war with the tribe of Judah, Baanah and Rechab may have been filled with a sense of dread about the future. Fearing for their own lives and the future of their kingdom, they may have acted out of this intense emotion and desperation, leading to the impulsive and violent act of assassinating their king. As soon as the crime has been committed, the KJV poignantly states that they *"gat them away through the plain all night"* (v. 7).

The two assassins bring the head of Ishboseth to David, echoing David's actions with the head of Goliath. By doing so, they acknowledge him as their new leader.

203

David's Response and Retribution (2 Samuel 4:9-12)

Contrary to what Baanah and Rechab might have expected, David does not receive the news of Ishbosheth's death with joy or gratitude. Instead, he responds with intense anger and indignation. He recalls the previous incident when an Amalekite brought him the news of Saul's death, thinking that David would reward him. However, that messenger was met with death as a reward (v. 10). Now, these two men, Baanah and Rechab, have committed a far more heinous act - they have slain a righteous person in his own house upon his bed (v. 11). Likely David's reference to Ishbosheth as righteous pertains mostly to his innocence in any matter worthy of death.

David's anger likely stems from multiple factors. One of them being the method used to deal with the problem - assassination. David recognizes that if these men were willing to assassinate Ishbosheth, they might someday be willing to do the same to him. They have shown themselves to be untrustworthy and dangerous, willing to commit murder for personal gain.

In response to this act of assassination, David takes extreme measures. He orders the execution of Baanah and Rechab, and not only that, he also orders for their hands and feet to be cut off, and their bodies to be publicly displayed over the pool in Hebron (v. 12). This brutal punishment serves as a stark and clear message to all - assassination is not the way the kingdom that bears God's mark conducts its business. It is a clear warning against anyone who might contemplate such an act in the future. David's swift and severe response underscores his commitment to justice and his determination to uphold the integrity of his rule.

In contrast, David *"took the head of Ishbosheth, and buried it in the sepulchre of Abner in Hebron"* (v. 12). He intended to honor Saul's family and respect authority, making his intentions clear.

King, At Last (2 Samuel 5:1-5)

We have come a long way since Samuel anointed David as the next king (1 Samuel 16:1-13). A lot of water has flowed under the bridge since that significant event. With the weakening and ultimate dissolution of Saul's house, the nation was left with virtually no place else to turn. It was amidst these circumstances that the nation in full recognized David as the rightful monarch. The scripture states, *"and they anointed David king over Israel"* (v. 3). This was David's third anointing as king. First, he was anointed by Samuel in private, then by the tribe of Judah after Saul's death, and now, finally, he was anointed by the entire nation of Israel. This progression marks the different stages in David's journey to kingship, each anointing signifying a step closer to the fulfillment of God's promise.

Throughout his journey to kingship, David has displayed a complex mix of patience, strategic thinking, and at times, a lack of trust in God's timing. He has displayed admirable restraint and respect for God's anointed, as seen when he refused to harm Saul despite having the opportunity. This shows a deep understanding of the sanctity of God's anointing and a willingness to wait for God's timing.

However, there were also times when David's patience wore thin and his trust in God seemed to waver. A prime example of this is when he aligned himself with Achish, the king of Gath, out of fear for his life. This decision, which led to him living among the Philistines, seemed to be more of a survival tactic than a move of faith.

205

Yet, despite these moments of wavering, God remained true to His promises. David's journey to kingship was not straightforward or easy, but it was marked by God's steady hand guiding him through every challenge and setback. Now, with David finally recognized as the king of all Israel, the stage is set for some of the most exciting, challenging, and significant moments of his life. As we continue to explore David's story, we will see how his faith, leadership, and character are tested and refined in the crucible of kingship.

In verses 4-5, the author provides us with some crucial chronology. We learn that David was thirty years old when he began to reign, and he reigned for forty years. A breakdown of his reign is provided, detailing that he reigned in Hebron over Judah for seven years and six months, and in Jerusalem, where he reigned over all Israel and Judah, for thirty-three years. This timeline offers valuable insights into the duration of David's reign and the stages of his leadership.

A Pastoral Thought

Life rarely follows the rose-colored or burdensome paths we often envision. Most of the time, it consists of a routine, akin to the famous 1970s commercial of *"making the donuts."* In times of unbelievable defeat, we should resist the urge to give up, just as in times of unbelievable victory, we should resist the belief that we have fully arrived.

Life is more the sum of all its parts than it is a single part. It's a blend of highs and lows, victories and defeats, joys and sorrows. It's important not to let a single moment, whether good or bad, define our entire life.

Let's strive to live with purpose in mind. Yet, let's do it slowly, allowing ourselves the grace to grow and learn. Let's do it gratefully, appreciating the blessings we have and the journey we are on. Let's do it graciously, extending kindness and understanding to others. And above all, let's do it faithfully, trusting that even in the ups and downs, we are being guided towards a greater purpose.

THE DAVIDIC CHRONICLES

Chapter 24:

THE CONQUEST OF JERUSALEM

2 Samuel 5:6-12

In the preceding chapters of 2 Samuel, we witnessed the waning strength of Saul's house and the unsettling dynamics of Israel's leadership under Ishbosheth. The political landscape was fraught with instability, marked by internal strife and a lack of decisive leadership. As David emerges from these tumultuous conditions, 2 Samuel 5:6-12 represents a critical turning point in his ascent to power. Here, we see David not just as a king contending with rivals, but as a visionary leader who begins to establish Jerusalem as the unified capital of Israel and Judah. This chapter transitions from the fragmented leadership under Saul and Ishbosheth to David's strategic consolidation of power, highlighting his capture of Jerusalem from the Jebusites and the establishment of the city as both his political and spiritual stronghold. Through these acts, David lays the foundational stones of a kingdom that seeks to embody the divine covenant, setting the stage for a new era of leadership characterized by God's favor and a renewed sense of national identity.

Conquering Jerusalem (2 Samuel 5:6-9)

Jerusalem, an ancient city with a history dating back more than 5,000 years, was originally a Jebusite city. The Jebusites were a Canaanite group that inhabited the region of Judah before the arrival of the Israelites. They were one of several cultural groups living in the region during the Bronze Age and early Iron Age, and are frequently mentioned in the Hebrew Bible.

209

The Davidic Chronicles

Despite its strategic importance, Jerusalem was not taken by the Israelites during Joshua's initial conquest of Canaan. The Book of Joshua (15:63) notes that the Jebusites could not be driven out of Jerusalem. The city's formidable natural defenses, coupled with the Jebusites' tenacity, likely contributed to this. The Jebusites continued to hold Jerusalem until David's time, symbolizing an incomplete conquest and unfulfilled promise that David would ultimately fulfill.

The city's strategic location and natural defenses made it an attractive site for any aspiring power. It was perched on a ridge encircled by valleys, posing a challenge for enemy attacks. Moreover, the city was centrally located between Judah to the south and the other tribes of Israel to the east, west, and north.

The taunting of the Jebusites, *"Except thou take away the blind and the lame, thou shalt not come in hither,"* reflects their confidence in the city's fortifications. They felt so secure that they believed even the blind and lame could defend the city against David's forces. This statement also serves to underline the significance of David's eventual victory, overcoming what the Jebusites believed to be an impregnable city.

In 2 Samuel 5:7, we encounter the inaugural biblical mention of *"Zion"* with the phrase, *"David took the stronghold of Zion."* Initially, Zion referred specifically to the Jebusite fortress, strategically located on the hill that would later underpin the city of Jerusalem, renowned in later periods as the site of the temple. Over time, the significance of *"Zion"* transcended its original geographical connotation, evolving into a potent symbol of the spiritual and political nucleus of the Jewish people.

The etymology of *"Zion"* is believed to derive from a Semitic root meaning *"fortress"* or *"protected place."* This origin profoundly reflects David's aspiration to forge a secure and unified kingdom, a sanctuary under the divine auspices, embodying both physical safety and spiritual refuge. This transformation of Zion into a symbol of divine protection and national unity underscores its enduring significance in Jewish history and scripture.

The text also notes that *"the same is the city of David."* This phrase was likely included to provide clarity and specificity for the first readers of the Hebrew Scriptures, which include the book of 2 Samuel. By referring to Jerusalem as the *"city of David,"* the authors were able to unequivocally identify the city in question. This designation is used 40 times throughout the Hebrew Scriptures, reinforcing the connection between David and the city of Jerusalem. The frequent use of this phrase also serves to emphasize David's significant role in establishing Jerusalem as the political and spiritual center of the Israelite kingdom.

In verse 8, we have a brief explanation of how the city was conquered. David issued a challenge with a reward: whoever could infiltrate the city through the *"gutter"* or water system would be made captain of the guard. It's important to note that the words *"he shall be chief and captain"* are supplied by the translators, coming directly from 1 Chronicles 11:6 where it is explicitly stated. Furthermore, the phrase *"Wherefore they said, The blind and the lame shall not come into the house"* can be understood as *"because they said..."* This challenge, and the subsequent victory, underscored David's tactical insight and strategic leadership. It cannot be known for sure, but it is possible that Araunah the Jebusite, a friend of David, had revealed to him that this was the *"weak link"* of the city's fortifications.

In 1 Chronicles we are informed that Joab, whom we have met before, met the challenge, and thus was made captain of the guard.

In the late 19th century, a significant archaeological discovery was made that further illuminated David's conquest of Jerusalem. The British Palestine Exploration Fund sent Charles Warren to conduct an excavation in Jerusalem between 1867 and 1870. During this expedition, Warren discovered an ancient shaft now known as *"Warren's Shaft,"* which is thought to be the *"gutter"* mentioned in the account of David's siege.

Warren's Shaft is a vertical tunnel hewn out of the rock, providing access from within the city to the Gihon Spring, the city's primary water source. The existence of this tunnel would have allowed the city's inhabitants to access fresh water even during a siege, which would have significantly boosted the city's defenses. The discovery of the shaft suggests a possible method by which Joab could have infiltrated the city, fulfilling David's challenge and leading to the city's capture.

While there is ongoing debate among archaeologists about the exact dating of the shaft and its relation to David's conquest, the discovery of such a tunnel system highlights the strategic importance of water access in ancient warfare and provides potential historical context for the biblical narrative.

In verse 9, the text reads *"David built round about from Millo and inward."* The term *"Millo"* is derived from a Hebrew word that means *"filling"* or *"rampart,"* and it is often associated with a fortification or structure used in defense. In the context of Jerusalem, Millo is generally thought to be a steep fortification that bordered the eastern side of the city, close to the Kidron Valley.

Establishing Jerusalem (2 Samuel 5:10-12)

In verse 10, we read a summary note of David's victories, with a glimpse into the future with the words, *"David went on, and grew great."* Both the conquering of Jerusalem and the continued success were due to the fact that *"the LORD God of hosts was with him."* This title for God is connected to the armies of heaven, highlighting the strength of God. This heavenly support is a recurring theme in David's narrative, consistently linked to his military and political successes. It serves to emphasize that David's strength and victories were not purely the result of his own might and skill, but were a manifestation of God's favor and guidance.

Following the capture of Jerusalem and the establishment of his rule, David's successes attracted the attention of neighboring kingdoms. Hiram, the king of Tyre, a prosperous city-state known for its skilled artisans and high-quality cedar, sent *"cedar trees, and carpenters, and masons"* to David for the construction of his palace. This action was not only a strategic political move to establish alliances but was also likely an obligation. Previously, Tyre might have been required, perhaps under Saul's reign, to send tribute to the Israelite kingdom. The tribe of Asher, in whose territory Tyre would have been, had failed to conquer the city, and thus, like the Jebusites with Jerusalem, Tyre existed independently. Seeing the fall of Jerusalem and the rise of David's influence, Hiram was likely determined to ensure good relations with the new power in the region.

213

Now, likely at least 15 years or more from Samuel's anointing, David could rest in the knowledge that God had indeed *"established him king over Israel."* Even more, David understood that God had not done this just to bless him, but *"for his people Israel's sake"* (v. 12). This moment marked the fulfillment of God's promise, and it also underscored the purpose of David's leadership - to serve and guide God's people. David's kingship was not merely a personal triumph but a manifestation of God's care and plan for the nation of Israel.

Conclusion

In these pivotal events, we see the establishment of David's house, setting a precedent for God's promise in the forthcoming chapters: *"Thine house and thy kingdom shall be established for ever "* (2 Samuel 7:16). Just as the promises made through Samuel did not find immediate fulfillment, so too the ultimate promise about the kingdom of David experiences a delay. However, we can trust in God's divine timing. His promise to establish David's throne forever may not occur immediately, but we know it will come to fruition, in His time.

Chapter 25

TRUSTING IN GOD'S GUIDANCE AND STRENGTH

2 Samuel 5:13-25

In the last chapter, we witnessed David's strategic consolidation of power with his capture of Jerusalem, a city that previously symbolized an incomplete conquest and an unfulfilled promise. This was a significant turning point, marking the transition from fragmented leadership to a unified kingdom under David's rule. David's victory over the Jebusites not only secured a political stronghold but also laid the foundation for Jerusalem becoming a spiritual sanctuary for the Israelites.

As we proceed to Chapter 25, we will dive deeper into David's expansion of his household and his encounters with the Philistines. We will explore how David, now firmly established in Jerusalem, navigates new challenges and further consolidates his power.

Expansion of David's Household (2 Samuel 5:13-16)

After conquering Jerusalem, David "took him more concubines and wives" (v. 13). This phrase reflects the cultural context of the time, where it was common for kings to have multiple wives and concubines. The wives were legally married to the king and had certain rights and privileges. The concubines, on the other hand, were women who lived with the king and bore him children, but they did not have the same legal status or rights as the wives. It's important to note that the Bible presents this information without a moral judgment. It is simply stating the facts of David's actions and the common practices of the era.

The Davidic Chronicles

Before the events of this chapter, the Bible tells us that David already had several wives. Michal, Saul's daughter, was David's first wife (1 Samuel 18:27). He then married Ahinoam of Jezreel and Abigail, the widow of Nabal of Carmel (1 Samuel 25:42-43). While in Hebron, David took additional wives, including Maacah, Haggith, Abital, and Eglah (2 Samuel 3:2-5). So, we know of at least seven wives and concubines that David had prior to his conquest of Jerusalem. However, the wives and concubines that David took in Jerusalem are not listed by name in the Biblical text. Later, of course, we will add Bathsheba to the list.

In the list of David's children born in Jerusalem, eleven sons are mentioned by name, although there were others, such as Absalom and Adonijah, who were born before David took Jerusalem. Among the sons listed here, two stand out for their prominence: Nathan and Solomon.

Nathan, though not as well-known as his brother Solomon, holds a significant place in the genealogy of Jesus. According to the Gospel of Luke (Luke 3:31), Nathan is the ancestor of Mary, Jesus' mother. This lineage establishes Jesus' legal right to David's throne, providing a strong link between the Old Testament promises made to David and their fulfillment in the New Testament with Jesus Christ.

Solomon, the most famous of David's sons listed here, succeeded David as king of Israel. His reign is known for its wisdom, wealth, and significant achievements, most notably the building of the First Temple in Jerusalem. Solomon's reign is considered the height of Israel's power and influence, and his wisdom is still celebrated today.

The text employs a technique called "chronological compression" to condense a significant amount of information into just a few verses. This method allows the author to give a broad overview of events or actions without going into extensive detail. For instance, Solomon, one of the most significant figures in the Bible, is mentioned here only in passing. His story, including his wisdom, his reign, and his relationship with his mother Bathsheba, will be given much more attention in later chapters. Interestingly, Bathsheba, despite her crucial role in the narrative, is not mentioned by name in this list. This is a common feature of chronological compression, where certain details are omitted in the initial summary but will be thoroughly explored later in the text.

The Philistine Challenge (2 Samuel 5:17-25)

Upon hearing the news of David's coronation by all of Israel, the Philistines, a long-time adversary of Israel, saw this as a threat. They likely harbored resentment towards David, who had once deceived them by feigning alliance with them. In response, they mobilized their forces, "spreading themselves in the valley of Rephaim" (v. 18), a maneuver that suggested preparation for a large-scale conflict.

David's reaction to this impending threat might seem unusual for a king. Instead of rallying his forces, he "went down to the hold" (v. 17). This does not reflect cowardice but rather a strategic move. The "hold" here is likely referring to a defensive stronghold or a fortified place, where David could assess the situation and make strategic plans to counter the Philistine threat. This act demonstrates David's wisdom and prudence in not rushing into battle unprepared. It underscores the importance of careful planning and strategic thinking in handling conflicts, a lesson that holds true in our lives today.

When the scripture says David "went down to the hold" (v. 17) in response to the Philistine threat, it does not suggest that David was hiding in fear. Instead, the phrase "went down" is likely referring to David's strategic movement southward, probably towards a military stronghold or fortress. Given that David had already been king in Hebron for over seven years, it is plausible that he had prepared such strategic locations in anticipation of potential threats.

The Valley of Rephaim, often equated with the modern-day Emek Haarazim, held strategic value. Today, it's part of Jerusalem, but during David's reign, it was miles away from the city. Currently, the valley lies on the main route from Jerusalem to Tel Aviv and has been an important battlefield for safeguarding Jerusalem throughout history.

David did not rely solely on his military expertise or intuition. Instead, he "enquired of the LORD" (v. 19). This likely involved the use of Urim and Thummim, sacred lots used by the priests to determine God's will. The act of consulting the LORD before going into battle underlines David's dependence on God's guidance, at least at this strategic moment. God's response was unequivocal. He commanded David to "Go up," (that is, northward towards the Philistine encampment). God assured David that He would "doubtless deliver the Philistines into thine hand" (v. 19).

"Rightly dividing the word of truth," as stated in 2 Timothy 2:15, is a critical aspect of understanding and applying the Scriptures. In the context of David's time, the "inquiry of the Lord" often involved the use of Urim and Thummim. However, in our current dispensation, the means through which we inquire of the Lord have changed.

Today, our primary means of inquiring of the Lord is through His Word - the Bible, in conjunction with prayer for wisdom and guidance. We don't have the Urim and Thummim, but we do have the complete canon of Scripture and the wisdom of the Holy Spirit. The Bible, as stated in 2 Timothy 3:17, is given to us so that we may be "thoroughly furnished unto all good works."

Therefore, while acknowledging the historical and cultural context of David's time, we should recognize that our approach to seeking God's guidance should be rooted in prayerful study and application of God's Word. This being the case, we should take time to be well-grounded in the Scripture before a crisis so that we are able to make good decisions when a crisis comes.

From the biblical account, we understand that the battle at Baal-perazim was both swift and decisive. The scripture tells us that "David smote them there" (v. 20), indicating a successful attack on the Philistines. This victory was not a result of David's military prowess alone, but was also a fulfillment of the Lord's promise. After the victory, David praised the Lord, saying, "The LORD hath broken forth upon mine enemies before me" (v. 20). This statement reflects David's recognition of God's hand in his victory, acknowledging that it was God who had gone before him, breaking through his enemies.

David named the place "Baal-perazim," which translates to "Lord (Master) of Breakthroughs," as a way to honor and acknowledge God's intervention in his victory. The term "Baal-perazim" metaphorically depicts God's power and might breaking through like an unstoppable flood of water, overwhelming and defeating David's enemies. This powerful imagery celebrates God's decisive action against the Philistines and attributes David's success not to his own abilities, but to God's aid and favor.

In addition to the physical victory, David also created a spiritual victory by burning the idols of the Philistines (v. 21). These idols were likely brought into battle by the Philistines as symbols of protection or power. However, in the face of their sudden defeat and retreat, they left these idols behind. David's act of burning these idols was not just a physical demonstration of victory, but also a spiritual statement. It undermined the power of the Philistine gods and reaffirmed the supremacy of the God of Israel. This act served as a powerful reminder to both the Philistines and the Israelites that the God of Israel was the true God, superior to any other. Indeed, this day was not just a great victory in a military sense, but also a significant spiritual triumph.

Philistines Regroup and Attack Again (vv. 22-25)

Verse 22 informs us that the Philistines regrouped and returned to the same location for a second confrontation with David's forces. The text doesn't specify, but there must have been a lapse of time between these two encounters. This unspecified period could have been used for regrouping, strategizing, or even recovering from the first defeat. It's noteworthy that the Bible, in this instance, clusters these two accounts thematically, focusing on the recurring threat from the Philistines and David's responses, rather than strictly following a chronological order.

David's second inquiry to the LORD resulted in a different strategy for the impending battle. Rather than a direct attack as before, David was instructed to "fetch a compass behind them." This phrase, "fetch a compass," does not refer to a navigational device as we might think today. According to the Oxford English Dictionary, "fetch a compass" means to take a circular or circuitous course, or to make a detour. In the context of this scripture (v. 23), it meant that David and his forces were to make a detour, going west, and approach the Philistines from behind.[4]

In verse 24, David is told to wait until he hears the "sound of a going in the tops of the mulberry trees." This must have been a certain sign, possibly a rustling or movement in the trees, that would indicate that the Lord was going ahead of him into battle. This sound was not just a natural phenomenon, but was the marching of the Lord's heavenly forces. Just imagine if one could have seen that which David heard! Once again, this highlights the assurance that the victory would come not by David's military might alone, but by the power of the Lord fighting on Israel's behalf.

David's obedience to the Lord's instructions was a defining factor in the victory over the Philistines. As per the Lord's specific instructions, David and his forces made a detour and positioned themselves behind the Philistines. They then waited for a distinct sound—a rustling or movement in the mulberry trees, which was the sign that the Lord was going ahead of them into battle. Following this divine signal, David launched the attack. The phrase

---

4 "compass, n.1". OED Online, Oxford University Press, accessed 11 May 2024, https://www.oed.com/dictionary/compass_n1?tab=meaning_and_use#8801424.

that the Lord "smote the Philistines from Geba until thou come to Gazer" (v 25) displays the comprehensive defeat, showing that the Israelites pursued the Philistines over a considerable distance, from Geba to Gazer. These two towns were, it is believed, strategically located to provide an western barrier between Jerusalem and the Philistines.

In Isaiah 28:21, the prophet Isaiah references the battles at Baal-perazim and Gibeon (where the sun stood still) in a warning to Judah. Despite the passage of hundreds of years, these battles were still seen as pivotal moments in Israel's history because they symbolized God's power and intervention for His people.

Although there's limited information about the battle at Baal-perazim compared to other biblical battle narratives, its significance in Israel's history was still strong in Isaiah's day. It stood as a lasting symbol of God's power and His readiness to intervene on behalf of His people.

Conclusion

In conclusion, this segment offers powerful insights into David's reign. We witness David's unwavering dependence on God for guidance, reinforcing the importance of seeking divine counsel in all our decisions. We celebrate God as the Breaker, leading His people to a decisive victory against a longstanding adversary, the Philistines. Finally, we observe David's leadership, marked by both personal and public responsibility, setting an example for leaders in every generation. These narratives continue to inspire and guide us in our journey of faith today.

Chapter 26:

A Spiritual Home for Israel

2 Samuel 6:1-23

In the last chapter, we observed David's increasing consolidation of power - both in his household and in his kingdom. Following his conquest of Jerusalem, David expanded his household, taking more wives and concubines and fathering more children, including Solomon and Nathan, who would later become significant figures in Biblical history. David's power also extended beyond Jerusalem, as he faced and overcame challenges from the Philistines, demonstrating his strategic prowess and further solidifying his rule.

As we transition to the study of 2 Samuel 6, we anticipate a shift in focus from David's political and domestic life to the spiritual realm. This chapter highlights the role of religion and the presence of God in David's kingdom, which sets the stage for the arrival of the Ark of the Covenant in Jerusalem, a significant event in Israel's history.

The Return of the Ark (2 Samuel 6:1-5)

David handpicked a group of 30,000 elite men for a special mission—to return the Ark of the Covenant to its rightful place of honor in Jerusalem. This was not a military operation but rather a ceremonial display of strength and reverence. The Ark of the Covenant, which symbolized God's presence and covenant with Israel, had been a significant religious artifact since the time of Moses. The last major mention of the Ark was in 1 Samuel 4, where it was taken into battle by the Israelites against the Philistines. Unfortunately, Israel was defeated, and the Ark was captured by the Philistines.

However, the presence of the Ark brought calamity upon the Philistines, causing plagues and misfortune wherever it was kept. After seven months, the Philistines decided to return the Ark to Israel to escape the divine retribution. They sent it back on a cart with offerings of gold, and it arrived at Bethshemesh. There, some Israelites irreverently looked into the Ark, resulting in a great slaughter. Consequently, the people of Bethshemesh decided to send the Ark to Kirjathjearim, to the house of Abinadab.

During this period, Israel underwent significant leadership changes. The Ark's stay in Kirjathjearim spanned the later years of Samuel's judgeship and the entire reign of King Saul, who ruled for 40 years. By the time David became king, the Ark had been at Abinadab's house for over 40 years. Recognizing the importance of the Ark both spiritually and politically, David decided to transport it to Jerusalem with much fanfare. This grand exhibition of regal authority and religious devotion was intended to consolidate his political power and fortify the nation's spiritual foundation. By bringing the Ark to Jerusalem, David aimed to establish the city not only as the political capital but also as the spiritual center of Israel, uniting the tribes under his leadership and reaffirming their covenant with God.

In verse 2, the term "Baale of Judah" refers to the same location as Kirjathjearim. It's one of the names used for this city in the Old Testament. So, when the Ark is mentioned as being moved from Baale of Judah, it indicates that it was being transported from the house of Abinadab in Kirjathjearim.

In verse 3, the phrase "they set the Ark of God upon a new cart" is significant. This mirrors what the Philistines had done when they returned the Ark, but it's important to realize that the Philistines were not under the Mosaic Law, while the Israelites were. According to the Mosaic Law, the Ark should be transported by the Levites (specifically the Kohathites) carrying it on their shoulders with poles that go through rings on the sides of the Ark, not on a cart. As we will see later, this seemingly minor deviation from God's instructions will put them in great danger, emphasizing the importance of following God's commands exactly as they are given.

Can you just imagine the scene on that day? The jubilation, the honor, the national pride, the spiritual high that must have characterized the occasion! Thirty thousand of the finest troops, the king leading the procession, the Ark of the Covenant finally coming to its rightful place of honor. The Philistines, their formidable adversaries, had been defeated not once but twice, miraculously. The air was filled with the sound of music playing royal songs. Truly, it was a day of days! It was a grand display of national unity, spiritual devotion, and divine favor. This was not just a historic event; it was a deeply spiritual moment that underscored God's presence and favor in their midst.

Uzzah's Death and David's Reaction (2 Samuel 6:6-11)

As the procession continued, an incident occurred that revealed the serious consequences of disregarding God's instructions. The Ark, as mentioned above, was to be cared for and carried only in a certain manner, as dictated by the Mosaic Law. This was not a mere suggestion but an explicit command from God, emphasizing the sacredness of the Ark. It was a principle that had severe implications if not followed, as the case of Aaron's sons offering strange fire before the Lord had previously demonstrated.

When the oxen pulling the cart stumbled, a man named Uzzah instinctively reached out to steady the Ark. Unfortunately, his well-intended act was a direct violation of God's command. As a result, Uzzah was struck dead by the Lord on the spot, a shocking incident that halted the joyful procession.

David's reaction to Uzzah's death was one of anger. Whether this anger was directed at himself, at the Lord, or at Uzzah for his impulsive act, we cannot be certain. However, what we do know is that this incident had a profound impact on David. He named the place "Perez-Uzzah," which means "the outbreak against Uzzah," echoing the term "Perezim" used in the previous chapter when God broke forth against the Philistines.

In the aftermath of this tragic event, David had to find a temporary home for the Ark. He chose the home of Obed-Edom the Gittite, where the Ark stayed for three months. Remarkably, during this time, Obed-Edom's household was blessed, a clear indication that when treated with the respect it deserved, the presence of the Ark (and by extension, the Lord) brought blessings and not calamity. This likely reassured David and the people of Israel that if they revered the Ark and the Lord correctly, they too would experience His blessings.

226

The Ark is Brought to Jerusalem (2 Samuel 6:12-19)

When David heard about the blessings that Obed-Edom's household was receiving because of the Ark's presence, he interpreted it as a divine sign that it was safe to resume the journey to Jerusalem. Before the Ark was moved, David made sure to offer a sacrifice to God every "six paces" (approximately 36 feet). This act of reverence and devotion likely served as a public affirmation of his faith and a reminder to the Israelites of the sacredness of their mission.

One of the most memorable parts of this journey, particularly for those familiar with the Bible, was David's dance before the Ark. Wearing a "linen ephod," David danced with all his might in a display of sincere and uninhibited worship. The ephod was a garment associated with the priests of Israel and was made of fine linen. It was a sleeveless, apron-like garment that was worn over the clothes. David wearing the ephod symbolized his role not only as a king but also as a spiritual leader leading his people in worship.

Finally, the Ark of the Covenant was brought into the City of David, also known as Jerusalem. This momentous occasion was marked by shouting and the sound of trumpets, a grand celebration fitting for such a significant event. The Ark's arrival in Jerusalem symbolized the fulfillment of David's ambition to establish Jerusalem as the spiritual center of Israel, reinforcing his leadership and the nation's covenant with God.

Psalm 87, a song of celebration of Jerusalem, is believed to have been composed either for or in light of this significant occasion of bringing the Ark of the Covenant to Jerusalem. The Psalm extols the city of Jerusalem, reflecting the joy and reverence associated with making it the spiritual center of Israel.

As the Ark of the Covenant was brought into the city, David, in his joy, danced and celebrated before the Lord with all his might. This celebration was not only a religious ceremony, but also a public festival for all the people of Israel, regardless of their gender or social status. Everyone was included in this celebration. David distributed among the entire population, to every man and woman, a loaf of bread, a piece of meat, a bottle of wine, and a cake of raisins. It was truly a day to remember, a day of joy and unity, a day of spiritual significance.

However, this scene of joy and celebration was marred by one person's disdain - Michal, the daughter of Saul and David's wife. As she looked out of the window and saw David's uninhibited and ecstatic dancing, she despised him in her heart. This is recorded in verse 16, which says, "Michal Saul's daughter looked through a window, and saw king David leaping and dancing before the LORD; and she despised him in her heart."

It seems not everyone was happy.

Michal Confronts David (2 Samuel 6:20-23)

Michal, Saul's daughter and David's wife, confronts David after the celebration. She sarcastically remarks, "How glorious was the king of Israel to day, who uncovered himself to day in the eyes of the handmaids of his servants, as one of the vain fellows shamelessly uncovereth himself!" (v. 20). This comment paints a picture in the public imagination that David was dancing nearly naked before the Lord, a notion that has often been chosen over the actual description provided in the scriptures. Contrary to this belief, we know that David was wearing a linen ephod (v. 14), which was not an immodest garment. This is an example of how sensational interpretations can sometimes overshadow the actual text.

It's likely that Michal, still smarting from past events, resented the victory celebration for David and believed that he should have been more dignified and royal in his behavior. She probably disapproved of David discarding his royal attire in favor of the humble garment of a priest and worshiper, thus aligning himself with the common man. This was not how her father, Saul, would have conducted himself.

David, deeply hurt by Michal's disrespect, let her know who was the real king. The text suggests that this confrontation had such a profound impact on their relationship that David never had relations with her again.

Chapter 27:

The Davidic Covenant:

The Genesis of the Kingdom of God

2 Samuel 7

Now that the Ark of the Covenant is securely in Jerusalem, David's focus shifts from consolidating political and spiritual power to creating a permanent dwelling for the Ark and the Jewish worship. In 2 Samuel 7, we see a significant shift from David's immediate actions to his long-term vision for Israel and its relationship with God. He expresses his desire to build a permanent house for the Lord, moving from his personal and national accomplishments to his spiritual aspirations for his people. This chapter represents a critical moment in Biblical history. God responds to David's plans by establishing an eternal covenant, promising to secure David's lineage and Israel's future in ways that extend beyond the physical construction of a temple.

David's Desire (2 Samuel 7:1-3)

In the time between 2 Samuel 6 and 7, a time of unknown duration, David achieves a position of personal victory and political power. It was a time in which David and his kingdom had "rest round about from all his enemies" (v. 1). Having successfully brought the Ark back to Jerusalem (2 Samuel 6), David is now able to shift his focus from his immediate challenges to more long-term, spiritual objectives.

In verse 2, we are introduced for the first time to Nathan the prophet. Nathan is set to become a significant figure in the narrative, serving as an advisor and counselor to both

David and his son Solomon. He will be present for some of the most significant events of their reigns. Despite his importance, we know little about Nathan himself. According to 1 Chronicles 29:29, he had a written record of David's reign, but this document has unfortunately been lost to history.

In this time of peace, David reflects on his own living conditions and compares them to where the Ark of the Covenant resides. He lives in a "house of cedar," which signifies a well-built, permanent structure - a stark contrast to the tent where the Ark is currently housed. David feels a sense of injustice; it doesn't sit well with him that the symbol of God's presence among His people is kept in a temporary and movable structure while he enjoys the comfort of a permanent dwelling.

Interestingly, the design God initially gave for the Tabernacle was intended to be "within curtains" (v.2), implying a temporary or movable nature. It would be intriguing to know more about David's thought process regarding this. Did he believe that building a more permanent structure for the Ark would offer a stronger symbol of God's unchanging and eternal nature? Or was it a desire to present a more honoring dwelling for God in response to the blessings and peace he had received? Unfortunately, the text does not provide further insights into David's contemplation on this matter.

Nathan, as the prophet of God, initially responds positively to David's intentions. He tells David to "Go, do all that is in thy heart; for the Lord is with thee" (v.3). This response seems to be a confirmation of David's plan, suggesting that the Lord is in agreement with David's desire to build a more permanent dwelling place for the

Ark. Nathan is essentially giving David the green light to proceed, assuring him that his intentions align with God's will and that he has God's blessing in this endeavor.

However, as it soon becomes apparent, the "short answer" Nathan initially provides doesn't turn out to be the "long answer" that God is about to give. This upcoming revelation will alter the plans but will also deliver such a tremendously positive message to David that it becomes difficult to categorize Nathan's initial response as "wrong". The shift in God's instructions represents the complexity and depth of His will. I hesitate to categorize Nathan's initial response as being hasty because, if anything, David comes out of the scene with more of God's "stamp of approval" than has been given any man since Abraham.

God's Affirmation (2 Samuel 7:4-11)

Following Nathan's confident response in verse 3, the Lord appears to Nathan with a question for David: "Shalt thou build me an house for me to dwell in?" (v. 5). The tone of this question is challenging to interpret. It can be perceived negatively, implying chastisement for David presuming to build God a permanent home without being asked. It can also be viewed positively, signifying honor to David, who has shown the initiative to propose a more permanent place of worship, unlike others in the hundreds of years since the need for a traveling tabernacle ended.

The context in verses 6 and 7 doesn't provide a definitive answer to this, and the interpretation can swing either way. Although many lean towards a negative interpretation, it's worth questioning this perspective. God ultimately accepts David's offer (though he commands a delay in the construction), and in doing so, affirms David in such a significant way that it surpasses any approval given to a man since Abraham. This level of affirmation suggests that God might indeed be honoring David's initiative rather than chastising his presumption.

The word "therefore" in verse 8 suggests a more positive interpretation of God's question. The subsequent verses, from 8 to 11, are affirming and positive in every aspect. God recognizes David's efforts, recounts what He has done for David, and promises to establish a permanent place for His worship. This means that the children of Israel won't have to shift their place of worship anymore - God will establish Jerusalem as their spiritual home. Moreover, in response to David's desire, God promises to build a "house" for David (v. 11). Given that David already has a "house of cedar" (v. 2), God's promise refers to a "house" in the sense of establishing a dynasty for David.

The Davidic Covenant (2 Samuel 7:12-17)

The verses from 2 Samuel 7:12-17 are some of the most significant covenantal verses in the entire Bible. They describe what is often referred to as the Davidic Covenant. It is a unilateral covenant, meaning it is entirely dependent on God for fulfillment and not on any human effort.

God begins by stating that when David's time comes and he passes away (v. 12), God will "set up thy seed after thee, which shall proceed out of thy bowels, and I will establish his kingdom" (v. 12). This is a prophetic declaration about the lineage of David, and it immediately applies to Solomon, David's son. Importantly, this prophecy refers to a child who has not yet been born ("which shall proceed out of thy bowels"), thus it does not pertain to any of David's already born sons. In its simplest interpretation, this is a prophecy about the reign of Solomon. However, could there be a deeper, more significant meaning, perhaps even a messianic prophecy? Many biblical scholars and students of the Word believe so.

The verses seem to have a dual fulfillment, a common occurrence in Hebrew prophecy. On one hand, they refer to Solomon, who will construct the "House for my name" (v. 13). This is a direct reference to Solomon's future role in building the physical temple in Jerusalem. On the other hand, these verses also point to the Messiah, who will build the dynastic "house" - an eternal throne that God promises to David. This dual interpretation provides a bridge between immediate historical events and the future messianic promises, revealing the depth and breadth of God's covenant with David.

Verse 14 appears is perplexing: "I will be his father, and he shall be my son." While this statement holds true for the Messiah, it doesn't seem to apply to Solomon. However, the subsequent words, "If he commit iniquity," appear to refer specifically to Solomon, not the Messiah. This presents a complex interpretation challenge.

Personally, I interpret these verses, including verse 14, as pertaining more to the Messiah than to Solomon. The mention of committing iniquity might seem to refer to Solomon at first glance. However, in a broader, prophetic sense, it could be indicative of the reality that the Messiah would bear the sins of humanity. This concept finds its resonance in the New Testament, specifically in 1 Peter 2:24, "Who his own self bare our sins in his own body on the tree, that we, being dead to sins, should live unto righteousness: by whose stripes ye were healed." This interpretation aligns the Davidic Covenant with the ultimate redemption brought about by the Messiah.

Verses 15-16 in 2 Samuel 7 establish the everlasting nature of the Messiah's throne. These verses state, "But my mercy shall not depart away from him, as I took it from Saul, whom I put away before thee. And thine house and thy kingdom shall be established for ever before thee: thy throne shall be established for ever." This divine promise seems unsuited to Solomon, whose kingdom was divided after his death and eventually fell to the Babylonians. This leaves the prophecy, seemingly, unfulfilled and awaiting a son of David to step into the role.

Christians believe that this prophecy will be fulfilled in the person of Jesus Christ, who is genealogically confirmed in Scripture to be a descendant of David. Jesus is the promised Messiah, the eternal King whose reign will be everlasting, fulfilling the prophecy in these verses.

Dispensational Christians refer to the Davidic Covenant as God's promise to King David about the future of the Israelite monarchy. According to this covenant, God promises to establish a kingdom for David's lineage, with an heir from David's line having an eternal kingdom. Dispensationalists believe this covenant is unconditional and literal, and they anticipate its fulfillment in the future millennial reign of Jesus Christ, who is understood to be the promised heir from David's line.

David's Response to God (2 Samuel 7:18-29)

In response to God's remarkable promise, David enters into a moment of profound reflection and prayer. Verses 18-29 capture David's humility, gratitude, and faith as he contemplates the magnitude of God's covenant with him. In fact, David's words are so positive that I think we can use them as confirmation that the Lord was entirely pleased with David's heart and desire to build a permanent Temple.

) David's Humility (Verses 18-21)

David begins by expressing his humility before God. He goes into the tent where the Ark of the Covenant is kept and sits before the Lord, a gesture of reverence and submission. He starts by acknowledging his unworthiness, asking, "Who am I, O Lord God? and what is my house, that thou hast brought me hitherto?" (v. 18). David is acutely aware of his humble beginnings as a shepherd and the extraordinary grace that has elevated him to kingship.

David continues by marveling at the future promise God has made, not just for him, but for his house. He is overwhelmed by the grandeur of God's plan, which extends far beyond his own lifetime. David recognizes that God's dealings with him are not merely about his personal achievements but about establishing a work that will impact future generations. He sees this promise as a reflection of God's greatness and faithfulness.

) David's Praise for God's Greatness (Verses 22-24)

David transitions from humility to praise, declaring, "Wherefore thou art great, O Lord God: for there is none like thee, neither is there any God beside thee" (verse 22). He acknowledges God's uniqueness and incomparability, emphasizing that no other god or power can match the Lord's greatness.

David then reflects on God's historical acts of deliverance for Israel. He recounts how God redeemed His people from Egypt, establishing them as a nation and making them His own. David recognizes that Israel's identity and destiny are

237

intricately linked to God's covenantal promises and mighty acts. This reflection underscores the continuity between God's past faithfulness and His future promises to Israel. The Davidic Covenant, as we call it, is a covenant with all the nation of Israel.

) David's Prayer for the Fulfillment of God's Promises (Verses 25-29)

David prays for the fulfillment of God's promises. He requests that the Lord establish the house of David and confirm His word forever, so that God's name may be magnified. David's prayer is centered on the glory of God, desiring that the fulfillment of the covenant will demonstrate God's faithfulness and bring honor to His name. He asks, "Do as thou hast said" (verse 25), showing his complete trust in God's promises.

David concludes his prayer by reiterating his faith in God's promise and seeking God's blessing upon his house. He acknowledges that it is God's revelation that has emboldened him to pray this prayer, expressing confidence that God's promise will indeed come to pass. David prays for God's blessing to rest upon his house forever, recognizing that true blessing comes from the Lord's favor and presence.

In this prayer, David demonstrates a deep understanding of God's sovereignty and faithfulness. He humbly submits to God's will, praises Him for His greatness, and earnestly prays for the fulfillment of His promises. David's response exemplifies a heart of worship, trust, and dependence on God.

238

The Beginning of the Kingdom of God

Prior to this point, there was no concept of the "Kingdom of God" in Biblical theology. Yes, God had made several promises: A Deliverer would come, born of a woman (Gen. 3:15), a prophet like Moses would arise (Deut. 18:15), and all the families of the earth would be blessed through the descendants of Abraham (Gen. 12:1-3). This blessing would specifically come through the line of Judah (Gen. 49:10). However, the notion of God establishing His kingdom on earth through this Deliverer was entirely unprecedented.

In fact, God's initial reaction to Israel's request for a king was negative, as seen in 1 Samuel 8. The people wanted a king to be like the other nations around them, but this was not God's original plan for His chosen people. Despite this, God granted their request, appointing Saul, and later David, as king.

Now, in 2 Samuel 7, God promises an everlasting throne with a Son of David upon it. This is the first time we see the concept of the "Kingdom of God" being introduced in Scripture. God is not just promising a king or a human kingdom, but an eternal dominion under the rulership of a Davidic descendant. This promise goes beyond any earthly monarchy—it introduces the theological idea of God's reign on earth, a concept that becomes central to both the Old Testament prophetic books and the New Testament.

This marks a significant shift in the narrative of God's covenantal relationship with His people. It introduces the idea that God's plan extends beyond individual leaders or nations to encompass a universal Kingdom under His rule. The Davidic Covenant, therefore, is the foundation for the Kingdom theology that unfolds throughout the rest of the Bible and is yet to be fully realized on earth.

The Davidic Chronicles

David certainly had a messianic expectation, as did all of Israel at the time. He anticipated that God would eternally care for Israel (v. 24) and that God would establish the House of David forever (v. 25). While it's difficult to pinpoint exactly how much David understood about these promises in a Messianic sense, it's reasonable to believe that he would connect his existing messianic expectations with this new revelation. So, even though we can't definitively say what David knew or understood, it's plausible to suggest that he likely grasped that these prophecies were, at least in part, about the Messiah.

Chapter 28:

THE WARRIOR KING & COMPASSIONATE FRIEND
2 Samuel 8:1-9:13

Having determined to build a permanent home for the Ark of the Covenant, and having heard the praise of God concerning David, along with a new covenant for Israel through the House of David, we now move to 2 Samuel 8 and 9, chapters which include military victories and a display of kindness toward Saul's legacy.

David's Victories (2 Samuel 8)

Chapter 8 of 2 Samuel provides a chronologically compressed update on David's reign, signifying his immense success up until this point. This chapter recounts various victories, including those over the Philistines (v. 1), the Moabites (v. 2) - where he killed two-thirds of the prisoners and enslaved the remaining third, and the Kingdom of Zobah (v. 3), which is modern Syria.

From Zobah, he seized "a thousand chariots, and seven hundred horsemen, and twenty thousand footmen" (v. 4). The phrase "David houghed all the chariot *horses*" refers to David hamstringing the horses, rendering them unfit for warfare. (Note: "houghed" is pronounced as "hocked").

Additionally, David defeated the Syrians of Damascus who came to aid Hadadezer (v. 5), and made them slaves (v. 6).

The summary of David's military victories is encapsulated in the phrase, "the LORD preserved David whithersoever he went" (v. 6). God's hand of favor was upon David, guiding his actions and granting him victory in all his battles. David's successes were not just a result of his own skills and strategies, but were also a manifestation of God's intervention and favor on his behalf.

Verses 7-12 speak of the spoils of war, both materially and politically, which David acquired from his victories. Notably, David dedicated these spoils to the Lord (v. 11), demonstrating his acknowledgement of God's hand in his victories and his commitment to honoring God with his successes.

Verses 13-18 detail more of David's victories and introduce several key figures in David's leadership. These include Joab, who served as the military chief; Jehosaphat, the recorder; Zadok and Ahimilech, who were priests; Seraihah, the scribe; and Benaiah, who was later introduced as one of David's mighty men.

The concluding verse of this section, "David reigned over all Israel; and David executed judgment and justice unto all his people" (v. 15), encapsulates the essence of David's reign - a reign marked by comprehensive control, fair and just leadership, and consistent victories, all under the favor and guidance of God.

David's Kindness to Mephibosheth (2 Samuel 9)

Despite his military successes, David didn't forget his deep friendship and commitments to Jonathan, Saul's son. As we step into chapter 9, we see David inquiring if there was anyone left from the house of Saul to whom he could show kindness (v. 1).

In 2 Samuel 4:4, we learned that Mephibosheth was only five years old when he became disabled due to an accident. By the time we meet him again in Chapter 9, Mephibosheth has a son of his own and is clearly a grown man. This suggests that a significant amount of time, likely at least 20 years or more, has passed between these two events.

A servant of Saul's household, Ziba, was found and brought before David (v. 2). Ziba informed the king about Mephibosheth, a son of Jonathan who was still alive but disabled. Mephibosheth was living in a place called Lodebar, a town located east of the Jordan River, known for its isolation and barrenness (v. 5).

Upon learning this, David immediately demonstrated kindness towards Mephibosheth. He restored to him all the land that had belonged to his grandfather Saul (v. 7), symbolizing the restoration of his family's honor. Furthermore, David invited him to live in the palace and dine at the king's table, an extraordinary act of kindness and acceptance that elevated Mephibosheth's status significantly. These actions showcased David's grace, compassion, and commitment to uphold his promise to Jonathan.

David further displayed his kindness by instructing Ziba, along with his fifteen sons and thirty servants, to work the land that had been restored to Mephibosheth (v. 12). This ensured that Mephibosheth's land would be productive and well-maintained. Despite this arrangement, Mephibosheth himself was not expected to work the land. Instead, he was to live in the palace and dine at the king's table, as if he were one of the king's own sons (v. 11). This was a significant act of honor and acceptance, further illustrating David's commitment to upholding his promise to Jonathan and his compassionate nature as a leader.

Mephibosheth, along with his son Micha, lived in Jerusalem and continually ate at the king's table (v. 13). They were treated as if they were part of the king's own family. It was a symbol of David's high regard for Jonathan, Mephibosheth's father, and Saul, his grandfather. It was also a mark of honor, as dining at the king's table was a privilege usually reserved for royalty and honored guests.

The story of Mephibosheth in 2 Samuel 9 can be compared to the story of *Oliver Twist* by Charles Dickens.

Mephibosheth, like Oliver, was an unfortunate child who lost his family and was living in unfavorable conditions. Mephibosheth was living in Lodebar, a place known for its barrenness and isolation, while Oliver was living in a workhouse under terrible conditions.

In both stories, a significant change of fortune happens. David, learning about Mephibosheth, shows great kindness and generosity to him, restoring his grandfather's land and inviting him to live in the palace and dine at the king's table. Similarly, Oliver's life changes dramatically when he is taken in by Mr. Brownlow, who treats him kindly and offers him a comfortable life.

In both stories there is also a notable deceased relative who "comes to the rescue" at the last. For Mephibosheth it was his deceased grandfather that caused good fortune to come his way. For Oliver it was his deceased father which brought him both misfortune, and, in the end, great fortune.

In both cases, the noble characters - David in the Bible and Mr. Brownlow in "Oliver Twist" - demonstrate compassion and generosity towards those who are less fortunate, significantly changing their lives for the better.

Conclusion

In these two chapters, we witness two contrasting yet complementary aspects of David's character. On one hand, we see David the military victor, who could at times be ruthless. On the other hand, we see David, the caring and compassionate friend, generous in every way. These two facets of David remind us that a single vignette of an individual, whether biblical or otherwise, is likely not the whole story. Humanity possesses an amazing capacity to be multifaceted, capable of displaying a wide range of characteristics and behaviors. When we hear "David was one of the most brutal kings of the Bible," it might be true. On the other hand, when we hear "David was one of the most compassionate kings of the Bible," it also might be true.

And such dichotomy is likely true of most people we know.

Chapter 29:

A Good Deed Gone Bad

2 Samuel 10:1-19

David's Kindness (2 Samuel 10:1-2)

Recall our earlier discussion in 1 Samuel 22 (Chapter 12 of this book), where David sent his parents to Moab for protection under the king of Moab (1 Samuel 22:3-4). There, we touched on a tradition that suggested the king of Moab murdered David's parents. However, the king of Ammon intervened and managed to save one of David's brothers. That king was named Nahash. If we are interpreting the connections correctly, then the Nahash who passes away in these verses is the same king. Consequently, David resolves to show kindness to Nahash's son, Hanun, just as Nahash "showed kindness unto me" (v. 2).

However, what is true for the common man is magnified for world leaders, and actions are often seen with suspicion or completely misinterpreted. That, as we shall see, is precisely what is going to happen. Partly, this misunderstanding can be attributed to David's reputation as a warrior king (see 2 Sam. 8). His position as a man of tremendous power can often lead to misinterpretations, especially when his actions are ambiguous.

The events of chapter 10 somewhat encapsulate chapters 8 and 9 together: in chapter 8, David is depicted as a warlord, while in chapter 9, he is a compassionate and benevolent king. Here, in chapter 10, he sets out to be compassionate and benevolent, but his actions will not be interpreted in that manner.

Misinterpretation and Insult
(2 Samuel 10:3-5)

The servants of Ammon were suspicious of David's intentions and gave Hanun some unfortunate advice. They suggested that David wasn't genuinely extending kindness, but instead, he came "to search the city, and to spy it out, and to overthrow it" (v. 3). This was a challenging judgment call on their part. When a known warlord comes bearing gifts, it's reasonable to approach the situation with a degree of skepticism. After all, it's akin to a stranger saying, "I'm from the government and I'm here to help!" These men had a significant responsibility to their country, and their suspicion, while misguided, was surely rooted in a desire to protect their homeland.

What is about to unfold serves as a powerful reminder that while suspicions can often be well-founded, they are not always reflective of reality. It's a precarious balance—naivety befalls those who have no suspicions, yet there is foolishness in acting on every single one. Discernment and investigation is key in distinguishing which suspicions warrant action and which ones are merely unfounded worries.

Unfortunately, the men did not investigate further, but instead, they acted upon their unfounded suspicions. They made a rash decision and took a drastic action that would have far-reaching consequences. They humiliated David's men by shaving off half of their beards. In addition to this, they "cut off their garments in the middle, even to their buttocks" (v. 4). Presumably, they cut off the bottom half of their garments, leaving the men exposed. This act was one of great disrespect and humiliation. They sent these men back to David, embarrassed and humiliated. This impulsive action, borne out of misguided suspicion, would escalate the situation into a major battle.

In their humiliated state, David's men were instructed to stay in Jerusalem until their beards could grow back. This wasn't because a shaven man would not command respect, but rather to avoid further shame and questions. The men who had departed with their beards intact would have had to explain why they returned shaved. This could lead to further humiliation as they would have to relive the incident repeatedly. Understanding the importance of their dignity, David showed wisdom by allowing them to wait in Jericho. This decision illustrates David's empathy and understanding as a leader, respecting the emotional well-being of his men.

Allow me to interject some personal opinion here. When a man is bullied, it seems to me that the right thing to do is to fight back, then and there. If he doesn't, he always goes home humiliated and the situation invariably escalates to circumstances far worse. Had David's servants immediately fought back, the matter might have been taken care of with just a small group. Of course, it's possible that there were circumstances of which we are not aware that prohibited them from doing so. However, it is my opinion that the only way to solve a bullying problem is by overpowering them quickly.

The Consequences of Actions (2 Samuel 10:6-14)

David, as king, is aware that even a "slight infraction" like this cannot go unanswered, especially within the context of a "power culture" such as that of the ancient Middle

East. A display of weakness through lack of response would likely invite further challenges in the future. This becomes evident rather quickly, as "the children of Ammon saw that they stank before David" (v. 6). In the aftermath of the incident, they resort to hiring mercenary warriors—a common practice of the time. Interestingly, some of these mercenaries were from the kingdoms David had previously defeated in chapter 8. This could be an indication of a weakening of David's kingdom over the region, and even within. We should see this as a "crack in the foundation" for the Kingdom, and I think we will see that crack widen in the events yet to unfold. In other words, this is a turning point in the Kingdom.

Joab, David's general, was acutely aware of the magnitude of the battle that lay ahead. In the midst of the conflict, he found himself in a predicament where "the front of the battle was against him before and behind" (v. 9). This situation required swift thinking and decisive action. Joab quickly devised a strategy to divide his army into two, in order to engage both fronts. He appointed Abishai, his brother, to lead the other group of soldiers (v. 10).

In the face of such daunting odds, Joab inspired his troops with a rousing speech, saying to Abishai, "Be of good courage, and let us play the men for our people, and for the cities of our God" (v. 12). The phrase "play the men" means to step up to the plate and fulfill their roles as men, to be brave and stand firm for their nation. This statement clearly reflects Joab's commitment to their cause and his willingness to fight to the end for their people and their cities.

In William Shakespeare's play *Henry V*, the king delivers one of the most stirring speeches in English literature on the eve of the Battle of Agincourt. Facing overwhelming odds, King Henry V addresses his outnumbered troops with words designed to inspire courage, unity, and a sense of honor.

The most memorable lines from this speech encapsulate his message of brotherhood and valor:

> "We few, we happy few, we band of brothers;
>
> For he to-day that sheds his blood with me
>
> Shall be my brother; be he ne'er so vile,
>
> This day shall gentle his condition."

In these lines, King Henry speaks directly to the hearts of his soldiers. He acknowledges their small numbers but transforms this into a source of pride and solidarity. He promises that the bonds formed in battle will elevate every man who fights alongside him, turning even the lowliest soldier into his equal—a brother in arms.

I suspect Joab's words had the same effect on his "band of brothers." They fought valiantly, causing the armies of the Ammonites and the Syrians to flee in fear.

Final Victory (2 Samuel 10:15-19)

Despite the initial retreat of the enemy, the conflict was far from over. When the Syrians saw their defeat, they regrouped and brought additional forces from beyond the river, led by Shobach, the captain of Hadarezer's army (v. 16). This was not merely a skirmish but a concerted effort to overthrow David's forces.

David, understanding the gravity of the situation, took command himself. He gathered all Israel and crossed the Jordan to confront the Syrians in Helam (v. 17). This decisive move demonstrated David's leadership and his strategic prowess in responding to renewed threats.

The ensuing battle was fierce. David's forces engaged the Syrians with determination and strength. The Bible records that David's army killed seven hundred charioteers and forty thousand horsemen, including Shobach, the commander of their army (v. 18). This devastating defeat broke the morale and the military strength of the Syrians, forcing them to sue for peace.

As a result, the Syrian kingdoms made peace with Israel and became their servants, unwilling to support the Ammonites further (v. 19). This victory reaffirmed David's dominance in the region and ensured the security of Israel from immediate threats.

This passage concludes a significant chapter in the history of David's reign. It illustrates the relentless challenges he faced from surrounding nations and his unwavering commitment to defend his kingdom. Joab's call to "play the men" resonates throughout the entire narrative, showing how courage, unity, and decisive leadership can lead to triumph even against formidable odds.

Chapter 30:
THE MOST INFAMOUS ADULTERY
2 Samuel 11:1-27

David's Sin With Bathsheba
(2 Samuel 11:1-5)

In the previous chapter (2 Samuel 10), the Ammonites had humiliated some of David's men, leading to a conflict between Israel and a coalition formed by the Ammonites and the Syrians. Despite this formidable coalition, Joab's leadership enabled the Israelites to drive both the Syrians and the Ammonites to retreat. David then brought his forces to join the conflict, striking the Syria so severely that the they were discouraged from further aiding the Ammonites and returning to loyalty to King David (2 Samuel 10:19). As chapter 11 commences, it is the time of year when kings typically went to war. However, David opts to send Joab and his troops to conclude the conflict with the Ammonites, instead of going himself (v. 1).

While David's decision to stay behind rather than join the battle is almost always interpreted negatively. However, it may also be viewed from a more positive perspective. It's possible that David recognized Joab's strategic prowess, having led the forces that caused both the Ammonites and the Syrians to flee at a moment when they seemingly had a great victory against Israel. Now, rather than take the glory for himself, David might have decided to step back and allow Joab to finish the battle with the Ammonites. Furthermore, David might have had personal reservations about going to war with the Ammonites due to the kindness they had shown his family in the previous generation, as noted in 2 Samuel 10:1. This showcase of empathy and strategic delegation could potentially cast David's decision in a more favorable light.

One evening, while at home in his palace, David took a walk on the roof. In the architecture of ancient Middle Eastern homes, the roof served as an outdoor living area, a place where residents could enjoy a cool breeze and a relaxing atmosphere. While on the roof, David saw a woman bathing. This observation would not necessarily have been the result of inappropriate spying or voyeurism on David's part. Given the topography of the City of David, with its hills and varying elevations, it would have been quite possible for such a view to be easily seen from the palace roof.

The scripture notes that she was "beautiful to look upon" (v. 1), a phrase used sparingly in the Bible and often denoting exceptional beauty. This is further supported by Jewish tradition, which includes Bathsheba among the five most beautiful women in the Bible. This illustrious list includes Sarah, Esther, Rachel, and Rebekah, women who were not only recognized for their physical beauty, but also their significant roles in biblical narratives.

David inquires about the woman and discovers her name: Bathsheba, who is also referred to as Bathshua in 1 Chronicles 3:5. She is described as "the daughter of Eliam, the wife of Uriah the Hittite" (v.3). This introduction suggests that there might be some degree of renown associated with her family. In fact, we learn in 1 Samuel 23:34 that she is the granddaughter of Ahithophel, one of David's advisors. It is Ahithophel who will later betray David and align with Absalom in a future narrative. Given this knowledge of what is to come, it is not surprising that Bathsheba's grandfather would not remain a loyal servant to the king.

Bathsheba's husband is introduced as Uriah the Hittite. The Hittites were an ancient civilization that had ceased to exist as a kingdom a few centuries before David's time. Their origins trace back to what is now modern-day Turkey, and the remnants of their empire can still be seen today at the UNESCO World Heritage site, Hattusa. Archaeology has unearthed many Hittite artifacts, including legal documents and treaties, offering valuable insights into that historical period.

Despite the dissolution of the Hittite kingdom, those of Hittite lineage survived through the generations, extending into David's era and beyond. It's important to note that they were not regarded as antagonists; they were not a nation-state posing a threat. In fact, Uriah's name, which translates to "Yahweh is my light," suggests that he was fully assimilated into Jewish society.

The narrative unfolds further as David and Bathsheba succumb to temptation, leading to an affair that is suggested to be a one-time event. Everything in the narrative looks to speak of mutually guilty parties. However, the repercussions of this act were immediate and profound. Bathsheba became pregnant and sent word to David informing him of this development. The scripture makes a point to mention that Bathsheba was "purified from her uncleanness" (v. 4).

This detail serves a dual purpose. On one hand, it highlights Bathsheba's faithfulness to Jewish ritual purity laws. On the other hand, it forms a stark contrast, reminding us that ritual purity and moral purity are not one and the same.

David's Sin With Uriah (2 Samuel 11:6-24)

David hatches a plan in his heart to bring Uriah home under contrived circumstances. The fact that Uriah was specifically called to give a report seems to communicate that Uriah was not a "private," but rather an officer of some kind. David showers Uriah with kindness, and encourages him to go to spend the night at home. Though David's plan is not spelled out in words, it is so much on the surface that everyone reading the story knows what David is trying to accomplish: a plan to make it look as if Uriah is the father of Bathsheba's unborn child.

Uriah, however, proves to be too loyal to his commander, Joab, and to his profession to "take a night off." He testifies strongly, "I will not do this thing" (v. 11). In a twist of irony, Uriah's loyalty and integrity in this moment stand in sharp contrast to David's actions.

Undeterred, David tried a second night, even getting Uriah drunk (v. 13), but his plan was unsuccessful. Uriah remained steadfast in his loyalty, refusing to go home to his wife while his fellow soldiers remained in the field. We can see the moral complexities of this chapter of David's life growing more and more tangled.

David's scheme then takes a darker turn. He sends a message to Joab, the battlefield commander, and chillingly, the message is carried by Uriah himself, a death warrant in his own hands. David's instructions to Joab are explicit: place Uriah at the forefront of the fiercest fighting, then pull back so that he is left alone and is killed. The instructions are given without any justification or explanation (v. 15).

Joab, a loyal servant, does not question these orders. He follows David's command and, in the heat of a subsequent battle, Uriah is left exposed and is killed, just as David had planned (v. 17). This act demonstrates the depths of David's desperation and the lengths he is willing to go to conceal his transgression. His actions have now escalated from adultery to orchestrated murder.

Joab sends a messenger back to David to report on the events of the battle, but his instructions to the courier reveal a deep understanding of David's character and military acumen. Joab expected David to berate him for poor strategy, for allowing his troops too close to the city walls, where they were vulnerable to attack. "Did you not know that they would shoot from the wall?" David would likely have asked (v. 20). Joab predicted that David would reference the story of Abimelech, son of Jerubbaal, also known as Gideon, a judge of Israel. After Gideon's death, Abimelech sought to make himself king, succeeding only in a small portion of Israel. His rule was contested, and during a battle, a woman fatally wounded him by dropping a millstone on him from a city wall. Rather than die from a woman's hand, Abimelech asked a servant to kill him with a sword, a slightly more honorable death (see Judges 9). Joab, having anticipated David's likely response, instructed the messenger to then reveal, "Uriah the Hittite is dead also" (v. 21). Joab knew this information would mollify David and justify the risky military tactic.

The messenger brings the news of the battle's progression and Uriah's death to David, as Joab instructed him to do (vv. 22-24). However, David's response is not what one might expect from a military strategist.

Instead of expressing anger or disappointment at what seemed like a poor military decision, his reaction is one of consolation and forgiveness towards Joab. This is a perplexing reaction for those who are not privy to the full story. David tells the messenger to say to Joab, "Do not let this thing displease you, for the sword devours one as well as another." (v. 25). This response reveals David's relief that his plan has worked and his sin is seemingly covered. His use of a common saying about the unpredictability of war serves to normalize Uriah's death and absolve Joab (and himself) of any wrongdoing.

Moving On (2 Samuel 11:26-27)

Upon hearing the news of her husband's death, Bathsheba mourns for Uriah. The details of David's plot are not revealed to her, leaving her to grapple with her grief and the reality of her pregnancy. Her emotions must have been a complex mix of sorrow, fear, and uncertainty. Despite the tragic circumstances of Uriah's death and the impending scandal of her pregnancy, the narrative takes a seemingly positive turn as "David sent and brought her to his house, and she became his wife and bore him a son" (v. 27).

This would appear to be a "happy ending" to a tale filled with deception and tragedy. David has seemingly managed to keep his sin concealed. Joab might have had suspicions about the unusual events, but he would not have known the full extent of David's machinations. Moreover, in the societal context of those times, the timing of Bathsheba's pregnancy could have been kept under wraps, further maintaining the illusion of propriety.

However, the final line of the chapter signals that this tale is far from over. Despite David's attempts to cover up his sins, "the thing that David had done displeased the LORD." This statement sets the stage for the consequences that will unfold in the next chapter, serving as a stark reminder that while one may deceive their fellow man, nothing can be hidden from God.

Lessons To Learn

From the narrative of 2 Samuel 11, we can glean several important lessons. First, no one is immune to sin. From the lowliest peasant to the mightiest king, each person is subject to the same temptations. Secondly, like David, most of us will attempt to hide our transgressions. Though announcing our wrongdoings from the hilltops may not be the best course of action, this story demonstrates the tangled web we weave when we try to cover up our sins. Thirdly, we must always be mindful of the potential consequences of our actions. In the next chapter, we will explore some of these consequences. However, it's important to note here that David is now beholden to Joab. After all, what would happen if Joab revealed the command he was given?

The fourth lesson is a reminder that God sees and knows everything. Whether or not He responds as He did in David's case, His knowledge is ever-present. Lastly, this story highlights the immense forgiveness that God extends to humanity. Despite our monumental mistakes, God, like with David, remains active in our lives. This serves as a reminder of the depth of God's love and forgiveness, even when we fail "royally."

Chapter 31:

CONSEQUENCES OF UNSEEN SIN
2 Samuel 12:1-14

In this chapter, we delve into the memorable narrative of King David's unseen sin, its exposure by the prophet Nathan, and the impactful consequences that followed. We explore the grace of God's forgiveness juxtaposed with the lasting effects of David's transgressions. As we journey through this chapter, we will gain a deeper understanding of the complexities of sin, the power of confrontation, and the boundless mercy of God.

Nathan Confronts David (2 Samuel 12:1-6)

Many students of the Word are at least somewhat familiar with the account of Nathan the prophet confronting David over his sin. What we often overlook is that Nathan's knowledge of David's sins, as revealed in verse 9, could only have come through prophetic revelation. Scripture gives no indication that Nathan learned of these events through any other means.

God, in His wisdom, chose not to let this sin go unnoticed. We can only speculate as to why. Was it due to the grievous nature of David's actions? Perhaps. But it may also have been to provide a profound example of repentance and renewal.

If this episode had remained hidden, we might have been spared the pain of witnessing this dark chapter in David's life. However, we would also have been deprived of Psalm 51, written in response to these events. This psalm has become a cherished "song of the soul" for those seeking repentance, illustrating the beauty and depth of God's forgiveness.

In 1 Samuel 7 (see chapter 27 of this book), we first met Nathan, a prophetic advisor to the king. Nathan was the one to reveal the prophecies about the future kingdom of God that would come through David. Now, it falls to Nathan to confront the honored king with the bad news. Whether God instructed him on how to approach David or he devised the means himself, Nathan delivered an ingenious story designed to elicit a strong response of anger.

The story Nathan told David involved a poor family and their little lamb, a narrative rich with elements of human nature that "tug at the heartstrings" and could only be dismissed by someone with the coldest of hearts. This parable was crafted to draw out David's sense of justice and compassion. As Nathan recounted the tale, anger welled up within David. Believing the story to be true, David pronounced a death sentence along with a fourfold financial penalty upon the man, unaware that the parable was a mirror reflecting his own transgressions.

The effectiveness of Nathan's approach lay in its ability to bypass David's defenses and self-deception, leading him to a place of genuine repentance. Whether the story was written by God or developed out of Nathan's personal insight, it was perfectly designed to bring David face-to-face with his own sin, prompting a profound and necessary transformation.

Nathan's Rebuke and Prophecy (Verses 7-12)

Nathan begins with a poignant story, but he quickly concludes with perhaps one of the most direct confrontations in history when he proclaims, "Thou art the man" (v. 7). This phrase has become famous, in its

KJV wording, for movies, poems, artwork, and even in regular conversation in almost all the English-speaking world. Edgar Allan Poe wrote a book by the title, *Thou Art the Man,* highlighting the phrase's enduring impact on literature and culture. William Shakespeare and Charles Dickens both use the phrase in their literature. It has been used from Poe to Shakespeare to Watergate.

This moment in 2 Samuel 12 is a dramatic climax where Nathan reveals David's hidden sin with Bathsheba and Uriah through a parable that stirs the king's sense of justice and compassion. The gravity of Nathan's proclamation cuts through the royal façade, exposing David's guilt and leading to his repentance.

The phrase "Thou art the man" has transcended its biblical origins, symbolizing the act of exposing hypocrisy and wrongdoing. It resonates with readers and listeners as a powerful declaration of truth and accountability. In literature, it has been used to underscore themes of justice, moral reckoning, and the uncovering of hidden truths.

Nathan's approach in delivering this rebuke is a masterclass in confrontation. He begins with a relatable story that disarms David, making him empathetic and ready to pass judgment on the injustice presented. Only then does Nathan turn the tables, revealing that the story is an allegory of David's own actions. This method not only ensures that David understands the severity of his sin but also that he feels the weight of his hypocrisy.

After the profound revelation, "Thou art the man," Nathan continues speaking on behalf of the Lord. He reminds David of the multitude of blessings that God has bestowed upon him. He mentions how God anointed him as king, safeguarded him from Saul, and granted him the houses of Judah and Israel (verses 7-8).

God even goes further to express, "I would moreover have given unto thee such and such things" (verse 8). This statement can be viewed as a 'blank check' from God, signifying that He would have willingly given David even more blessings. This phrase holds significant weight as it is perhaps one of the most open-ended promises in the entire Bible, underscoring the vastness of God's generosity and willingness to bless David.

In verse 9, Nathan brings the sin into the open with a clear and direct accusation, leaving David with no room for denial or rationalization. Nathan asks David, "Wherefore hast thou despised the commandment of the LORD, to do evil in his sight?" This question, while directed at David, is rhetorical in nature. There is no satisfactory response that David could offer. What could he say? That he was misguided? That he temporarily lost sight of his values? Any attempt at an explanation would be woefully inadequate. The truth is, David sinned. He turned away from his faith and his moral compass. His actions mirror those of Adam and Eve, and indeed, every instance of deliberate sin committed by humanity. At times, we simply choose to reject God's guidance. This question, although posed to David, serves as a stark reminder of the senseless nature of sin.

In verses 10-12, Nathan delivers a heartbreaking prophecy for David. He states, "The sword shall never depart from thine house" (v. 10). This prophetic pronouncement signifies that conflict and strife will continuously plague David's family. The rest of David's life would be marked by discord within his own house, a painful consequence of his sins.

In a striking twist, Nathan declares that this division within David's household will not be hidden, unlike David's initial transgressions. Instead, it will occur in the fullness of daylight, for all to see. This visibility of the consequences stands in stark contrast to David's secretive sins.

As we explored in the previous chapter, David's sins of adultery with Bathsheba and the orchestration of Uriah's death were carried out with calculated secrecy. The biblical narrative makes it clear that David took great pains to ensure his actions remained hidden. Now that Nathan has confronted David, an intriguing question arises: did David's sin ever become public knowledge during his lifetime?

While many assume that everyone must have known, the evidence suggests that it could have been kept private. 2 Samuel 12 records what appears to be a private confrontation between Nathan and David. Nathan, a man of integrity, might have understood that there wasn't always merit in exposing every sin to the public. There is nothing in the remainder of the Davidic narrative to suggest that others within the family or the kingdom were fully aware of David's sin, beyond Nathan and David himself.

Psalm 51's title states that it was written "when Nathan the prophet came unto him, after he had gone in to Bathsheba." However, it is likely that this title was added (under the guidance of the Holy Spirit) after David's death, during the later compilation of the Psalms. Therefore, it is speculative but possible that the entire matter of David and Bathsheba remained unknown to the general public until long after David's death, possibly even after Solomon's death.

If privacy is indeed the case, then the upcoming divisions within the House of David would only have the matter of David and Bathsheba as a secondary and unknown cause. As we have previously discussed, there were existing cracks in the foundations of David's house that would only grow wider as time passed. There is a marked shift from the earlier days when David could seemingly do no wrong, and the hand of God was continually upon him, to this day of confrontation and the time following it. David would now struggle to keep his kingdom, and his family, intact.

Sin's Long Shadow (2 Samuel 12:13-14)

Verse 13 of 2 Samuel 12 is one of the most remarkable verses of grace in the entire Bible. David's cry, "I have sinned against the LORD," is immediately followed by the reassuring declaration, "The LORD also hath put away thy sin." This exchange vividly demonstrates that, even before the dispensation of God's grace was revealed to the Apostle Paul (Ephesians 3:2), God has always been swift to forgive.

This theme of God's forgiveness echoes throughout the scriptures. Consider Cain, to whom God said, "If thou doest well, shalt thou not be accepted? And if thou doest not well, sin lieth at the door. And unto thee shall be his desire, and thou shalt rule over him" (Genesis 4:7). Or consider the story of the Prodigal Son, who said, "I will arise and go to my father, and will say unto him, Father, I have sinned against heaven, and before thee" (Luke 15:18). In response, "when he was yet a great way off, his father saw him, had compassion, and ran, and fell on his neck, and kissed him" (Luke 15:20).

These examples, among many others, underscore the boundless compassion of God the Father toward humanity.

This is not to say that we have always been in the dispensation of grace, as such a statement would contradict Paul's testimony. Rather, it highlights that the character of God has always been one of forgiveness. This is why an unforgiving heart is so harshly dealt with by Jesus on several occasions - unforgiveness goes against the character of God Himself.

Verse 14, however, shows that while God "put away" David's sin (v. 13), it would still have consequences. Not only were there the ones already mentioned in verses 10-12, but there was also the tragic declaration that "the child also that is born unto thee shall surely die" (v. 14). In the next chapter, we will delve into the death of this child and the birth of Bathsheba's second child, shedding light on the lasting repercussions of David's actions.

But before we leave this segment, we should consider the words of verse 14 concerning David's sin, "By this deed thou hast given great occasion to the enemies of the LORD to blaspheme." At first glance, this seems to go against my previous speculation that the sin was kept private. However, let me say two things concerning this before we go.

First, the deed did indeed open up many opportunities for the enemies of the Lord to blaspheme the Lord, even without the details of the affair and murder being known. Second, the text itself is difficult in this passage. There is a linguistic case to be made that the Hebrew says that David himself blasphemed the Lord by this occasion.

In short, I would recommend against making any arguments based on the text of verse 14 since all translations of v. 14 require a great deal of interpretation.

Some Practical Considerations

As we close this chapter, there are several considerations we can ponder.

1. Even familiar stories have possibilities we may not have considered. For instance, the sin of David might have remained a secret throughout his lifetime, a perspective that offers a fresh understanding of the narrative.

2. Nathan revealed David's sin in a manner that appears to be gracious in itself. Instead of immediately condemning him, Nathan designed his approach to speak to David's "better side," enabling a transformative recognition of wrongdoing.

3. Not all sin needs to be made public for all the world. It rarely helps anyone in their faith. Instead, the focus should be on personal repentance and transformation.

4. God is a God of forgiveness. We can rejoice that through the cross, God has now ushered in a time of grace in which He is not imputing our trespasses to us (2 Corinthians 5:19).

5. Even with forgiveness, sin sometimes has a long shadow. When we live in that shadow, the best we can do is make the best of it, for God's glory. This involves learning from our mistakes, seeking to rectify our wrongs when possible, and moving forward with a commitment to live righteously.

Chapter 32:

LESSONS FROM A HAUNTING DEATH

2 Samuel 12:15-25

2 Samuel 12 is a pivotal chapter in the narrative of King David's reign, marking both God's judgment and the complexities of David's character. The chapter opens with the prophet Nathan confronting David with a parable, exposing David's sin with Bathsheba and the murder of her husband, Uriah. This confrontation leads to David's heartfelt repentance, but also to severe consequences decreed by God.

The narrative then shifts to the illness and eventual death of the child born from David and Bathsheba's adulterous union. This tragic event underscores the gravity of David's sin and God's punishment, despite David's heartfelt prayers and fasting. Following the child's death, David's response demonstrates a striking blend of acceptance and continued faith in God.

The chapter concludes on a note of hope with the birth of Solomon, whom God names Jedidiah, meaning "beloved of the LORD." This signifies God's enduring grace and the future legacy of David's line, which ultimately leads to the establishment of Solomon as king and the builder of the temple.

The Death of David and Bathsheba's Child (Verses 15-19)

Verse 14 ended in a clear prophetic punishment: "the child also that is born unto thee shall surely die." Now the Lord delivers on that punishment, and He "struck the child...and it was very sick." Such a scenario brings a plethora of questions to our minds. Why would God strike

269

the child rather than the parents? There are questions we cannot answer, and in the end we must recognize that "now we see through a glass, darkly" (1 Corinthians 13:12).

It is important to recognize, of course, that this is not a standard punishment for out-of-wedlock pregnancies. But additionally, we must recognize that there is no "standard punishment" for this nor any sin. God's response to sin has been, at times, direct and announced. Most other times it has been indirect, or sometimes even completely overlooked, even in the Old Testament.

I am convinced that in the "dispensation of the grace of God" (Eph. 3:2) that all punishment for sin is indirect. That is, there are consequences that God has worked into actions so that those actions bring their own self-punishment. For example, Colossians 2:21-22 gives a parenthetical thought about prohibitions of activities, saying, "(Touch not; taste not; handle not; Which all are to perish with the using;)" that last phrase, "which are all to perish with the using" means that "things take care of themselves." In addition to punishments that may be "baked into the cake" of certain activity, there are cultural punishments that change from time to time and can be based on scriptural values but are sometimes just societal norms.

I am not a fan of those who associate every bad experience directly to sin. There were times in the scripture when God was working directly in circumstances to bring about a desired end. However, my theological view is that in this parenthetical dispensation in which we live, such is not happening today. After the rapture, God's direct work in human living will return.

270

David sought God, fasted, and, it seems, repented by laying "all night upon the earth" (v. 16). His display of remorse was so visible and dramatic that his advisors were concerned for his wellbeing (v. 17). A keen student of the Word would notice that David is doing things often taught for success in prayer life, including fasting, persistence, repentance, and concern for others. However, we will soon see that David's prayer will not be answered. This reminds us that some of the great prayer promises, like Matthew 21:22 - "And all things, whatsoever ye shall ask in prayer, believing, ye shall receive" - are not blanket promises to everyone.

One wonders: could this have been the time in which the cry of Psalm 51 was first voiced? David's remorse in 2 Samuel 12:16-17, where he fasted and lay upon the earth, echoes the sentiments expressed in Psalm 51. In the midst of his child's illness, David's actions demonstrate a heart burdened by guilt and seeking divine forgiveness. Psalm 51:1-2 mirrors this desperation: "Have mercy upon me, O God, according to thy lovingkindness: according unto the multitude of thy tender mercies blot out my transgressions. Wash me throughly from mine iniquity, and cleanse me from my sin." These verses reflect David's awareness of his sin and his plea for God's cleansing, a plea likely intensified by the immediate consequences of his actions involving Bathsheba and Uriah.

David's acknowledgment of his sin in Psalm 51:3-4, "For I acknowledge my transgressions: and my sin is ever before me. Against thee, thee only, have I sinned, and done this evil in thy sight," aligns closely with the broken spirit he displayed in 2 Samuel 12. His laying all night upon the earth signifies a man deeply troubled by his wrongdoing and seeking reconciliation with God. The depth of his

271

repentance is further captured in Psalm 51:10-12, "Create in me a clean heart, O God; and renew a right spirit within me. Cast me not away from thy presence; and take not thy holy spirit from me. Restore unto me the joy of thy salvation; and uphold me with thy free spirit." These pleas for a renewed heart and spirit resonate with the sorrow and humility David exhibited during his child's illness, underscoring a sincere moment of repentance that likely influenced the composition of this penitential psalm.

When the child died after seven days of life, David's servants clearly feared for his life. They were not sure how he would respond to the news. This is a sign of how tremendously deep the pain was in David's life.

David observed the behavior of his servants and realized that the child had died. His direct question received a direct answer: "He is dead" (v. 19). At times, the most difficult truths come with the fewest words. The harshest realities of life often require no embellishment: *You're dying. He's dead. You're fired.*

David's Response to the Child's Death (Verses 20-23)

Verses 20-21 show a complete reversal of behavior for David after the death of the child. He both "washed and anointed himself" (v. 20). The word translated "anointed" is used nine times in the scriptures, and appears to have some visible nature in which others can tell if you are anointed or not (see 2 Sam. 14:2). It seems to be done with olive oil (Deut. 28:40) and a sign of blessing and prosperity that was withheld during times of mourning (Dan. 10:3).

David "came into the house of the LORD, and worshipped" (v. 20). The House of the Lord at this time

272

was the tabernacle (see 2 Samuel 6:17). His worship likely involved the bringing of a sacrifice, and perhaps joining with others in singing and prayer.

The term "house of the Lord" is used 234 times in the Hebrew scriptures. It is never used in the New Testament, though there are some similar phrases, such as references to the temple, "My Father's house," etc. To refer to the local church as "the Lord's house" is somewhat foreign to the pages of scripture. There is no "Lord's house" on earth today. Rather, there are places that people have set aside for worship, either permanently (like a church building) or temporarily (like a living room used in a home church).

When a person experiences severe grief after a time of begging God for mercy, we often expect their behavior to be much more somber after losing the battle than before. This expectation stems from the natural process of mourning and the deep sorrow that typically follows such a profound loss.

A historical example that illustrates this is Calvin Coolidge's depression after the death of his son. Calvin Coolidge, the 30th President of the United States, faced a devastating personal tragedy when his younger son, Calvin Jr., died from a staph infection in 1924. The loss deeply affected Coolidge, who had been a devoted father. Despite his public duties and stoic demeanor, those close to him noticed a significant change in his behavior and outlook on life.

Coolidge's grief was profound and long-lasting. He became more withdrawn and melancholic, and many historians believe that the death of his son cast a shadow over the remainder of his presidency. The tragedy

273

illustrates how the loss of a loved one, especially after fervent prayers and hopes for their recovery, can lead to a deep and enduring sorrow, often altering a person's behavior and outlook on life.

But the change in David's activity and outlook was so different that the servants were perplexed and had to ask David, "What thing is this that thou hast done?" (v. 21). This question highlights the stark contrast between David's intense mourning during the child's illness and his sudden return to normal activities after the child's death. The servants expected David's grief to continue or even intensify, but instead, he washed, anointed himself, and went to worship in the house of the LORD. This unexpected behavior baffled them, prompting their inquiry.

David explained himself in verses 22-23. His grief was for the potential of God's mercy, which did not come. Now David is resolved that there is nothing more he can do, "can I bring him back again?" (v. 23).

This is really not a crass response. It is actually deeply rooted in reality. At times, typically at the worst of times, we have to "remake" ourselves and determine to move forward, because moving forward is really the only option. This is tremendously difficult in grief and shows that David really is trying to act responsibly.

The phrase "I shall go to him, but he shall not return to me" (v. 23) has elicited much discussion. In its simplest terms, it means that David admits he will die someday but the child will not come back to life. However, it is used in such a degree of reassurance and comfort that one who takes a pure death point of view (rather than an afterlife point of view) would have to explain why this thought would bring such comfort to David. The thought of going to his deceased child seems to be a strong comfort for David.

Scripture provides only limited details about the theology of afterlife in David's time, a concept that was more fully developed in later Old Testament writings and especially in the New Testament. During David's era, the idea of "Sheol" as the abode of departed spirits was a consistent belief. Sheol was perceived as the destination for all the dead, irrespective of their moral conduct during life. It was a realm disconnected from the activities of the living, such as work (Ecclesiastes 9:10) and worship (Psalm 6:5).

Despite the somber depiction of Sheol, it was also viewed as a place of reunion for the dead, as suggested in Genesis 37:35, where Jacob expresses his intention to go down to Sheol to be with his son Joseph. This indicates a belief in some form of continued existence and familial connection after death.

Moreover, there are early indications of a belief in resurrection. Job 19:25-26 reveals a hope in a future bodily resurrection: "For I know that my redeemer liveth, and that he shall stand at the latter day upon the earth: And though after my skin worms destroy this body, yet in my flesh shall I see God." Similarly, Psalm 16:10-11 reflects a hope in deliverance from Sheol and a continued presence with God: "For thou wilt not leave my soul in hell; neither wilt thou suffer thine Holy One to see corruption. Thou wilt shew me the path of life: in thy presence is fulness of joy; at thy right hand there are pleasures for evermore."

The Birth of Solomon (Verses 24-25)

This sad story has a happy ending in the birth of Solomon. The text tells us that Solomon was born to David

275

and Bathsheba, and "the LORD loved him" (v. 24). This puts Solomon in the ranks of those like Abraham (Is. 41:8), Jacob (Mal 1:2-3), Daniel (Dan. 10:11), and the nation of Israel itself (Deut. 7:7-8).

As we all know, in time Solomon will inherit the kingdom and will build the temple as well as bring the kingdom to its zenith in ancient history.

Though his parents called him Solomon, the Lord called him Jedidiah, "beloved of the Lord" (v. 25). There are no other places in Scripture in which the name Jedidiah is used.

Could it be that this "I love you" from God was God's way of saying, "forgiveness has been granted"? What a beautiful way to say the story of David is not over!

Chapter 33

DAVID'S HOUSE IN TURMOIL

2 Samuel 12:26-13:39

In 2 Samuel 12:10-11, we read the solemn words: "Now therefore the sword shall never depart from thine house..." This prophecy, delivered to David by the prophet Nathan, foreshadows the continuous strife and turmoil that would plague David's reign. This chapter encapsulates both the external battles with the Ammonites and the internal battles within David's own household. As we delve into the narrative, we witness the siege of Rabbah, a significant military campaign, juxtaposed against the intimate and tragic events that unfold in David's family. The consequences of David's actions reverberate through these verses, illustrating the enduring impact of sin and the complex dynamics of leadership, power, and family.

Joab Captures Rabbah (Verses 26-29)

Earlier we learned that David stayed home during "the time when kings go forth to battle" (2 Sam 11:1) (see Chapter 30). There we speculated as to why David may have stayed home. Now, after the Bathsheba interlude, we immediately jump back into the story of the siege of Rabbah. In fact, you could almost put 2 Sam 11:1 back to back with 2 Sam 12:26 and get the story without Bathsheba.

Rabbah, also known as Rabbath Ammon, was the capital city of the Ammonites. It is located in present-day Amman, the capital of Jordan. The city was strategically significant due to its location and fortifications, making it a critical target during military campaigns.

The entire account of 2 Samuel 11-13 includes a digression into the saga of Bathsheba. This saga is completed while on the digression, and then the narrative returns back to the framework story of the siege of Rabbah. Therefore, it appears that 2 Samuel 13:26 actually backs up in time to the same spot as 2 Samuel 11:1.

As David "tarried still at Jerusalem" (2 Sam. 11:1), Joab "took the royal city" (2 Sam 12:26). Joab sent a message to David letting him know he had taken the city (v. 27).

But that is not all that was in the memo from Joab. He gave David the opportunity to come take the city, "lest I take the city, and it be called after my name" (v. 28). But wait... He had taken the city (v. 27) and then suggested that David should come and take the city, "lest I take the city" (v. 28). This looks like a psyops[5] move. Joab, in deference to David, is allowing him to come give a visual appearance of taking the city. So "David gathered all the people together, and went to Rabbah, and fought against it, and took it" (v. 29). Notice that he "gathered all the people," confirming our suspicion that this is all for show.

Because we do not know the timing of this, it is difficult to know for certain if this was before or after the instruction to have Uriah killed, but I suspect it was prior to. The timeline was likely as follows:

1. Joab went to battle, David stayed home and had an affair.

2. Joab won the battle and called David for the psyops victory photo-op.

---

5 Psychological operations (psyops) refer to various techniques used by military and other organizations to influence the emotions, motives, objective reasoning, and behavior of individuals, groups, and governments. These operations are aimed at conveying selected information and indicators to audiences to influence their emotions, motives, and objective reasoning, ultimately leading to behavior favorable to the originator's objectives.

3. Bathsheba learns she is pregnant and the story goes from there.

Spoils of War and Subjugation (Verses 30-31)

As David was in Rabbah, they had a coronation of sorts, as David had conquered their territory and the land of the Ammonites was now occupied by the Kingdom of Judea. David took the tremendous spoils of this once-great kingdom, including crown jewels made of "a talent of gold with the precious stones" (v. 30), back to his kingdom.

Then David participated in what appears in English to be total brutality. However, it is likely our understanding of the Hebrew is influenced by middle-ages torture devices rather than the Hebrew words themselves. The word translated "under," when used with weapons or implements, is always understood as "with." In this light, verse 31 can be seen as follows:

◊ **Put them under saws:** David subjected the captured Ammonites to labor with saws, which may have been used for cutting wood or stone, indicating forced labor.

◊ **Under harrows of iron:** The Ammonites were forced to work with iron harrows, which are agricultural tools with sharp teeth used for breaking up soil.

◊ **Under axes of iron:** David used iron axes on the Ammonites, likely indicating forced labor involving heavy and dangerous tasks.

◊ **Made them pass through the brickkiln:** The Ammonites were made to pass through brick kilns, which were used for baking bricks. This likely suggests forced labor. It could even be understood as "make them pass through the place of the Molechs" (ancient Ammonite gods).

279

In short, David subjugated the people of Ammon, not incorporating them into his kingdom, but using them for laborious tasks in the kingdom. Incidentally, in 2 Samuel 17:27 these same people are going to come out to support David during the time of the coup of Absalom.

While the people saw a victory, those "in the know" saw that David's house was becoming a house of cards. The external triumphs masked the internal decay, as David's moral failings and familial strife began to undermine the stability of his reign. The apparent success in battle could not conceal the growing cracks within his household, foreshadowing the eventual family struggles and turmoil that would plague his legacy. And with that we move into the tragic story of Ammon and Tamar in 2 Samuel 13.

Amnon's Obsession and Sin (2 Samuel 13:1-14)

Amnon, the eldest son of David, becomes infatuated with his half-sister Tamar, a beautiful virgin. His obsession grows to the point where he becomes physically malnourished because he believes it is impossible to be with her. Amnon's cousin Jonadab, who is described as a very shrewd man, devises a deceitful plan to help Amnon fulfill his desires.

Jonadab advises Amnon to pretend to be sick and request that his father, King David, send Tamar to take care of him and prepare food for him in his sight. Amnon follows Jonadab's advice and feigns illness. When King David visits him, Amnon asks that Tamar come to his house to make him some food. David agrees and sends Tamar to Amnon's house.

280

Once Tamar is in his house, Amnon dismisses everyone else and asks Tamar to bring the food into his bedroom. When she does, he grabs her and tries to force her to lie with him. Tamar pleads with Amnon, urging him not to commit such a disgraceful act. She points out that such behavior is not done in Israel and asks him to speak to the king, suggesting that David might allow them to marry. However, Amnon refuses to listen to her and, being stronger, he overpowers her and rapes her.

This act of violence against Tamar is not only a grave sin but also a selfish and needless action driven by Amnon's uncontrollable lust. It sets off a chain of tragic events within David's household, contributing to the internal turmoil and strife that had been prophesied to plague David's family.

Amnon's Despicable Reaction (2 Samuel 13:15-17)

Once Amnon had what he wanted, he "hated her exceedingly; so that the hatred wherewith he hated her was greater than the love wherewith he had loved her" (v. 15). This was either a sign of a tremendous character flaw or mental illness, or perhaps Tamar insisted, for honor, that she be taken as his wife. The latter seems the most likely, in light of Tamar's words upon being sent away, "this evil in sending me away is greater than the other that thou didst unto me" (v. 16).

None of the options for Amnon's response does anything other than make him look worse than he did in the beginning. Amnon appears to be no good in every way. Unless this is mental illness, which is doubtful, it speaks of the chaos of family life that appears to be cracking the foundation of David's home.

281

The Public (And Private) Response (2 Samuel 13:18-22)

Tamar had a particular colorful garment worn by virgin princesses. Upon being expelled, she gave a very public display of grief, tearing the garment, putting ashes on her head, and crying out. Tamar's virtue appears strong in every way through all of this, as she responds in a way that is responsible: grieve, and tell others (vv. 18-19).

However, Absalom, her brother, saw what was happening and seemed to immediately know what had taken place, likely knowing the character flaws of his brother. Bullinger suggests that at the time of this event, Amnon was 22 and Tamar 15, while Absalom was 20 and David 53, occurring two years after the birth of Solomon (*The Companion Bible*, note on 2 Samuel 13:1).

David came to know of the events, either through Absalom or Tamar herself, or perhaps through one of the servants (v. 21). Ultimately, it was David's job to execute judgment in his kingdom, and that responsibility began within his own household. However, when your own life is not in order, it becomes incredibly difficult to administer justice for others.

Absalom's Revenge (2 Samuel 13:24-29)

Having no justice, Absalom's heart grew more angry, and he devised a plan. Absalom waited two full years, harboring his anger and resentment towards Amnon. He then formulated a scheme to avenge his sister Tamar. Absalom invited all the king's sons to a sheep-shearing event, a festive occasion that would not raise suspicion. He specifically instructed his servants to wait until Amnon was in high spirits from drinking wine and then strike him down.

As planned, during the feast, Absalom's servants struck Amnon as he was merry with wine, killing him. The other sons of the king, fearing for their own lives, fled the scene in terror. This act of vengeance fulfilled Absalom's desire for retribution but also set off a chain of events that would further destabilize David's household and reign.

Confusion In The Aftermath (2 Samuel 13:30-39)

In the immediate aftermath of Amnon's murder, there was significant confusion and fear among David's sons. News reached David that Absalom had killed all of his sons, causing the king to tear his garments and lie on the ground in grief. However, Jonadab, the same cousin who had earlier advised Amnon, quickly clarified that only Amnon was dead, killed by Absalom's servants.

David's heart was deeply grieved for the loss of Amnon, but he also longed for reconciliation with Absalom, who fled to Geshur to escape retribution. Despite his sorrow, David's desire to see Absalom again revealed the complexity of his emotions and the tension between justice and familial love.

This tragic event and its aftermath heightened the animosity within David's family, creating a breeding ground for further strife and rebellion. The unresolved tension and the king's inability to enforce justice impartially would sow seeds of discord that threatened the stability of his reign and the unity of his household.

Conclusion

We have seen a vivid depiction of the fulfillment of Nathan's prophecy to David regarding the continuous strife that would plague his house as a consequence of his sins. The intertwining of the external military triumphs with the internal familial tragedies, highlighting the complexity of leadership, power, and the enduring impact of personal actions. David's "photo-op" victories on the battlefield contrast sharply with the moral decay and turmoil within his own household. The tragic story of Amnon and Tamar, followed by Absalom's vengeful act, underscores the prophecy's haunting accuracy. The narrative serves as a somber reminder of the consequences of sin and the intricate dynamics that influence both personal and political realms.

Chapter 34:

THE RETURN OF ABSALOM

2 Samuel 14:1-33

Absalom had killed Amnon in revenge for the rape of his sister Tamar and then fled to Geshur. King David had not sent for Absalom to return. After three years, however, David longed to see Absalom again (2 Sam. 13:39).

Joab's Plan (2 Samuel 14:1-11)

Joab, having served King David for about two decades in Jerusalem, "perceived that the king's heart was toward Absalom" (v. 1). As the story unfolds, we see that Joab knew his boss well. While David probably wouldn't respond to a direct inquiry about his feelings, he would respond to a good story. David, a man of steel on the outside and a heart of gold on the inside, was more receptive to indirect approaches. So, Joab devised a story.

Throughout his life, David was often moved by tender stories or settings. One notable instance is when the prophet Nathan confronted him with a parable about a rich man who took a poor man's only lamb (2 Samuel 12:1-7). David, angered by the injustice in the story, declared that the rich man deserved to die, only to be told by Nathan that he was that man, leading to David's repentance for his sins with Bathsheba.

Another moment is found in David's deep lamentation over the deaths of Saul and Jonathan. His heartfelt eulogy (2 Samuel 1:17-27) shows his capacity for deep emotion and tenderness, even towards Saul, who had sought his life.

David also showed great compassion when he sought out Mephibosheth, the crippled son of Jonathan, to show him kindness for Jonathan's sake (2 Samuel 9:1-13). David's actions here stemmed from his deep friendship with Jonathan and his desire to honor that bond.

These instances reflect David's complex character, where his strong exterior often gave way to profound emotional responses to stories and situations that touched his heart.

This time, Joab decides to bring in an actress: a wise woman from Tekoah, a town near Bethlehem. Joab enlisted her help to tell "her story," complete with the appearance of having been in mourning for quite some time. We are not told who she is, whether Joab knew of her in advance, if David knew her, or any other details, but it does seem that Joab had this well planned.

The woman of Tekoah approached King David with a fabricated story, as instructed by Joab. She claimed to be a widow with two sons. According to her tale, one of her sons had killed the other in a field, and now her entire family was demanding the life of the surviving son as vengeance for the murder.

Hmmm... all that sounds vaguely familiar!

She expressed her deep fear and anguish to David, explaining that if her remaining son were to be executed, her family line would be extinguished, and her husband's legacy would be erased. This plea mirrored David's own situation with Absalom, stirring his compassion and leading him to promise protection for her remaining son. David assured her that her son would not be harmed, demonstrating his sensitivity to the plight of a grieving mother and his inclination to show mercy.

Joab's Secret Revealed (2 Samuel 14:12-20)

Having received what she wanted, the woman pressed her luck and begged to say one more thing (v. 12). When she received permission, she "let into" King David. She implied that David not receiving Absalom back was a sin against the "people of God" (i.e.: Israel) (v. 13) since Absalom was the next in line for the throne. The woman then implored him to bring Absalom home. She pleaded logically, saying, "we must needs die, and are as water spilt on the ground" (v. 14), implying that life is too short to live without forgiving those who hurt you. Then she argues spiritually, saying that God allows all the banished to come to Him (v. 14).

It is a profound blessing that "yet doth he [God] devise means, that his banished be not expelled from him." This verse highlights the incredible lengths to which God goes to bring back those who are estranged from Him. Throughout the Bible, there are numerous stories that exemplify God's relentless pursuit of the lost and His divine strategies to restore them to His fold.

One such story is that of the prodigal son (Luke 15:11-32). Despite the son's decision to leave his father's house and squander his inheritance, the father devises a means to welcome him back with open arms. The father's unwavering love and readiness to forgive mirror God's heart toward us.

Similarly, the story of Jonah (Jonah 1-4) showcases God's willingness to go to great lengths to bring a wayward prophet back to His purpose. Despite Jonah's initial disobedience and attempt to flee from God's calling, God orchestrates events, including a storm and a great fish, to redirect Jonah back to Nineveh.

287

The account of Peter's denial and subsequent restoration (John 21:15-19) also illustrates God's redemptive plan. After Peter denies Jesus three times, Jesus seeks him out after the resurrection, offering forgiveness and reaffirming Peter's role in His mission.

These stories only touch the surface, and the greatest is the means which God devised to allow every man, woman, boy and girl to come to Him!

In verses 15-20, the woman of Tekoah continues her plea by revealing her true purpose. With the King's insistence, she explains that Joab orchestrated the entire scenario to persuade King David to reconcile with Absalom.

Absalom Returns (2 Samuel 14:21-27)

King David responds to Joab's scheme by granting his request to bring Absalom back to Jerusalem. David instructs Joab to go and bring Absalom from Geshur. Joab, grateful for the king's decision, bows and thanks David, expressing his appreciation for the favor. Joab is likely grateful for two reasons: first, he got what he wanted (which was best for his boss and the kingdom); second, the king didn't punish him (and he likely could have been punished with death).

Absalom returned to Jerusalem, but for unstated reasons, David did not meet with his son. Instead, he allowed Absalom to live in Jerusalem without seeing him.

In all of Israel, there was no one praised as much for his beauty as Absalom. From the sole of his foot to the crown of his head, there was no blemish in him (v. 25). Absalom's hair was particularly notable. When he cut his hair at the end of each year because it became too heavy for him, the weight of the hair from his head was two hundred shekels by the king's standard, which is about five pounds (v. 26). This striking physical appearance contributed to Absalom's charismatic personality and significant influence among the people.

The term "polled" in the context of verse 26 means "cut" or "trimmed." In historical and biblical usage, "poll" as a verb means to cut or clip, especially hair or wool. The etymology of "poll" traces back to Middle English, originating from the Old English word "polle," which referred to the top part of the head. Over time, "poll" came to be associated with cutting hair, particularly the hair on the head, thus extending to the act of trimming or cutting hair.

In modern English, the term "poll" is more commonly associated with voting or surveys, where it refers to the counting of heads or gathering of opinions. However, the older usage as seen in the Bible carries the meaning of cutting or trimming hair.

Cutting hair only once a year was not a common practice for young Jewish men during biblical times. It is mentioned in the context of Absalom to highlight his extraordinary and notable appearance, as well as his distinctiveness and perhaps even vanity. Most Jewish men would have adhered to more regular grooming practices, and specific religious vows—such as the Nazirite vow—sometimes included not cutting hair for a certain period, but these were exceptions rather than the norm.

Absalom also had three sons and a daughter named Tamar, who was described as a beautiful woman (v. 27).

289

David and Absalom Reconciled (2 Samuel 14:28-33)

Absalom spent two years in Jerusalem without seeing his father, King David, face to face. Prior to that, he had lived in Geshur for three years after fleeing from Jerusalem.

Eventually, this situation upset Absalom, and his patience ran out. He had his servants set Joab's fields on fire, indicating that perhaps Joab wasn't providing him with much information about the issue or was dragging his feet. This act got Joab's attention, and Absalom lamented that he would have been better off in Geshur if he had known he would not be able to see David (v. 32). So Joab told David and pleaded with him, and David finally invited Absalom into his presence. Absalom is now back in good stead with David. ...but for how long?

Conclusion

The story of David and Absalom reveals a father's reluctance to reconcile with his estranged son, contrasting sharply with the parable of the prodigal son where the father eagerly welcomes his wayward child back home. David's hesitation and the complex dynamics of his relationship with Absalom illustrate the challenges and emotional struggles that can accompany forgiveness and reconciliation in human relationships.

However, the parable of the prodigal son provides a powerful depiction of God's unconditional love and readiness to forgive. In this parable, the father represents God, who waits patiently and eagerly for all who are lost to return to Him. Unlike David, who needed persuasion and time to embrace Absalom again, God is always ready to welcome us with open arms, regardless of our past mistakes.

This comparison reminds us of the incredible grace and mercy God extends to each of us. We can be thankful that, like the father in the parable, God is always watching and waiting for our return, ready to forgive and restore us to His family. His patience and love are boundless, offering us hope and assurance that no matter how far we stray, He is always there to welcome us back.

THE DAVIDIC CHRONICLES

Chapter 35:
Absalom's Rebellion (Part 1)
2 Samuel 15:1-37

In 2 Samuel 14, Absalom is brought back to Jerusalem after three years of exile for killing his brother Amnon. Joab, David's commander, orchestrates Absalom's return through a devised plan involving a wise woman from Tekoa, who persuades David to reconcile with his estranged son. Despite being allowed back into the city, Absalom remains in partial isolation, unable to see the king's face for two more years. Eventually, he is fully restored to David's favor, but the chapter hints at Absalom's growing ambition and dissatisfaction, setting the stage for the events of 2 Samuel 15.

Absalom's Conspiracy (2 Samuel 15:1-12)

Absalom prepared an entourage to display his strength and power (v. 1). This entourage is part of a long-range plan in Absalom's mind to become the king of Israel. He first prepared "chariots and horses." Kings of Israel were not to rely on horses (Deut. 17:16), but David had spared 100 chariots and horses from his battle with one of the Assyrian kings, Hadadezer, in 2 Samuel 8:4 (see Chapter 28). Perhaps it is these same chariots and horses Absalom now uses.

In addition to the chariots and horses, Absalom had "fifty men to run before him." All this was part of the "show" to solidify the public persona of Absalom, who is no doubt wanting people to see him as "king material" rather than a "conniving murderer" (2 Sam. 13).

Rashi, a medieval Jewish commentator from the 11th century, notes that these men "all had their spleen and the flesh of the soles of their feet cut off." This comment reflects Jewish tradition and provides insight into the scientific thinking from the 2nd century through the 10th century AD, spanning the time of the Talmud to the era of Rashi. There was an ancient belief that removing the spleen could make a man run faster. Additionally, it was thought that by cutting a pattern in the soles of the feet and allowing scar tissue to grow over, one could run barefoot for long distances.

In 2013 the International Journal of Surgery had this to say,

> The spleen had long been associated with the ability to run, with references in ancient literature to splenectomy being performed to allow men and horses to run faster; as Pliny asserts has the characteristic of slowing down the race of men, for this reason, runners were subordinated to its burn with a red-hot iron". In 1922 this myth was tested in the laboratory at Johns Hopkins University, where Macht and Finesilver observed that asplenic mice were able to run faster than mice with an intact spleen.[6]

Absalom, always charming and always cunning, wasted no time in setting up a little charade to win over the people of Israel. He stationed himself conspicuously by the city gate, the prime spot for intercepting those who had legal disputes to present before the king. Like a seasoned charmer, Absalom would call out to the troubled citizens, "Of what city art thou?" (v. 2). Upon hearing their grievances, he would lament, oh so sympathetically, that there was no one deputed by the king to hear them.

---

6 Renzo, Dionigi, et al. "History of splenectomy." International Journal of Surgery, vol. 11, no. S1, 2013, pp. S42-S43, ScienceDirect, https://www.sciencedirect.com/science/article/pii/S1743919113600138#bib8. Accessed 27 July 2024.

And then, with a flair for the dramatic, Absalom would declare, "Oh that I were made judge in the land, that every man which hath any suit or cause might come unto me, and I would do him justice!" (v. 4).

Such a selfless act of public service, isn't it? And just to seal the deal, he would stretch out his hand, take hold of the complainer, and kiss him. All this to show how much he cared about their woes.

Through these calculated gestures, Absalom "stole the hearts of the men of Israel" (v. 6). With each act, he chipped away at David's authority, positioning himself as the true "people's advocate."

So, while Absalom's father, King David, was busy with the affairs of the kingdom, Absalom was busy undermining him, one kiss at a time.

After forty years (v. 7), Absalom was ready to move to the second phase of his plan. The reference to "forty years" is confusing because Absalom himself was not even forty years old, and he certainly did not spend forty years executing this plan. Most scholars believe this refers to forty years into the kingdom, starting from Saul's coronation. Others suggest it might be forty years from David's anointing. The latter interpretation fits the timeline much better, especially considering Acts 13:21 states that Saul reigned for forty years, although there are various interpretations of that verse.

The conspiracy began when Absalom requested permission to "go and pay my vow" (v. 7) in Hebron. Since this was a vow to the Lord, it likely means he wanted to go to Hebron to offer a choice sacrifice. King David granted permission (v. 9), seemingly taking Absalom at his word.

But Absalom had other plans. In verses 10-12, we see the culmination of years of careful planning and manipulation. Absalom sent secret messengers throughout all the tribes of Israel, instructing them to proclaim, "Absalom reigneth in Hebron" as soon as they heard the sound of the trumpet (v. 10). This was a calculated move to create the appearance of widespread support and to give his claim to the throne an air of legitimacy.

Absalom didn't stop there. He invited two hundred men from Jerusalem to accompany him, who went in their innocence, knowing nothing of the conspiracy (v. 11). These men were likely prominent figures, and their presence would lend further credibility to Absalom's claim. Their unwitting participation would also make it more difficult for them to later oppose him, as they could be seen as complicit in the coup.

Additionally, Absalom sent for Ahithophel the Gilonite, David's counselor, from his city Giloh, while he was offering the sacrifices (v. 12). Ahithophel was a man of great influence and wisdom, and his defection to Absalom's side was a significant blow to David. It indicated that even within David's inner circle, there were those who believed in Absalom's cause or who were dissatisfied with David's rule.

Ahithophel the Gilonite was the grandfather of Bathsheba, the woman with whom King David committed adultery. Bathsheba is the daughter of Eliam (2 Samuel 11:3), and Eliam is identified as the son of Ahithophel the Gilonite (2 Samuel 23:34). This connection might have contributed to any animosity or dissatisfaction Ahithophel held against David.

The conspiracy grew strong, and Absalom's following kept increasing (v. 12). This was not a sudden rebellion but the result of years of Absalom's careful efforts to undermine David and position himself as the preferred leader. His charm, manipulation, and strategic alliances all played a part in building the foundation for this moment, where he would openly declare his intent to seize the throne.

David's Flight from Jerusalem (2 Samuel 15:13-30)

In verses 13-14, a messenger comes to David with alarming news: "The hearts of the men of Israel are after Absalom" (v. 13). Absalom's conspiracy has gained significant support, posing an immediate and serious threat to David's reign. Recognizing the gravity of the situation, David acts swiftly. He tells all his servants who are with him in Jerusalem, "Arise, and let us flee; for we shall not else escape from Absalom: make speed to depart, lest he overtake us suddenly, and bring evil upon us, and smite the city with the edge of the sword." (v. 14).

David made a swift decision to flee for one or both of the following reasons. First, he was likely exhausted and demoralized, feeling utterly drained of the will to fight. This could stem from sheer physical fatigue and the emotional burden of the chaos he had contributed to, possibly compounded by efforts to keep certain matters concealed. Second, David may have been significantly influenced by Absalom's strategic and effective psychological operations, which created the appearance that men throughout the kingdom had abandoned him.

David's servants desired to be loyal to David, willing to do whatever he asked (v. 15). But David insisted on getting out and "left ten women, which were concubines, to keep the house" (v. 16). Leaving behind these women displays the poor decision-making on David's part during this time. They will be seen again in a tragic event in 2 Samuel 16.

David and his loyal followers fled the city and "tarried in a place that was far off" (v. 17). In Hebrew, the "place that was far off" is Beth-hammerḥah, and could be a proper noun rather than a description.

Verse 18 states: "And all his servants passed on beside him; and all the Cherethites, and all the Pelethites, and all the Gittites, six hundred men which came after him from Gath, passed on before the king."

In this verse, several groups are mentioned: the Cherethites, the Pelethites, and the Gittites. These groups were part of David's personal bodyguard and loyal followers.

1. **Cherethites and Pelethites:** These were elite troops who served as David's personal guards. The Cherethites are often associated with the region of Crete, while the Pelethites are thought to be a similar group, possibly also of foreign origin. They were fiercely loyal to David and played crucial roles in protecting him and enforcing his rule.

2. **Gittites:** This group refers to the people from Gath, one of the major cities of the Philistines. The six hundred men mentioned here were part of a group that had followed David when he fled from Saul and lived among the Philistines in Gath (1 Samuel 27:2-3). These men had remained loyal to David and continued to serve him faithfully even after he became king.

This loyalty of these groups is especially notable given that many of these men were originally non-Israelites, yet they chose to stand by David in his time of need.

In verses 19-22, David speaks to Ittai the Gittite, a foreigner who had recently joined David. David suggests that Ittai should stay in Jerusalem, as he is a newcomer and doesn't need to share in David's hardship (v. 19). However, Ittai pledges his allegiance to David, expressing his willingness to follow him wherever he goes, even if it means facing death (v. 21).

The mention of these groups and this individual seems to be some anecdotal evidence that perhaps David should have stayed and fought. However, this is not what he chose to do.

In verse 23, David's departure takes place, as Israel mourns.

The text continues with David's departure from Jerusalem, carrying with him the Ark of the Covenant, a symbol of God's presence and favor (v. 24). Zadok and Abiathar, the priests, also accompanied David, bringing the Ark along, its presence a constant source of encouragement and direct connection to God (v. 25).

However, in a moment of deep resignation, David instructs Zadok to return the Ark to the city, expressing a forlorn hope that if he finds favor in the Lord's eyes, he will be brought back to see both the Ark and the place where it dwells (v. 25). This act is filled with sorrow, as it signifies David's acceptance of his banishment and his relinquishment of God's direct protection.

David's words reveal his despair and submission to whatever fate might befall him, showing a lack of the

299

kingly resolve and trust in God's promises that once defined him (v. 26). He seems to be surrendering to his circumstances rather than fighting for his rightful place.

He then instructs Zadok and Abiathar to return to Jerusalem with their sons, Ahimaaz and Jonathan, and act as his eyes and ears, relaying any news back to him (vv. 27-28). This move, while strategic, underscores David's sense of isolation and loss, as he relies on others to keep him informed about the very kingdom he once ruled with confidence.

The priests comply, taking the Ark back to Jerusalem and remaining there (v. 29). This scene leaves a lingering sadness, as it feels like David is abandoning his spiritual anchor, the Ark which he had once so victoriously ushered into Jerusalem.

In verse 30, David ascends the Mount of Olives, weeping as he goes, with his head covered, and barefoot. This act of mourning and humility displays the deep sadness and emotional turmoil he feels as he flees from his own city and his own son, Absalom.

Jerusalem Falls, Hope Remains (2 Samuel 15:31-37)

As David approached the top of the Mount of Olives, he learns that "Ahithophel is among the conspirators with Absalom." Showing a bit of resolve and a glimmer of hope, David prays, "I pray thee, turn the counsel of Ahithophel into foolishness" (v. 31).

Having reached the top, David worshiped the Lord, with perhaps one last and dreary look at his beloved Jerusalem. As he was there, his servant Hushai joined him, arriving "with his coat rent, and earth upon his head" (v. 32).

Up to this point, we have not known Hushai the Archite, but he is going to play a pivotal role in overcoming Absalom's rebellion. An Archite is a person from the town of Archi, located near the border of the tribes of Ephraim and Benjamin in ancient Israel.

David, recognizing Hushai's loyalty and value, devises a cunning plan to counter Absalom's rebellion. In verses 33-34, David tells Hushai that if he follows him, it will only be an additional burden. Instead, David instructs Hushai to return to Jerusalem and offer his services to Absalom, pretending to be loyal to him. By doing so, Hushai can act as a double agent, providing David with valuable intelligence and working to undermine Ahithophel's counsel to Absalom.

In verses 35-37, David instructs Hushai to collaborate with the priests Zadok and Abiathar, who will relay any information to their sons, Ahimaaz and Jonathan. These sons will then act as messengers to inform David of any developments in Jerusalem. Hushai returns to the city as David's spy, while Absalom enters Jerusalem as its new King, setting the stage for the impending conflict.

The Psalm 3 Connection

Psalm 3 is notable for being the first psalm to include a title and a stated author. The title attributes the psalm to David and specifically mentions that it was written during his flight from Jerusalem when he was fleeing from his son Absalom. This context makes it especially pertinent to the events described in 2 Samuel 15, as it reflects David's thoughts and prayers during this tumultuous period in his life.

In the Psalm, David begins by expressing his distress over the increasing number of enemies rising against him, feeling besieged by those who doubt his deliverance (vv. 1-2). In contrast, the Lord becomes "a shield for me; my glory, and the lifter up of mine head" (v. 3). The strength of the Lord comes upon David, and he concludes with a strong note of celebration, "Salvation belongeth unto the LORD: thy blessing is upon thy people" (v. 10).

A Note of Hope

2 Samuel 35 paints a somber picture of Absalom's rebellion and David's subsequent flight from Jerusalem. The chapter is filled with tension and sorrow as David, once a mighty king, finds himself fleeing from his own son. The betrayal by trusted advisors and the support Absalom garners from the people highlight the fragility of David's reign and the personal cost of his earlier transgressions.

However, amidst the sadness and despair, there is a glimmer of hope. David's strategic decisions, such as sending Hushai to counter Ahithophel's counsel, demonstrate his resilience and wisdom. Moreover, the connection to Psalm 3 offers a profound insight into David's mindset during this difficult time. Despite the overwhelming odds and the betrayal he faces, David's faith in the Lord remains unwavering. He finds solace and strength in his relationship with God, trusting that salvation and blessing ultimately come from Him.

While the immediate circumstances are bleak, the chapter ends on a note of hope, reminding us that even in the darkest of times, faith and resilience can pave the way for eventual restoration and redemption.

Chapter 36:

ABSALOM'S REBELLION (PART 2)

2 Samuel 16:1-23

Chapter 16 of 2 Samuel continues the dramatic and turbulent events of Absalom's rebellion against his father, King David. This chapter delves deeper into the deceptive and treacherous actions surrounding David, highlighting the challenges he faced from both trusted allies and outright enemies.

In the previous chapter, 2 Samuel 15, we witnessed the beginning of Absalom's revolt. Absalom, having won the hearts of the people of Israel through deceit and manipulation, declared himself king in Hebron. David, realizing the gravity of the situation, fled Jerusalem to avoid confrontation with his son, taking his loyal followers with him. The chapter ended with David's departure from the city, a moment filled with sorrow and uncertainty.

As we move into Chapter 16, the narrative unfolds with more intense and perilous moments. We see the cunning of Ziba, the loyalty test of Hushai, and the bold but bad counsel of Ahithophel.

Ziba's Deception (Verses 1-4)

Ziba was a former servant of Saul. David had called upon him when he was looking to see if any of Saul's descendants were left, and Ziba told him about Mephibosheth. David gave Ziba a very nice position of running Saul's vast estate, now bequeathed to Mephibosheth.

Ziba came to David loaded with gifts. He brought donkeys, bread, summer fruits, and wine, all in an effort to make himself look trustworthy to David. But what he said to David when David asked about Mephibosheth was the startling part: "he abideth at Jerusalem: for he said, To day shall the house of Israel restore me the kingdom of my father" (v. 3). David, incensed that Mephibosheth would treat him that way, gives all Mephibosheth's vast holdings to Ziba.

This looks like a sad day for David, as yet another beloved one has turned against him. And it is sad, but what the reader does not know (nor does David), is that none of it is true. Ziba is the only one turning against David, while making it look like he is taking care of him. The situation will not be resolved until 2 Samuel 19:24-30.

This passage offers a few valuable lessons:

1. **Beware of "free lunch" out of nowhere:** When someone offers something too good to be true, it often comes with hidden motives or consequences. Always be cautious and consider the possible reasons behind such generosity.

2. **Be discerning:** It's crucial to investigate and ask questions before making judgments or decisions. David's lack of discernment led to a hasty decision based on false information. Taking the time to verify facts can prevent misunderstandings and misguided actions.

Shimei Curses David (Verses 5-14)

As David and his men continued their journey, they came to Bahurim, where a man named Shimei, from the house of Saul, came out. Bahurim is a village in the territory of Benjamin, near the Mount of Olives, which played a role in several biblical narratives. Shimei cursed

David continually and threw stones at him and his servants. Shimei accused David of being a "man of blood" and a "man of Belial" (v. 7). The term "Belial" is often used in the Bible to signify worthlessness or wickedness, essentially labeling David as a man without value or morality. Shimei claimed that the Lord had returned upon David all the blood of the house of Saul, in whose stead David had reigned, and that the Lord had delivered the kingdom into the hand of Absalom, David's son. Shimei declared that David was caught in his own mischief because he was a "bloody man" (v. 8).

This encounter was highly distressing for David, who was already burdened with the betrayal of his son Absalom and the deception of Ziba. The humiliation took place while "all the people and all the mighty men were on his right hand and on his left" (v. 6).

In response to Shimei's cursing, Abishai, the son of Zeruiah, came forward with very strong words, suggesting to David that Shimei should be put to death for cursing the king (v. 9). However, David was in no mood for the strength of character that Abishai was showing. Instead of agreeing with Abishai's suggestion, David chose to endure the curses, believing that they might somehow be part of God's will.

In verses 10-12, David's response to Shimei's cursing reveals a man who is emotionally spent and morally weakened. David says, "So let him curse, because the Lord hath said unto him, Curse David. Who shall then say, Wherefore hast thou done so?" (v. 10). He continues, "Behold, my son, which came forth of my bowels, seeketh my life: how much more now may this Benjamite do it? let him alone, and let him curse; for the Lord hath bidden him" (v. 11). David even hopes that enduring these curses might lead to some form of divine mercy: "It may be that the Lord will look on mine affliction, and that the Lord will requite me good for his cursing this day" (v. 12).

David's attitude here is not one to be praised or emulated. Instead of standing up against the ungodly behavior of Shimei, David misinterprets this moment as a form of humility and submission to God's will. He wrongly believes that by accepting these false curses, he might work his way back into God's favor. However, this is a misplaced humility. Shimei's curses are not from God but are actually against the very work that God accomplished in removing Saul and placing David on the throne. David's failure to recognize this and his passive acceptance of Shimei's words reflect a man who has lost the "fight" in him, both emotionally and morally. This is not an example of righteous suffering but rather a flawed attempt to seek redemption through unwarranted suffering.

In verses 13-14, the narrative continues with David and his men enduring Shimei's relentless cursing and stone-throwing as they travel. The scripture states, "And as David and his men went by the way, Shimei went along on the hill's side over against him, and cursed as he went, and threw stones at him, and cast dust." Shimei's actions were not merely verbal; he was physically manifesting his disdain by throwing stones and dust at David and his entourage.

Despite the hostility, David and his people continued on their journey. Verse 14 highlights the exhaustion and emotional toll this ordeal took on them: "And the king, and all the people that were with him, came weary, and refreshed themselves there." This verse underscores the physical and emotional fatigue experienced by David and his followers. Unfortunatly, by not dealing with Shimei, the physical and emotional fatique was worse than it needed to be. And the reason David did not deal with it, it seems to me, is a false interpretation of how to get into right-standing with God.

The Tale of Two Advisors (Verses 15-23)

In verses 15-19, we see Absalom entering Jerusalem with all the men of Israel and Ahithophel, notably with him. This marks a significant and symbolic moment as Absalom takes over the city, seemingly completing his rebellion against his father, King David.

) Hushai (Verses 16-19)

When Hushai the Archite, a friend of David, approached Absalom, he offered a surprising pledge of loyalty by greeting him with a cheer for the king. Absalom, curious about Hushai's loyalty, asked why he wasn't with David, his friend. Hushai cleverly responded that he would serve whoever the Lord and the people of Israel chose, and since they had chosen Absalom, he would remain by his side. He added that just as he had served David, he would now serve David's son, Absalom.

Hushai's words served to reassure Absalom of his loyalty while cleverly positioning himself to remain close and potentially influence events in favor of David. This pledge of loyalty by Hushai is a rare positive note in this chapter, offering a glimmer of hope in an otherwise dark and tumultuous time for David.

) Ahithophel (Versess 20-23)

In verses 20-22, Ahithophel offered strategic counsel to Absalom, suggesting a bold and odious move to solidify his rebellion against his father, David. Ahithophel advised Absalom to take his father's concubines, whom David had left to keep the house, and lie with them in a public display. This act would signal to all Israel that Absalom had completely severed ties with David and had no intention of reconciling with him.

By doing this, Ahithophel believed that Absalom would strengthen the resolve of his followers. He said, "the hands of all that are with thee be strong" (v. 21). The public nature of this act would ensure that Absalom's supporters would not fear being abandoned or labeled as traitors if Absalom later changed his mind and sought reconciliation with David. It was a move designed to cement Absalom's leadership and commitment to the rebellion.

Absalom followed Ahithophel's counsel, and a tent was pitched for him upon the top of the house. There, in the sight of all Israel, Absalom went in unto his father's concubines. This act of defiance was a powerful statement, reinforcing his claim to the throne and his break from David.

This event may be history's all-time "Gold Medal" in the "burning bridges" category.

Verse 23 provides critical insight into the high regard in which Ahithophel's counsel was held. It states, "And the counsel of Ahithophel, which he counselled in those days, was as if a man had enquired at the oracle of God: so was all the counsel of Ahithophel both with David and with Absalom." This verse emphasizes that Ahithophel's advice was considered exceptionally wise and almost divinely inspired. People treated his counsel as though it came directly from God, showcasing the tremendous respect and authority he commanded in both David's and

Absalom's courts. This high level of esteem underscores the gravity and influence of his recommendations, making his support for Absalom particularly impactful.

Conclusion

Governments throughout history have invariably been rife with drama and political intrigue, and David's government is no exception. The political machinations and power struggles can be both enticing and disgusting to witness. In this chapter, we are given a rare glimpse inside the workings of a government, revealing the often unsavory process of "how the sausage is made." It isn't a pretty picture, filled with deception, betrayal, and ruthless tactics. This serves as a poignant reminder that our trust should be placed in God, not in the flawed and fallible institutions of human government.

Chapter 37:

ABSALOM'S REBELLION (PART 3)

2 Samuel 17:1-18:33

In 2 Samuel 16, King David faced a series of challenges. Ziba, the servant of Mephibosheth, brought provisions to David and falsely claimed that Mephibosheth had betrayed him. Shimei, from the house of Saul, cursed David and threw stones at him, but David restrained his men from retaliating. Meanwhile, Absalom entered Jerusalem and, following Ahithophel's advice, publicly slept with his father's concubines to assert his claim to the throne.

And the rebellion of Absalom continues.

Competing Counsel (2 Samuel 17)

Ahithophel's Counsel (17:1-4)

Ahithophel, who had already gained the king's attention as seen in chapter 16, now suggests that an army of 12,000 men be led—by him, of course—to make a sneak attack while David and his men are tired. His plan is to capture the king and force the rest to surrender. Such tactics were not uncommon in ancient warfare. Contrary to the notion that warfare in those days was more "gentlemanly," surprise attacks and strategies aimed at capturing or killing key leaders were often employed to ensure a swift and decisive victory.

Hushai's Counter-Counsel (17:5-14)

Hushai has the unenviable task of standing before the new king and going against his most trusted advisor plus all the elders of Israel (v. 4). Hushai presents David in all his strength. Even though he knows that David is currently weak, Absalom doesn't know that, and everyone sees David as the manly, vibrant warrior that he once was. Hushai uses colorful language, drawing a frightening word picture. Hushai continues in dramatic fashion, explaining what should be done: taking all of Israel and going in mighty force against David. Moreover, Hushai encourages Absalom to be the one leading the troops (v. 11).

Hushai made what must have been one of the most rhetorically strong persuasive speeches in history up to that time. His words resonate with what we might call Churchillian qualities today. Hushai's speech was masterfully crafted to inspire confidence and evoke a sense of fear and urgency. He painted a vivid and intimidating picture of David as a formidable and experienced warrior, which likely stirred Absalom's imagination and played on his insecurities. By emphasizing the need for a massive show of force and suggesting that Absalom personally lead the troops, Hushai cleverly appealed to Absalom's vanity and ambition, making his plan seem both grand and necessary.

) Absalom's Decision (17:14)

In verse 14, Absalom and all the men of Israel decide that Hushai's counsel is better than Ahithophel's. Despite Ahithophel's reputation for giving sound advice, Absalom is swayed by Hushai's dramatic and persuasive rhetoric.

Absalom is confident that he has saved himself from what he perceived as the Lord's work to undo him and honor David, which he believed was unknowingly embeded by God into Ahithophel's plan. However, in reality, he was merely deceived by Hushai's great speech.

Hushai's Counter Intelligence Operation (17:15-22)

Hushai speaks to Zadok and Abiathar, the priests who are secretly on David's side, just as Hushai is. He informs them of both Ahithophel's and his own counsel to Absalom, urging them to send word to David immediately about the danger. Jonathan and Ahimaaz, the sons of Zadok and Abiathar who were stationed for this purpose, receive the message through a young lady who acts as a covert messenger. They then pass the information on to David (v. 15). Note that the King James Bible uses the term "wench," which, in 1611 had a neutral meaning for "young lady," thought it has taken on a negative meaning today.

In verses 16-20, there is a close call when Jonathan and Ahimaaz are discovered by Absalom's supporters. They hide in a well, and a woman covers the well with grain to conceal them. When Absalom's men arrive and ask if anyone has seen the two messengers, the woman misleads them, allowing Jonathan and Ahimaaz to escape and deliver the message to David.

David and those with him manage to escape beyond the Jordan River, putting a safer distance between themselves and Absalom's forces. They await the coming battle from this more secure location.

The Fall of Ahithophel and David's Provision in Mahanaim (17:23-29)

When Ahithophel realizes that Absalom has not followed his counsel, he comprehends the gravity of the situation. Knowing that his advice was not heeded and predicting the eventual failure of Absalom's rebellion, Ahithophel sees no future for himself. In ancient times, an advisor whose counsel was rejected, especially in such critical matters, often faced severe consequences. Understanding the potential backlash and disgrace, Ahithophel returns to his hometown, sets his affairs in order, and hangs himself. This act of suicide signifies his complete loss of hope and his anticipation of the impending doom.

Absalom appoints Amasa as the commander of his army in place of Joab. Amasa is a relative of David, being the son of Abigail, who is David's sister. This change in military leadership indicates Absalom's desire to solidify his position and distance himself from those loyal to David, like Joab. Joab had been a significant military leader under David, and his replacement signifies a shift in loyalty and strategy within Absalom's camp.

Shobi, the son of Nahash, is mentioned as one of the individuals who provides support to David. Shobi is from Rabbah of the Ammonites, indicating that he is likely an Ammonite prince or a person of influence. Along with others such as Machir and Barzillai, Shobi brings provisions and supplies to David and his men in Mahanaim. Their support is crucial for David, as it helps sustain his followers and boosts their morale during this challenging time. Shobi's actions demonstrate loyalty and the importance of alliances in times of crisis.

The Battle in the Forest of Ephraim (2 Samuel 18)

David Prepares for Battle (2 Samuel 18:1-5)

David organizes his troops and prepares for the imminent battle against Absalom's forces. David divides his men into three groups, placing them under the command of Joab, Abishai (Joab's brother), and Ittai the Gittite. David initially expresses his intention to lead the troops personally, but his men strongly advise against it. They argue that David's life is far more valuable than any of theirs, and that he should remain in the city to provide support and strategize.

In verse 5, David gives a specific and poignant command to his commanders: "Deal gently for my sake with the young man Absalom." Despite Absalom's rebellion and the pain it has caused, David's paternal love for his son is evident. He instructs his commanders to capture Absalom alive and to treat him with care, hoping to avoid the death of his son. This command underscores the intense personal conflict David faces, torn between his duties as a king and his emotions as a father.

The Battle in the Forest of Ephraim (2 Samuel 18:6-8)

The battle takes place in the forest of Ephraim, east of the Jordan River. This location is significant because it gives David's forces a strategic advantage. David's men are already positioned in the forest when Absalom arrives. The dense woods hinder Absalom's larger army, giving David's men an edge in combat.

A total of 20,000 of Absalom's men fell in battle. In verse 8, the scripture notes that "the wood devoured more people that day than the sword devoured." This phrase means that the difficult and treacherous terrain of the forest caused more casualties than the actual fighting did. Soldiers likely got lost, trapped, or injured by natural obstacles such as dense underbrush, steep ravines, and possibly even wild animals. The chaotic environment of the forest played a critical role in the high number of casualties, illustrating the hazards of fighting in such a setting.

Absalom's Death (2 Samuel 18:9-18)

As the battle rages, Absalom finds himself in a dire situation. Riding a mule, Absalom passes under the thick branches of a large oak tree. His hair gets caught in the branches, and his mule continues running, leaving Absalom hanging helplessly in mid-air. One of Joab's men sees Absalom suspended in the tree and reports it to Joab.

Despite King David's explicit command to deal gently with Absalom, Joab decides to take matters into his own hands. Upon hearing the report from his man, Joab expresses frustration that Absalom was not immediately killed. Joab then goes to Absalom and personally thrusts three darts (or javelins) into Absalom's heart while he is still alive. Following Joab's initial attack, Joab's ten armor-bearers surround Absalom and finish him off, ensuring his death.

Joab blows the trumpet to signal the end of the battle, and his troops cease their pursuit of the fleeing Israelites. Absalom's body is then taken and thrown into a large pit in the forest. To mark the grave, they heap a great pile of stones over it. This act not only serves as a burial but also as a symbolic gesture of disgrace, as unmarked graves and stone heaps were often associated with dishonor.

Interestingly, prior to his rebellion, Absalom had set up a monument for himself in the Valley of the Kings, known as Absalom's Monument, because he had no son to carry on his name. This pillar was intended to preserve his legacy, but his untimely and ignominious death stands in stark contrast to his aspirations for lasting renown.

Ahimaaz's Request and Joab's Decision (2 Samuel 18:19-23)

After the battle concludes, Ahimaaz, the son of Zadok, eagerly requests permission from Joab to deliver the news of the victory to King David. Ahimaaz, known for his loyalty to David, is keen to be the bearer of what he assumes will be good news. However, Joab, understanding the complexity of the situation, refuses Ahimaaz's request. Joab is aware that while the victory is significant, the death of Absalom—David's son—would cause David great distress.

Instead, Joab sends a Cushite servant to carry the message to David. The Cushite, likely chosen for his ability to deliver the news more objectively, is tasked with informing the king of the battle's outcome, including the sensitive news about Absalom.

Ahimaaz, undeterred by Joab's initial refusal, persists in his request. Eventually, Joab relents and allows Ahimaaz to run as well. Ahimaaz, being faster, takes a different route and outruns the Cushite, arriving first at the city where David awaits news.

Ahimaaz's Incomplete Report (2 Samuel 18:24-29)

David, anxious to hear news from the battlefield, is stationed at the city gate. When a watchman sees a runner approaching, he informs the king, who recognizes the significance of a lone messenger. As the watchman spots a second runner, David anticipates that both carry important messages.

Ahimaaz arrives first and enthusiastically reports the victory, emphasizing the LORD's deliverance of David's forces. However, when David asks directly about Absalom, Ahimaaz hesitates and avoids delivering the painful news. He vaguely mentions that there was "much tumult" but does not disclose Absalom's fate, likely out of fear of the king's reaction or a desire to soften the blow.

The Cushite's Message and David's Grief
(2 Samuel 18:30-33)

Following Ahimaaz's incomplete report, the Cushite arrives with the full news. The Cushite tactfully conveys the outcome of the battle, stating that the LORD has avenged David of those who rose up against him. When David again inquires specifically about Absalom, the Cushite confirms that Absalom is dead, phrasing it as a victory for David over his enemies.

Upon hearing of his son's death, David is overwhelmed with grief. He retreats to the chamber over the gate and laments deeply, crying out, "O my son Absalom, my son, my son Absalom! would God I had died for thee, O Absalom, my son, my son!" This outpouring of sorrow reveals the depth of David's love for his son, despite Absalom's rebellion. The intensity of David's grief underscores the tragic nature of the conflict, where the personal loss far outweighs the political victory.

Chapter 38:
RESTORATION AND RECONCILIATION
2 Samuel 19:1-43

Mourning for Absalom (2 Samuel 19:1-8)

A lot is going on in the king's mind and heart, but in the end, he had won a victory. However, the victory to others felt like a defeat because of David's tremendous mourning for Absalom. Those who were with him snuck into the city of Jerusalem, back to their homes, "by stealth" (v. 3) rather than marching in a grand victory parade.

Joab (who had been the one who killed Absalom) came as captain of the guard and played the role of realist for David. He accused him to his face, saying, "thou lovest thine enemies, and hatest thy friends" (v. 6). His accusation that if they had died and Absalom lived the king would have been glad (v. 6) seems to be accurate. And such a condition simply cannot work when you are the king, a role in which personal feelings have to be kept under cover and dealt with personally.

Joab came with some solid advice: "If you do not act like the King, before the day is over you'll have more problems than your lifetime has ever presented you, combined" (v. 7). Fortunately, David took the advice and sat at the gate, displaying himself as King (v. 8).

David's Return and the Reconciliation Process (2 Samuel 19:9-15)

David's problems are not over. Despite his return to his duties and his efforts to reestablish his kingship, the people of Israel are still divided and in turmoil. The people in all the tribes of Israel began to argue among themselves, saying, "The king saved us from our enemies, but he fled from Absalom. Now he has returned; what should we do?" (v. 9, paraphrased).

The people recognize that Absalom, whom they had made king, is dead, while the king they had been under is in exile. They begin to ask one another why they have not yet invited David back to be their king once again (v 10).

The king, knowing he must go back and aware that the people's hearts have turned toward him, now speaks to the elders of his own tribe, Judah, who seemingly have not yet given the word for his return. He uses Zadok and Abiathar as the spokesmen, asking them to, in a sense, shame the elders into asking David to return (vv. 11-12).

In a surprising twist, David then sends word to Amasa, who had become the captain of the host (army) under Absalom, to replace Joab (v. 13). We do not know if David is aware that Joab was the one who killed Absalom against his orders, but he may be. Alternatively, this move could be seen as a strategic effort to solidify both sides of the kingdom: those loyal to Absalom and those loyal to David, into a cohesive unit once again.

How does this intrigue with Amasa and Joab play out? Stay tuned, we will address the outcome in the next chapter!

In verses 14-15, the efforts to reconcile and reunite the people prove successful. The hearts of all the men of Judah turn toward David as one, and they send word to the king, inviting him to return with all his servants. David accepts their invitation and crosses the Jordan River, finally bringing an end to this period of division and uncertainty.

Encounters on the Way Back (2 Samuel 19:16-39)

) Shimei And Ziba Come Groveling (vv. 16-23)

Verses 16-17 reintroduce Shimei, who now hurried down with the men of Judah to meet King David. This is the same Shimei who had the audacity to curse David and pelt him with stones as he fled from Absalom (2 Samuel 16:5-13). Now, in a dramatic twist, Shimei has realized David's triumphant return to power and comes seeking forgiveness. He brings along a thousand men from Benjamin, indicating his significant support and influence. Ziba, the servant of Mephibosheth, also comes to meet the king. Remember Ziba? He's the one who deceived David, falsely claiming that Mephibosheth stayed in Jerusalem to seize the throne (2 Samuel 16:1-4). Their presence here adds another layer to the complex relationships David must navigate upon his return.

Verses 18-20 give the detail of Shimei's groveling before David.

Verses 21-23 introduce Abishai, the son of Zeruiah, who recommends that Shimei should be put to death for cursing the king. David rejects this advice swiftly and curtly, emphasizing that this is not a day for executions but for healing and unity. It should be remembered that Abishai is the brother of Joab, who has just been demoted. Abishai, it seems, was a loyal warrior for David (as was Joab), but the entire family may have been more swift to bloodshed than David was comfortable with, especially on this day in which there is so much turmoil and so much need for healing.

321

) Mephibosheth's Defense (vv. 24-30)

Mephibosheth, Saul's grandson and Jonathan's son, comes to meet David. In verse 24, it's noted that Mephibosheth had not taken care of his feet, trimmed his mustache, or washed his clothes from the day the king left until the day he returned safely. This implies that Mephibosheth was in a state of mourning and distress during David's absence, showing his loyalty and grief for the king's departure.

It's important to recall the deception by Ziba, Mephibosheth's servant, who had previously told David that Mephibosheth had stayed in Jerusalem to claim the throne for himself. David had believed Ziba's lies and granted him all of Mephibosheth's possessions (2 Samuel 16:1-4). But now Ziba's chickens are about to come home to roost!

In verses 25-27, Mephibosheth explains to David how he was deceived and left behind, only to be slandered by Ziba, his King-appointed caretaker. Mephibosheth acknowledges David's goodness and tells him to do whatever he thinks is best. In gratitude, he recognizes that the king has done so much for him that he cannot ask for anything more.

In verses 29-30, David decides to split the land between Ziba and Mephibosheth. This action demonstrates the benevolence of the king, balancing justice and mercy. However, it also reflects the honor culture of ancient biblical times, where being deceived did not absolve one from keeping their word. Even if fooled, a man was expected to maintain his integrity and adhere to his promises.

Several biblical examples illustrate this principle:

◊ **Joshua and the Gibeonites (Joshua 9:15-21):** Joshua made a treaty with the Gibeonites, who had deceived him into believing they were from a distant land. Despite the deception, Joshua honored the treaty, showing his commitment to his word.

◊ **Jephthah's Vow (Judges 11:30-39):** Jephthah made a vow to the Lord that if he was given victory over the Ammonites, he would sacrifice whatever came out of his house to greet him. Tragically, his daughter was the first to greet him. Despite the personal cost, Jephthah kept his vow.

◊ **Saul and the Oath (1 Samuel 14:24-45):** King Saul rashly vowed that anyone who ate before evening would be cursed. His son Jonathan, unaware of the vow, ate honey. When Saul discovered this, he was prepared to put Jonathan to death to fulfill his oath, although the people intervened to save Jonathan.

These examples underscore the importance within the ancient near east culture of integrity and the value placed on keeping one's word, even when it involved personal sacrifice or challenging circumstances.

The incident in 2 Samuel 19:29-30 effectively concludes Mephibosheth's story within the biblical narrative. His refusal to accept the land demonstrates his loyalty to David, and this scene marks the last significant interaction involving Mephibosheth. Although he is mentioned again in 2 Samuel 21, it is only in passing, and there are no further developments or stories involving him after this point.

) Barzillai's Farewell (vv. 31-39)

Barzillai the Gileadite, whom we met in 2 Samuel 17:27-29, comes down from Rogelim to escort King David across the Jordan River. Barzillai is described as a very wealthy eighty-year-old man who had provided for the king during his stay in Mahanaim. David invites Barzillai to come to Jerusalem and be cared for, but Barzillai declines, citing his old age and desire to die in his own city near the grave of his parents. Instead, he suggests that Chimham, presumably his son, go with the king in his place. David agrees and promises to do for Chimham whatever Barzillai wishes.

Barzillai is mentioned briefly again in 1 Kings 2:7, where David, on his deathbed, instructs Solomon to show kindness to the sons of Barzillai, allowing them to eat at his table because they supported David during Absalom's rebellion.

Chimham is also mentioned in Jeremiah 41:17, where a place near Bethlehem is referred to as the "habitation of Chimham," possibly indicating that David granted him land there. Some have taught that "Chimham's Inn" is the inn at which there was no room, in Luke 2, but this is pure speculation.

Contention Between Judah and Israel (2 Samuel 19:40-43)

The final verses of the chapter highlight the growing contention between the tribes of Judah and Benjamin and the rest of Israel. As David returns to Jerusalem, tensions flare between the men of Judah and the northern tribes, who feel slighted in the celebration of the king's return. This tension is not new; there has been a longstanding rift between the northern and southern kingdoms, as seen in the early days of David's reign when Ishbosheth reigned over the northern tribes.

The northern tribes felt particularly aggrieved because they had been the first to suggest David's return as king (v. 11), yet it seemed that the men of Judah had taken over the rejoicing and the honor of bringing the king back. This slight was enough to stir up resentment and conflict.

This division foreshadows the eventual split of the united monarchy into two separate kingdoms: the northern kingdom of Israel and the southern kingdom of Judah. While this division would take many years to fully manifest, the seeds of discord were already being sown in these moments of perceived injustice and rivalry.

Conclusion

Chapter 19 of 2 Samuel details the aftermath of Absalom's rebellion and King David's return to power. The chapter begins with David's mourning for his son Absalom, which prompts Joab to remind him of his duties as king. David heeds Joab's advice and resumes his role, addressing the divisions among the tribes of Israel and Judah. He initiates a reconciliation process, replacing Joab with Amasa to unify the kingdom. Various individuals, including Shimei and Ziba, come seeking forgiveness, while Mephibosheth defends his loyalty. The chapter also highlights Barzillai's farewell and the growing contention between Judah and Israel, foreshadowing future divisions within the kingdom. Thematically, the chapter emphasizes reconciliation, loyalty, and the challenges of leadership in the face of personal loss and political strife.

Chapter 39

SHEBA'S REBELLION AND DAVID'S RESTORATION

2 Samuel 20:1-26

Sheba's Rebellion (Verses 1-2)

We are introduced for the first time to "Sheba, the son of Bichri, a Benjamite." He hasn't been mentioned before in the biblical narrative, so little is known about his past. His Benjamite heritage is significant because this tribe was historically loyal to the house of Saul, Israel's first king, who was also a Benjamite. As we know, there was ongoing tension between the houses of Saul and David, and such tensions often arise during times of political instability.

Sheba was "a man of Belial." The word "*Belial*" (בְּלִיַּעַל) can be broken down into two parts: "beli," meaning "without," and "ya'al," meaning "usefulness" or "profit." Together, the term literally means "worthlessness" or "lawlessness." In 2 Samuel 16:7, Shimei called David "a man of Belial," but in Sheba's case, the words are divinely inspired.

Sheba called for insurrection, saying, "We have no part in David, neither have we inheritance in the son of Jesse" (v. 1).

It may seem surprising that "every man of Israel went up from after David, and followed Sheba" (v. 2) except for David's own tribe of Judah. This serves as a reminder that we often view our biblical heroes like David as moving from one victory to the next, glossing over this kind of turmoil—from one insurrection to another. Moreover, it reminds us that just because crowds turn away from one man to follow another doesn't mean God has blessed the man with the crowds.

An interesting aspect of Sheba's instruction is his call

for "every man to his tents" (v. 1). Since the people didn't literally live in tents, this is either a figure of speech or, as many conservative scholars suggest, an "emendation of the Sopherim." This phrase appears three times in scripture (also in 1 Kings 12:16 and 2 Chronicles 10:16). In Hebrew, "tents" can be formed by transposing the two middle letters of "gods." If true, this phrase might be a purposeful euphemism, implying Israel's turn to polytheism, with only Judah remaining faithful to God. Whether these verses describe a purely political problem or a spiritual one as well is open to interpretation, but it's possible that the nation, almost as a whole, was rejecting their God. (See also note on verse 22).

David's Return and Response (Verses 3-7)

Verse 3 indicates that Sheba's rebellion occurs before David's return to Jerusalem. This timing raises interesting questions. In 2 Samuel 19, Israel had initially welcomed David back, with Judah following later. However, after Judah escorts David home, Israel feels slighted—they had proposed his return but weren't included in the celebration. Their discontent is expressed in 2 Samuel 19:41-43. Sheba appears to have exploited this dissatisfaction, rallying the northern tribes to secede and form their own kingdom. After all, if they received so little recognition, why remain united? This entire scene displays the fickle nature of people and their politics!

Rather than deal with Sheba's rebellion immediately, David returned to Jerusalem to reestablish authority. Part of this was to address the situation of the concubines who had been left behind and then used to solidify Absalom's rebellion. These women were placed in seclusion, though cared for, for the rest of their lives. It's challenging for us to fully grasp the cultural issues at play here, but this approach was likely both politically prudent and gracious.

Amasa, whom you may recall as the new captain of the host, having replaced Joab in a purely political move (2 Sam. 19:13), is given his first instruction as captain in verse 4. However, Amasa "tarried longer than the set time" (v. 5). Worried about Sheba's rebellion, the king called for Abishai to pursue him due to Amasa's delay (v. 6). Abishai had been quick to suggest violent solutions, as seen when he recommended executing Shimei for cursing David. David often had to restrain Abishai's inclination towards violence, preferring more moderate approaches, especially in times of reconciliation. Now, it seems, David wants a man of swift action, and Abishai leads the warriors of Israel in pursuit of Sheba.

Joab's Killing of Amasa (Verses 8-13)

As the men pursued Sheba, Amasa caught up and intercepted David's forces, which included Joab, the former captain of the host who had been sidelined by the political decision that put Amasa in his position. Joab, anticipating this encounter, came prepared. He had hidden a sword strategically in his military clothing, likely tied by a belt to his lower back, so that when he knelt, the sword would not move with him, allowing him to secretly grasp it. Taking hold of the weapon, he gave Amasa "the kiss of death," striking him "in the fifth rib" (see note, *The Davidic Chronicles ~ Consolidated Edition, pg. 197*). Immediately, "Joab and Abishai his brother pursued after Sheba" (v. 10). One of Joab's men stood by Amasa's body and called for the troops to "*go* after Joab" (v. 11). After a hasty and bloody

329

roadside burial, "all the people went on after Joab, to pursue after Sheba" (v. 13). We can see from this that although David has not officially reinstated Joab, circumstances are strategically aligning for his return to power.

The Siege at Abel of Bethmaachah (Verses 14-22)

The pronouns in verses 14-15 can be tricky, so let's examine them carefully. Verse 14 describes Sheba's actions: "he went through all the tribes of Israel," successfully gathering support. However, Joab and his men pursued Sheba: "they were gathered together, and went also after him" (v. 14). Subsequently, "they" (Joab and his forces) "besieged him" (Sheba) in the town of Abel (v. 15).

Joab and his men employed a sophisticated siege tactic to breach the walls of Abel. They constructed a ramp, likely using earth, stones, and timber, to create an inclined plane leading up to the city wall. This ramp served as a path for their siege equipment, particularly the battering ram. The text states that they "battered the wall, to throw it down" (v. 15), indicating the use of a powerful battering ram to repeatedly strike the wall until it weakened and collapsed.

Interestingly, this siege technique foreshadows the tactics that would be employed by the Romans centuries later during their siege of Masada in AD 70-73. At Masada, the Romans famously constructed a massive earthen ramp to breach the seemingly impregnable fortress. This parallel demonstrates the enduring effectiveness of such siege tactics in ancient warfare, spanning from the time of David to the Roman Empire.

The use of such advanced siege techniques by Joab's forces highlights the military prowess and strategic capabilities of David's army. It also underscores the seriousness with which they pursued Sheba's rebellion, willing to go to great lengths to capture him and quell the insurrection.

In 2 Samuel 20:16-18, we encounter a wise woman who intervenes in a tense situation. She calls out to Joab, the commander of David's army, and shares what seems to be an old proverb: "They shall surely ask counsel at Abel: and so they ended the matter" (v. 18). This cryptic statement has been interpreted in several ways, but the core message remains consistent across interpretations: seek the counsel of the citizens before taking drastic action.

The woman's advice aligns with the principle found in Deuteronomy 20:10-11, which instructs the Israelites to offer terms of peace to a city before attacking it. By invoking this proverb, the wise woman is essentially telling Joab to consult with the people of Abel before proceeding with any military action.

The wise woman of Abel demonstrates her diplomatic skills by appealing to Joab's sense of respect for the people of Israel. In verse 19, she asks Joab to approach the situation with consideration for the city's inhabitants rather than resorting to bloodshed. This clever tactic shifts the focus from military aggression to peaceful negotiation.

Joab, recognizing the wisdom in her words, responds with clear peace terms. He states in verse 21, "deliver him [Sheba] only, and I will depart from the city." This offer shows Joab's willingness to resolve the conflict without further violence, provided his primary objective - capturing Sheba - is met.

The wise woman, proving herself to be both shrewd and decisive (indeed, a "tough cookie"), doesn't hesitate in her response. She boldly declares, "Behold, his head shall be thrown to thee over the wall" (v. 21).

The wise woman's persuasive skills and quick thinking led to a swift resolution of the siege. She convinced the men of the city to execute Sheba, cutting off his head and throwing it over the wall to Joab and his army. This decisive action effectively ended the rebellion, as Joab had promised to withdraw if Sheba was handed over.

Upon receiving Sheba's head, Joab blew the trumpet (shofar), signaling the end of the conflict. The text states that "they all departed, every man to his tent" (v. 22). This phrase is significant when compared to the similar phrase in verse 1.

The phrase "every man to his tents" in verse 1 is considered by many scholars to be an emendation, possibly a euphemism for returning to polytheistic practices. However, the phrase "every man to his tent" in verse 22 is generally accepted as a literal description of the army dispersing after the battle.

The distinction between these two phrases and their interpretations is primarily based on the Jewish oral tradition, specifically the Talmud. The Talmud provides a list of 18 emendations made by the scribes to the biblical text, and the phrase in verse 22 is not included in this list. This omission suggests that it should be taken literally.

If we accept this oral tradition, we can interpret verse 1 as a euphemism for spiritual or political rebellion, while verse 22 describes the literal act of soldiers returning to their temporary dwellings after the conflict. This interpretation is further supported by the context of verse 22, which follows the conclusion of a military engagement where soldiers would indeed be returning to their camp.

The Officers in David's Kingdom (Verses 23-26)

Verses 23-26 provide an overview of the key officials in David's administration after his return to power:

◊ **Joab:** Reinstated as commander over all of Israel's army. Joab's reinstatement suggests his continued importance to David's reign, despite their complex relationship.

◊ **Benaiah:** In charge of the Cherethites and Pelethites, David's personal bodyguard. We will see Benaiah play a crucial role in Solomon's rise to power in the future.

◊ **Adoram:** Overseer of forced labor or tribute. This is his first mention, indicating David's expanding administrative structure.

◊ **Jehoshaphat:** The recorder or chronicler, maintaining the same position he held before Absalom's rebellion (2 Samuel 8:16).

◊ **Sheva:** The royal secretary, replacing Seraiah who held this position earlier (2 Samuel 8:17).

◊ **Zadok and Abiathar:** Continuing as priests, maintaining their roles from before the rebellion.

◊ **Ira the Jairite:** A new addition as one of David's chief advisors. This appointment might indicate David's efforts to broaden his base of support.

This list demonstrates the reestablishment of David's rule over a reunited kingdom.

Chapter 40:

DAVID MAKES A COMEBACK

2 Samuel 21:1-22

David has been through unbelievable struggle and turmoil, and the previous chapters have largely been one bit of bad news after another, both for David and the kingdom. However, having returned to the throne, Chapter 21 shows David solidly reigning as monarch once again. This is evident in two ways: first, through a restoration of national blessing, and second, through a display of the valor we once knew from David but had largely lost, along with the strong support of his warriors.

In chapter 21, it is time to say, "Welcome back!"

Restoration of National Blessing (2 Samuel 21:1-14)

A famine had persisted for three years, and David sought insight from the Lord as to why this punishment had come upon the nation (v. 1). It is important, first of all, to recognize that not every weather pattern is directly from God, and so we remember a cardinal rule: don't make a doctrine out of an historical account. However, in this case the famine was sent from God, who told David clearly, "It is for Saul, and for his bloody house, because he slew the Gibeonites" (v. 1).

The Lord's response do David must be read carefully, or a key part of the passage will be missed. Thre are *two*, not one cause of the famine. First of all, "It is for Saul." That is, the nation had done something that dishonored Saul, and they were being punished for it. But also for Saul's persecution of the Gibeonites, going against the oath of the nation given by Joshua (Joshua 9). At some point in his reign Saul breached this ancient covenant by attacking the Gibeonites. This act not only violated the agreement made by Israel's forebears but also defied God's command to honor such oaths.

The text is going to deal with the issue with the Gibeonites before dealing with the issue of the nation's disrespect of Saul, as we shall soon see.

David, recognizing the gravity of the situation, first sought to make amends for Saul's transgression. He approached the Gibeonites and asked them directly, *"What shall I do for you? And wherewith shall I make the atonement, that ye may bless the inheritance of the LORD?"* (v. 3). It seems that David expected to pay a financial remuneration, but that is not what came about.

The Gibeonites' response was unexpected and severe. They rejected any form of monetary compensation, stating, *"We will have no silver nor gold of Saul, nor of his house"* (v. 4). Instead, they demanded a form of blood justice, requesting *"seven men of his sons be delivered unto us, and we will hang them up unto the LORD in Gibeah of Saul"* (v. 6).

This request for the execution of Saul's descendants as atonement for the bloodshed committed against them reflects the ancient Near Eastern concept of an honor culture and blood vengeance. While this may seem harsh to western readers, it's important to understand it within its historical and cultural context. The Gibeonites saw this as a way to balance the scales of justice for the wrongs committed against their people. In fact, David's kingdom probably would have dealt with retaliation by a coalition of its neighbors had it not "paid its dues" for the past sins.

David's agreement to this request (v. 6) demonstrates his recognition of the need for resolution to end the famine afflicting the land.

David did not hesitate to fulfill the Gibeonites' request, with one notable exception. He spared Mephibosheth, the son of Jonathan, due to the oath of protection he had sworn to Jonathan (v. 7).

Without further delay, David delivered seven of Saul's descendants to the Gibeonites. These men were Saul's two sons by Rizpah (Armoni and Mephibosheth - not to be confused with Jonathan's son) and five grandsons born to Merab, Saul's daughter (vv. 8-9). The Gibeonites then carried out their stated intention, hanging these seven men as an act of retribution.

In verse 10, David recognizes an opportunity to address the nation's disrespect towards Saul, whom he always regarded as the Lord's anointed. When David hears that Rizpah is protecting the bodies of the deceased, he is reminded that these Jewish men haven't received a proper Jewish burial. Moreover, he realizes that Saul and his sons also lack such a burial.

Jewish burial practices are guided by several key principles that come from the Torah, and include:

◊ **Prompt burial:** The Torah emphasizes the importance of burying the deceased as soon as possible, ideally within 24 hours of death (Deuteronomy 21:23).

◊ **Respect for the body:** The human body is considered sacred, as it houses the soul. Therefore, it must be treated with utmost respect and dignity (Genesis 1:27).

337

◊ **Simplicity:** Jewish law promotes equality in death. Regardless of social status, all are buried in simple shrouds and plain wooden coffins.

◊ **Natural return:** The body should be allowed to return to the earth naturally, as stated in Genesis 3:19: "For dust you are, and to dust you shall return."

◊ **No embalming:** Traditional Jewish law prohibits embalming or cremation, as these practices are seen as interfering with the natural process of decomposition.

◊ **Burial in the ground:** The deceased should be buried in the earth, not in above-ground mausoleums (Genesis 23:19).

These practices reflect the Jewish belief in the sanctity of human life and the body, even after death, and the importance of honoring the deceased in accordance with divine commandments.

However, neither Saul, nor his sons, nor the seven just executed had received the respect that was due them. Verse 12 refers to David's actions to remedy the situation: "*And David went and took the bones of Saul and the bones of Jonathan his son from the men of Jabeshgilead, which had stolen them from the street of Bethshan, where the Philistines had hanged them, when the Philistines had slain Saul in Gilboa.*"

To understand this verse, we need to revisit the events following Saul's death:

◊ **Battle of Mount Gilboa:** Saul and his sons, including Jonathan, were killed in battle against the Philistines on Mount Gilboa (1 Samuel 31:1-6).

◊ **Desecration by the Philistines:** After the battle, the Philistines found Saul's body and those of his sons.

They cut off Saul's head and stripped him of his armor. They then hung the bodies of Saul and his sons on the wall of Beth Shan (also known as Beit Shean) as a display of victory (1 Samuel 31:8-10).

◊ **Rescue by the men of Jabesh Gilead:** When the people of Jabesh Gilead heard what the Philistines had done, they sent a group of valiant men to retrieve the bodies. These men traveled all night, took down the bodies from the wall of Beth Shan, and brought them back to Jabesh. There, they burned the bodies and buried the bones (1 Samuel 31:11-13).

Now, years later, David is rectifying the situation by giving Saul and Jonathan a proper burial in their family tomb. This act serves multiple purposes:

◊ It shows respect for Saul as the Lord's anointed and for Jonathan as David's beloved friend.

◊ It demonstrates David's commitment to honoring the royal family, even after their deaths.

◊ It helps to unify the nation by showing respect for the previous dynasty.

◊ It completes the proper burial process according to Jewish customs.

By retrieving these bones and ensuring a proper burial, David is addressing both the disrespect shown to Saul's lineage and fulfilling religious and cultural obligations, thus paving the way for the restoration of national blessing, which God grants in verse 14.

Display Of Valor And Support (2 Samuel 21:15-22)

Before delving into the events of 2 Samuel 21:15-22, it's important to recall David's previous victories over the Philistines, which established his reputation as a formidable warrior and leader:

- ◊ **Goliath's defeat:** David's first major victory was as a young shepherd when he defeated the Philistine giant Goliath with a sling and stone (1 Samuel 17).

- ◊ **Early military successes:** As a commander in Saul's army, David repeatedly led successful campaigns against the Philistines (1 Samuel 18:5, 18:30).

- ◊ **Victories as king:** After becoming king, David defeated the Philistines at Baal-perazim (2 Samuel 5:20) and in the Valley of Rephaim (2 Samuel 5:25).

- ◊ **Subjugation of Philistia:** David eventually subdued the Philistines, taking control of Gath and its surrounding territories (2 Samuel 8:1).

These victories established David's military prowess and helped secure Israel's borders against one of its most persistent enemies.

Despite David's previous victories, the Philistine threat resurfaces in 2 Samuel 21:15. This time, however, we see a different side of the aging warrior-king. As David engages in battle, the text tells us that he "waxed faint" (v. 15). David, once the epitome of strength and valor, is now showing signs of fatigue and vulnerability.

At this moment, the reader might anticipate a dire turn of events. David's weariness in battle could spell disaster for him and for Israel. However, just as the situation seems most precarious, help arrives in an unexpected form.

As David felt the weight of his years (Bullinger suggests David was 60 at this time), a new threat emerged: Ishbibenob, a previously unknown giant. He was described as one of the "sons of the giant," though the identity of this progenitor remains a mystery. Could it have been Goliath? One might speculate that Goliath's own son had come seeking vengeance, but this is mere conjecture, albeit an interesting one. Ishbibenob wielded a new sword—recall that David had claimed Goliath's—and appeared poised for battle.

At this critical moment, Abishai, the son of Zeruiah, came to David's aid. Abishai had been a loyal and fierce warrior throughout David's reign, playing significant roles in recent events. He had accompanied David when they infiltrated Saul's camp (1 Samuel 26), he had been instrumental in the war against Abner and Ishbosheth (2 Samuel 2-3), and he had led troops against the Ammonites (2 Samuel 10). Most recently, Abishai had stood by David during Absalom's rebellion, commanding a third of David's forces (2 Samuel 18).

In this instance, Abishai's timely intervention proved crucial. He struck down Ishbibenob, saving David from potential harm or even death. This close call prompted David's men to take action to protect their king and, by extension, the nation.

Following this incident, David's warriors made a significant decision. They approached David, saying, "*Thou shalt go no more out with us to battle, that thou quench not the light of Israel*" (v. 17). This statement was both a mark of deep respect and a strategic move for national protection. By encouraging David to remain behind during battles, they were acknowledging his invaluable leadership and the importance of preserving his life for the sake of the entire nation.

The Davidic Chronicles

This moment marked a transition in David's role. While he had been known as a warrior-king, his men now urged him to focus on leadership from a safer position. Their words, referring to David as "the light of Israel," underscore the high esteem in which he was held and the recognition that his life was crucial to the nation's wellbeing. This shift in David's role also demonstrated the strength and capability of his warriors, who were now ready to take on the frontline battles themselves.

2 Samuel 21:18-22 describes three more encounters with Philistine giants, each defeated by one of David's mighty warriors. These battles demonstrate the strength and valor of David's men, as well as God's continued protection over Israel.

The first giant mentioned is Saph (also called Sippai in 1 Chronicles 20:4), who was slain by Sibbechai the Hushathite. This battle took place at Gob, a location otherwise unknown but presumably in Philistine territory. Sibbechai was one of David's mighty men, mentioned in 2 Samuel 23:27 and 1 Chronicles 11:29.

In another battle at Gob, Elhanan the son of Jaare-oregim, a Bethlehemite, killed the brother of Goliath the Gittite. The parallel account in 1 Chronicles 20:5 clarifies that the brother's name was Lahmi.

The third encounter occurred in Gath, the hometown of the original Goliath. This giant was particularly notable for having six fingers on each hand and six toes on each foot, totaling 24 digits. Such polydactyly (extra digits) is a real genetic condition, often associated with gigantism. He was struck down by Jonathan, the son of Shimea, David's brother.

These accounts serve multiple purposes in the narrative:

◊ They demonstrate God's continued protection of Israel against formidable enemies.

◊ They showcase the bravery and skill of David's warriors, highlighting their ability to protect the nation even without David's direct involvement in battle.

◊ They provide a sense of closure to the threat posed by the Philistine giants, which began with Goliath and now ends with these final encounters.

◊ They reinforce the idea that David's kingdom is secure and blessed by God, able to overcome even the most intimidating foes.

These victories over the giants mark the end of an era, symbolizing the final defeat of the seemingly invincible Philistine threat that had once terrorized Israel. Through these accounts, we see how God used not just David, but also his loyal and capable warriors, to secure Israel's safety and establish the kingdom's strength.

THE DAVIDIC CHRONICLES

344

Chapter 41:

DAVID'S MIGHTY MEN

2 Samuel 23:8-39

As we concluded Chapter 40, we left David in a place of triumph after a season of trials and tribulation. 2 Samuel 21 highlighted David's return to the throne, the restoration of national blessing, and a demonstration of valor that rekindled memories of his earlier feats. It was a moment where we could all say, "Welcome back, David!" The king, once beleaguered by enemies and internal strife, has now reclaimed his role as the protector and leader of Israel.

Now, before diving into the next chapter, we need to make a brief note on how we're going to structure the remainder of our study. We'll be skipping over 2 Samuel 22:1-23:7 for the time being. This section includes a psalm of victory and David's last words, a fitting capstone to his life. However, rather than tackling them right now, we're going to save these for our final chapter as the grand conclusion. They're placed here in the text for good reason—likely as a reflection on his life's victories—but we'll see them as a reflection on his entire reign and legacy when we finish the series.

With David firmly back on the throne, 2 Samuel 23:8-39 shifts gears from David's personal victory to celebrating the men who helped make it all possible—David's mighty men. These warriors weren't just muscle-bound bodyguards; they were the backbone of David's reign, men who fought beside him throughout the peaks and valleys of his kingship. Their loyalty and courage were instrumental in establishing David's kingdom as one of strength, unity, and faithfulness to God.

But before we jump into the tales of their heroism, it's worth noting the Hebrew word used to describe these men: **gibbor**. This term, often translated as "mighty" or "valiant," carries the connotation of being a strong and courageous warrior. These were men marked by exceptional physical and moral strength. The word **gibbor** previews the type of warriors we're about to meet—men who didn't flinch in the face of overwhelming odds and whose strength wasn't just physical, but deeply rooted in their faithfulness to their king and God.

Interestingly, **Gabriel**, the angel who appears later in biblical history, shares a connection to this word. His name means "God is my strength," drawing from the same root, **gbr**. Just as Gabriel is a messenger of God's strength, these mighty men were instruments of God's strength in David's kingdom.

Now, as we move forward, we're not just recounting their heroic feats; we're celebrating the community that surrounded David and helped make his kingdom amazing. Without these men, David's comeback might have ended prematurely. Instead, they helped secure his legacy as one of Israel's greatest kings.

With that in mind, let's dive into their stories!

The Three Chief Heroes (23:8-12)

Adino the Eznite – Chief of the Captains (23:8b)

Adino the Eznite is introduced in 2 Samuel 23:8 as the chief of David's mighty men, though his role remains somewhat mysterious. The verse describes him as a warrior who single-handedly defeated 800 men with his spear. His title, "chief of the captains," denotes his high rank among

346

the elite warriors. However, some translations use "three" instead of "captains," reflecting a textual variation. This could suggest his leadership over the first trio of mighty men, renowned for their exceptional feats. Adino's name was likely changed from an original Baal reference, similar to Ishbosheth and Mephibosheth (see note on these names in *The Davidic Chronicles ~ Consolidated Edition, chapter 23*). Various translations and references offer slightly different versions of his name and title.

Little else is known about his background or family, but his single-handed slaughter of 800 men speaks volumes about his prowess in battle. This warrior had amazing strength or unbelievably good circumstances, or both. His victories set him forever in "the best of the best" category.

Eleazar, Son of Dodo the Ahohite (23:9-10)

Eleazar, the son of Dodo the Ahohite, stands out as one of David's elite warriors, second in the list of the mighty men. His most notable feat is recorded only here and 1 Chronicles 11:12-14, where he stood firm with David against the Philistines at a battle in Pasdammim. As the rest of the Israelite forces fled in retreat, Eleazar held his ground, wielding his sword until his hand grew so weary that it "clave unto the sword." His perseverance paid off as the Lord brought about a great victory that day, and the Israelites returned only to strip the dead of their spoil.

Despite overwhelming odds and the desertion of his fellow soldiers, Eleazar fought on, driven by a determination that could only be matched by his formidable skill in combat. He reminds us that the time for true courage is when all others have deserted you and you stand alone against the enemy. As Kipling so memorably

347

wrote, "*If you can keep your head when all about you are losing theirs...,*" you prove the mettle of a true warrior. And like Tennyson's famous charge, Eleazar's duty was not to question the odds but to fight on: "*Theirs not to reason why, theirs but to do and die.*"

Shammah, Son of Agee the Hararite (23:11-12)

Shammah, son of Agee the Hararite, completes the trio of David's top mighty men. His moment of glory came when the Philistines gathered at Lehi to raid a lentil field. As the rest of the Israelite army fled, Shammah stood his ground in the middle of the field, single-handedly defending it against the Philistines. Through his courage and determination, the Lord once again brought about a great victory.

This account, found only in this passage, highlights Shammah's tenacity and willingness to defend even a humble field of lentils. Interestingly, "Hararite" isn't the name of a clan but rather means "mountain man," as *har* in Hebrew means "mountain."

A Notable Event Involving the Three (23:13-17)

One of the most memorable stories involving David's mighty men occurs when David was hiding in the cave of Adullam during harvest time. The Philistines had set up camp in the valley of Rephaim, and a Philistine garrison was stationed at Bethlehem, David's hometown. Amid the pressures of battle and survival, David expressed a seemingly casual longing, wishing aloud for water from the well near Bethlehem's gate. This wasn't just any request for water—it was a nostalgic and emotional cry for something tied deeply to his roots, likely reflecting his weariness of conflict and desire for home.

In an astonishing display of loyalty, three of David's mighty men (likely from the group of "the three") heard David's words and immediately sprang into action. Without hesitation, they broke through enemy lines, risking their lives to fetch water from the well of Bethlehem and return it to their king. When they presented David with the water, however, he did something unexpected—he refused to drink it. Instead, David poured it out as an offering to the Lord, saying, "Be it far from me, O Lord, that I should do this: is not this the blood of the men that went in jeopardy of their lives?" (v. 17). David recognized the extreme sacrifice these men had made, equating the water with their very blood, and thus felt it was too precious for personal consumption.

This event is a vinget that displays both the extraordinary devotion of David's warriors and David's deep reverence for their lives and for God. These men were willing to risk everything for what might seem a small request, highlighting their unwavering loyalty. David's response, in turn, demonstrates his humility and recognition that such sacrifices were not to be taken lightly.

The Second Tier of Mighty Men (23:18-23)

Abishai, Brother of Joab (23:18-19)

Abishai, the brother of Joab, was the captain of the second group of mighty men. His most notable feat mentioned here is lifting up his spear against 300 men, slaying them in a single battle. This incredible display of combat prowess earned him great renown among David's warriors, placing him just below the first group of three mighty men in terms of distinction. However, as the text notes, he did not quite attain to their level of legendary status, though he was undoubtedly a fearsome warrior in his own right.

But Abishai's valor wasn't limited to this one act. Throughout David's reign, Abishai frequently appeared at key moments in battle and in times of crisis. For instance, it was Abishai who saved David's life when the king grew faint in battle against a Philistine giant (2 Samuel 21:17). He was also one of the commanders during Absalom's rebellion, leading one-third of David's forces (2 Samuel 18:2). His loyalty to David was unwavering, but his fiery temperament often caused David to hold him back from rash actions.

Abishai's hotheadedness is most evident in several instances where David had to restrain him. In 1 Samuel 26, when David and Abishai infiltrated Saul's camp, Abishai was ready to kill Saul on the spot, saying, "God hath delivered thine enemy into thine hand this day" (v. 8). David had to stop him, reminding him that Saul was still the Lord's anointed. Again, in 2 Samuel 16:9, Abishai offered to kill Shimei, a man who cursed David as he fled from Absalom. David, again, had to pull him back, saying, "What have I to do with you, ye sons of Zeruiah?"

Despite these moments of rashness, Abishai was a warrior at heart—bold, fearless, and fiercely protective of David. His passion and zeal often needed tempering, but his loyalty and courage were never in question. He consistently stood at David's side in battle, and his leadership among the mighty men speaks to his abilities and the respect he commanded. While not quite in the upper echelon of the three greatest warriors, Abishai's contributions to David's reign were invaluable.

Benaiah, Son of Jehoiada (23:20-23)

Benaiah, the son of Jehoiada, was a valiant man from Kabzeel, a town in southern Judah. His exploits were so remarkable that they earned him a place of high honor among David's mighty men, even though he did not reach the level of the top three. Benaiah's reputation was built on his courage, combat skill, and loyalty, and his story stands out for its vivid examples of bold, almost cinematic feats of bravery.

Among his most notable achievements are the following:

◊ **Slaying two lion-like men of Moab:** These two fierce warriors, described as "lion-like," were likely formidable opponents, and Benaiah's victory over them speaks to his incredible prowess in hand-to-hand combat.

◊ **Killing a lion in a pit on a snowy day:** As if killing a lion weren't challenging enough, Benaiah did it in a pit during difficult winter conditions, where the ground would have been slick and the cold could have hampered his movements. This feat highlights his tenacity and skill, no matter the circumstances.

◊ **Slaying a giant Egyptian warrior:** The Egyptian is described as "a goodly man," (v. 21), or, more literally, "a sight to see." He is described in 1 Chronicles 11:23 as standing five cubits tall (about 10 feet, using the Pyramid as the standard for a cubit), was armed with a spear, but Benaiah approached him with a staff, disarmed him, and then killed him with the Egyptian's own spear. This act demonstrates not only Benaiah's strength but also his cleverness and ability to turn the tide of battle through quick thinking.

Benaiah's series of victories and his proven loyalty earned him a high standing among David's mighty men. While he did not attain the status of the top three, his achievements placed him among the most respected warriors in David's army. As a result, David entrusted him with an important position: head of his personal guard. This role would have made Benaiah responsible for the king's safety, further highlighting David's trust in his abilities and integrity.

Benaiah later became even more prominent under Solomon's reign, where he continued to demonstrate his loyalty and leadership. His story is one of steadfast courage, and he remains a figure known for his impressive feats, resourcefulness, and unwavering commitment to his king.

The Remaining Mighty Men of David (23:24-39)

) The Remaining Mighty Men of David
(2 Samuel 23:24-39)

This section lists the rest of David's mighty warriors, totaling **37 men**. While many of these men remain obscure beyond this listing, a few are mentioned elsewhere in the narrative of David's reign, offering glimpses into their contributions and loyalty to the king.

◊ **Asahel, Brother of Joab** (23:24)
Asahel, famously fleet of foot, was killed by Abner in battle (2 Samuel 2:18-23). His death sparked a long-standing feud between Joab and Abner, leading to Abner's eventual assassination by Joab.

◊ **Elhanan, Son of Dodo of Bethlehem** (23:24)
Likely the same Elhanan mentioned in 1 Chronicles 20:5 who slew the brother of Goliath, Lahmi, marking him as a giant-killer like David.

◊ **Shammah the Harodite** (23:25) &
Elika the Harodite (23:25)
Little is known of these two warriors except their
inclusion in this list.

◊ **Helez the Paltite** (23:26)
Also mentioned in 1 Chronicles 11:27, not much else is
recorded about Helez.

◊ **Ira, Son of Ikkesh the Tekoite** (23:26)
Possibly from the town of Tekoa (later known as the
hometown of the prophet Amos), Ira was a key figure
among David's men, mentioned also in 1 Chronicles 11:28.

◊ **Abiezer the Anethothite** (23:27)
From Anathoth, a town known later for producing
the prophet Jeremiah. Abiezer is mentioned in
1 Chronicles 11:28.

◊ **Mebunnai the Hushathite** (23:27)
Likely the same as Sibbechai in 1 Chronicles 11:29, who
was known for slaying a Philistine giant in battle
(1 Chronicles 20:4).

◊ **Zalmon the Ahohite** (23:28)
Likely connected to Eleazar, Son of Dodo the Ahohite.
He is mentioned in 1 Chronicles 11:29.

◊ **Maharai the Netophathite** (23:28)
Another of David's great warriors, also mentioned
in 1 Chronicles 11:30. His hometown of Netophah is
near Bethlehem.

◊ **Heleb, Son of Baanah the Netophathite** (23:29)
Another warrior from Netophah, listed also in
1 Chronicles 11:30.

353

- **Ittai, Son of Ribai of Gibeah, of the Children of Benjamin** (23:29)
  His association with Gibeah places him among Saul's kinsmen, adding significance to his loyalty to David.

- **Benaiah the Pirathonite** (23:30)
  From Pirathon, in the territory of Ephraim, he is listed in 1 Chronicles 11:31.

- **Hiddai of the Brookes of Gaash** (23:30)
  Also mentioned in 1 Chronicles 11:32, his location near Mount Gaash places him in Ephraimite territory.

- **Abi-albon the Arbathite** (23:31)
  His town of origin is likely Beth-Arabah near the Dead Sea, also mentioned in 1 Chronicles 11:32.

- **Azmaveth the Barhumite** (23:31)
  Likely from Bahurim, the town where David encountered Shimei during Absalom's rebellion (2 Samuel 16:5).

- **Eliahba the Shaalbonite, of the Sons of Jashen** (23:32)
  Likely from Shaalbon, mentioned in 1 Chronicles 11:33, though little else is known about him.

- **Jonathan, Son of Shammah the Hararite** (23:32)
  Shares the same lineage as Shammah listed earlier, suggesting a familial connection between these warriors.

- **Ahiam, Son of Sharar the Hararite** (23:33)
  Also mentioned in 1 Chronicles 11:35, not much more is known about him.

- **Eliphelet, Son of Ahasbai, the Son of the Maachathite** (23:34)
  His lineage likely connects him to the people of Maacah, a region near Geshur.

◊ **Eliam, Son of Ahithophel the Gilonite** (23:34)
Eliam was the son of Ahithophel, David's counselor who later betrayed him. Eliam was also the father of Bathsheba, David's wife, making this an interesting family connection to David's life and reign.

◊ **Hezrai the Carmelite** (23:35)
Possibly from Carmel in Judah, a town associated with Nabal and Abigail.

◊ **Paarai the Arbite** (23:35)
Mentioned also in 1 Chronicles 11:37, from Arab in Judah.

◊ **Igal, Son of Nathan of Zobah** (23:36)
Likely from Zobah, a kingdom David conquered, marking Igal as a man from outside Israel's traditional tribal lines.

◊ **Bani the Gadite** (23:36)
One of the few listed men from the tribe of Gad, highlighting the breadth of geography from which David's forces came.

◊ **Zelek the Ammonite** (23:37)
A foreigner, Zelek was from Ammon, a neighboring enemy nation, yet served loyally under David.

◊ **Naharai the Beerothite, the Armor-bearer of Joab** (23:37)
He was Joab's armor-bearer, showing his close connection to the commander of David's army.

◊ **Ira the Ithrite** (23:38) & **Gareb the Ithrite** (23:38)
Both Ira and Gareb were from Ithra, a region or clan that remains somewhat mysterious.

◊ **Uriah the Hittite** (23:39)
Uriah, famously the husband of Bathsheba, was one of David's most loyal soldiers. His death was orchestrated by David after the king's sin with Bathsheba, a dark stain on David's reign.

These 37 men represent a diverse and fiercely loyal group of warriors from various regions and backgrounds, united under David. They fought valiantly to secure his kingdom and establish the strength of Israel during David's reign.

A Nation of Mighty Men

No king does it all himself. While history and Scripture alike often focus on the deeds of King David, the Bible reminds us that David's story is, in fact, the story of many men. These warriors, fighters, and supporters stood by his side through triumph and trial. Many of them remain unsung heroes, their names long forgotten except for those who knew them personally or remembered their stories. But their collective impact on David's reign reminds us of the immense value of people— whether their names are famous or lost to history, their contributions shaped the course of a nation.

In the same way, history is filled with individuals whose contributions were crucial but largely forgotten. Take, for example, the story of Peter Robinson, the speechwriter who penned one of the most iconic lines of the 20th century: "*Mr. Gorbachev, tear down this wall.*" Robinson wasn't a famous statesman or public figure. In fact, he was just a nobody—a college student at the time—who camped out on Ronald Reagan's lawn hoping to meet him. That chance encounter led him to become part of Reagan's team, eventually writing some of the most influential words of the Cold War era. While most people may never remember Robinson's name, his words helped shape the course of history. He may be forgotten, but his work endures.

Much like Robinson, the mighty men of David's reign were instrumental in the success of his kingdom, but few of their names are widely remembered. Some of these men were loyal to David for life, standing by him in every season of his kingship. Others served only for a time, perhaps at a critical moment, before fading from the narrative. And then there's the sobering reminder that David himself was not always loyal to some of his men— most notably, Uriah the Hittite, whose tragic end came not at the hands of an enemy but through David's betrayal.

The Bible presents these stories with a frank honesty, offering "the facts of life" in a factual way. It doesn't gloss over the failings of even its greatest heroes, but instead highlights the complexity of human nature. We see David's strengths and weaknesses, just as we see the loyalty, bravery, and occasional tragedy among the men who fought for him. Through these narratives, we are reminded that every great leader is shaped by those who stand with him, whether their names are remembered or forgotten. Together, these mighty men helped forge David's reign and secure his place in history—not as a solitary hero, but as the leader of a nation built by many mighty hands.

Chapter 42

A CENSUS AND ITS CONSEQUENCES

2 Samuel 24:1-24

In this chapter, we delve into a pivotal moment in King David's reign - the controversial census of Israel and its far-reaching consequences. This event, recorded in 2 Samuel 24:1-24, provides insight into the complex relationship between God, His chosen leader, and the people of Israel. It serves as a stark reminder of the weight of leadership decisions and the importance of humility before God.

As we explore this narrative, we'll witness the interplay of God's anger, David's pride, and the consequences of disobedience. We'll also see David's heart of repentance and God's mercy in action.

God's Anger and David's Census (2 Samuel 24:1-9)

The Lord's anger can be kindled! In this passage, we're not told why He's angry, but He is. In His anger, He decides to leave David to his own devices.

This is where the story becomes intriguing.

2 Samuel 24:1 suggests that the Lord prompted David to "Go, number Israel and Judah." To a modern reader, this might seem like a morally neutral act—even a typical kingly duty. However, we'll soon discover it's problematic.

The more significant issue in verse 1 is the question: "Who initiated the census?" Would God instigate something sinful that would lead to punishment? This seems troubling, but the real conundrum arises when we compare the parallel passage in 1 Chronicles 21:1. There, it clearly states that "Satan stood up against Israel, and provoked David to number Israel." How can 2 Samuel attribute to the Lord what Satan did?

What's the resolution? I believe that the Lord, angry with Israel, withdraws His protection and allows Satan to act as he wishes, leaving David to make his own choice. This situation resembles Job's story in some ways. God, who had been blessing and protecting David, removes those blessings and protections, and we witness how swiftly things deteriorate.

In verses 2-3, David instructs Joab to take the census, and we get the first indication that something is amiss. Joab's reaction is telling: "Why would you want to do such a thing? The number of Israel is the Lord's doing, not ours." This response likely stems from Israel's understanding of Moses' original instruction about census-taking. Exodus 30:12 states, "When you take a census of the Israelites to count them, each one must pay the Lord a ransom for his life at the time he is counted. Then no plague will come on them when you number them." The key point here is that each person was to "pay a ransom for his life." This ransom, set at half a shekel per person, was meant to acknowledge that the nation belonged to the Lord. In essence, it said, "We are His; He alone has the right to count us."

Joab tried to persuade the king, but in the end, "the king's word prevailed against Joab, and against the captains of the host" (v. 4). Verses 5-9 describe the nine months and 20 days of census work (imagine the expense!). The final tally of warriors is given: "there were in Israel eight hundred thousand valiant men that drew the sword; and the men of Judah were five hundred thousand men" (v. 9).

God's Judgment for the Census (2 Samuel 24:10-14)

Once again, we aren't given the "back story," but we are told the results: David expresses remorse for his actions and confesses, "I have done very foolishly" (v. 10). In his confession, he pleads with the Lord to "take away the iniquity of thy servant" (v. 10).

Following this, we're reintroduced to Gad. In chapter 12 (vol. 1), we noted that Gad was a prophet and seer who played a crucial role during King David's reign. Here's what we know about him from the biblical accounts:

1. **Advisor to David:** Gad first appears in 1 Samuel 22:5, advising David to leave the stronghold and enter the land of Judah. This suggests Gad served as a divine counselor to David during his flight from King Saul.

2. **Historiographer:** Gad is recognized as a historian who documented events during David's reign. 1 Chronicles 29:29 states that the "acts of David the king, first and last" were recorded in the writings of Samuel the seer, Nathan the prophet, and Gad the seer.

3. **Divine Messenger:** In 2 Samuel 24, Gad appears after a long absence and, as David's seer, presents him with three options for divine retribution.

4. **Writings:** While the Bible mentions Gad's writings, they aren't part of the biblical canon, and no such texts are known to exist today. They may have served as sources for compiling the Books of Samuel or Chronicles.

In verses 12-13, Gad gave David a choice of three punishments for his sin:

1. **Seven years of famine** in the land.

2. **Three months of fleeing from enemies**, during which David would be pursued.

3. **Three days of pestilence** (plague) in the land, sent by the hand of the Lord.

These three options reveal the severity of David's sin. Each option posed significant suffering and devastation to Israel, and David had to weigh which form of judgment would be most bearable.

In verse 14, David's response is notable: "I am in a great strait: let us fall now into the hand of the LORD; for his mercies are great: and let me not fall into the hand of man."

The Plague (2 Samuel 24:15-17)

The plague swept from north to south, sparing only Jerusalem. In this brief period, 70,000 men perished. Verse 16 reveals that an "angel"—a messenger of God—was carrying out the Lord's work. This angel "stretched out his hand upon Jerusalem to destroy it," seemingly leaving Jerusalem for last. However, at this point, "the LORD relented from the calamity, and said to the angel who was destroying the people, 'Enough! Withdraw your hand.'" While the King James Version uses "evil," the term originally meant "calamity." Similarly, "repented" in this context means exactly what it does today: the Lord changed His mind and altered His course of action.

Can God do this? We must accept it at face value: *the Bible says what it says and means what it says.* If we struggle with the concept of God changing His mind, it's our preconceived theology that needs adjustment, not the text.

By the end of verse 16, we discover that this is not just any angel, but "the angel of the LORD." There's compelling reason to interpret this phrase, when used in the Old Testament with the definite article, as a Christophany—a pre-incarnate appearance of the Son of God.

This event occurred "by the threshing floor of Araunah the Jebusite," a location that will prove significant later in the narrative.

Upon witnessing the devastation, David pleaded for the punishment to fall on him rather than on the people (v. 17).

David's Altar and Sacrifice (2 Samuel 24:18-25)

Upon the command of the Lord through the prophet Gad, David determined to build an altar to the Lord at the very place the plague was stopped. He approached Arauna, the landowner, to purchase the property. Araunah graciously offered not only the land, but also oxen and everything needed for an altar and a sacrifice. But David would not take it, giving some of the most famous words of his life, insisting that he would not offer to the Lord "that which doth cost me nothing" (v. 24). David purchased the property, built the altar, offered the sacrifice, "and the plague was stayed from Israel" (v. 25).

It's worth noting that verse 24 states David paid 50 shekels of silver for the threshing floor, while 2 Chronicles 21:25 mentions 600 shekels. How can we reconcile this difference? Rather than assuming an error in the text, we can reasonably conclude that the two accounts refer to different aspects of the same purchase. Bullinger suggests that the 50 shekels were for the threshing floor alone, while 600 covered the entire "place," as worded slightly differently in 1 Chronicles 21:25. Jewish tradition offers another interpretation: 50 shekels per tribe, totaling 600.

David's Attempted Temple (2 Chronicles 22:1-8)

At the climax of 2 Samuel 24, David builds an altar to the Lord on the threshing floor of Araunah the Jebusite—the very place where the plague was stopped. This location becomes deeply significant in Israel's history, as it would later be the site of the Temple, the focal point of Israel's worship for centuries.

In 1 Chronicles 22:1, David declares, "This is the house of the LORD God, and this is the altar of the burnt offering for Israel." This moment marks the recognition that this site, where God's mercy was shown by halting the plague, would become the future location of the Temple—where God's presence would dwell and sacrifices for Israel's sins would be offered.

David immediately began gathering workers and "set masons to hew wrought stones to build the house of God" (2 Chron. 22:2). He also "prepared iron in abundance for the nails for the doors of the gates, and for the joinings; and brass in abundance without weight; Also cedar trees in abundance: for the Zidonians and they of Tyre brought much cedar wood to David" (2 Chron 22:3-4).

All of this work was preparatory, however, and David knew it. In 2 Samuel 7:13 (see chapter 27), the Lord had already told David that it would be his son, not himself, who would build the Temple. In 1 Chronicles 22:5 the Scripture says, "I will therefore now make preparation for it. So David prepared abundantly before his death." Verse 8 goes on to reveal that God did not allow David to do so because he had shed so much blood during his reign.

Though David had, dreamed the dream (2 Sam. 7:1-14), purchased the property (2 Sam. 24:24-25), and prepared the material (2 Chron. 22:1-19), the cornerstone of the Temple would be laid by Solomon four years after David's death (1 Kings 6:1)

THE DAVIDIC CHRONICLES

Chapter 43

THE SUCCESSION CRISIS

1 Kings 1:1-53

As we move from 2 Samuel to 1 Kings, we selve into the final days of King David's reign and the tumultuous succession of his son Solomon to the throne.

Before we explore these events, it's important to recall the events of 2 Samuel 24. In that chapter, David, driven by pride, conducted a census of Israel against God's will. This act of disobedience resulted in a severe plague upon the nation. David's repentance and sacrifice at the threshing floor of Araunah the Jebusite ultimately halted the plague, but not before it had taken a significant toll on the people.

Now, as we enter 1 Kings 1, we find an aging David, weakened by the years, coming to his final act as King: naming a successor.

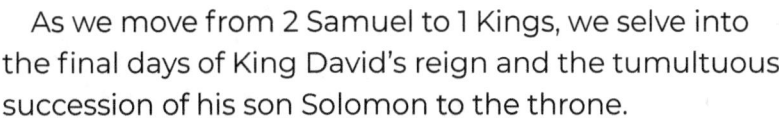

David's Declining Health in Old Age (1 Kings 1:1-4)

David, now described as "old and stricken in years" (v. 1), is about 70 years old. This age can be calculated by comparing 2 Samuel 5:4-5, which states he began his reign at about 30 and ruled for 40 years—7 in Hebron and 33 over all Israel.

The text doesn't specify David's ailment, but he may have had a fever, as those around him were unable to keep him warm with clothing and blankets.

David was warmed by the body of a young virgin named Abishag, from Shunem, a town in the tribe of Issachar's territory. This sounds incredibly odd to us today, but it appeared to be well-accepted by his advisors as a way to heat the body. The text clearly states that there was no sexual activity.

Adonijah's Self-Proclaimed Kingship (1 Kings 1:5-10)

Adonijah, the fourth son of King David, was born in Hebron (2 Samuel 3:4). His mother, Haggith, was one of David's wives. Following the deaths of his older brothers— Amnon, Chileab (presumed dead as he's not mentioned after 2 Samuel 3:3), and Absalom—Adonijah viewed himself as the rightful heir to the throne, being David's eldest surviving son.

Remarkably, Adonijah's bid for power mirrored that of his half-brother Absalom, who had previously attempted to usurp David's throne. Despite their different mothers, both sons employed strikingly similar tactics in their quest for kingship:

- **Preparation of chariots and horsemen:** Adonijah "prepared him chariots and horsemen, and fifty men to run before him" (1 Kings 1:5). Similarly, Absalom "prepared him chariots and horses, and fifty men to run before him" (2 Samuel 15:1). It's believed these 50 men had their spleens removed and the soles of their feet scraped to increase their running speed (see *Chapter 35*).

- **Self-exaltation:** Adonijah declared, "I will be king" (1 Kings 1:5), exalting himself. Absalom likewise sought to elevate his status, as shown in 2 Samuel 15:2-6, where he "stole the hearts of the men of Israel."

- **Gathering supporters:** Adonijah "conferred with Joab the son of Zeruiah, and with Abiathar the priest: and they following Adonijah helped him" (1 Kings 1:7). Similarly, Absalom amassed supporters, including David's counselor Ahithophel (2 Samuel 15:12).

Adonijah, it seems, suffered from his father's adoration and inability to discipline him. As verse 6 tells us, "his father had not displeased him at any time in saying, Why hast thou done so?" This could be attributed to Adonijah being David's eldest surviving son, his handsome appearance (v. 6), or simply David's own weakness as a parent.

Solomon's words in Proverbs about disciplining children may have been influenced by his recollection of this experience. He later wrote:

⬧ **Proverbs 13:24** "He that spareth his rod hateth his son: but he that loveth him chasteneth him betimes."

⬧ **Proverbs 19:18** "Chasten thy son while there is hope, and let not thy soul spare for his crying."

⬧ **Proverbs 22:15** "Foolishness is bound in the heart of a child; but the rod of correction shall drive it far from him."

⬧ **Proverbs 29:15** "The rod and reproof give wisdom: but a child left to himself bringeth his mother to shame."

⬧ **Proverbs 29:17** "Correct thy son, and he shall give thee rest; yea, he shall give delight unto thy soul."

A retrospective passage (1 Chronicles 22:9-10) explicitly says that David had previously been instructed that Solomon would be the next king. Knowing this, David bears greater responsibility for not quelling Adonijah's early rebellion from the outset, presuming he had the health to do so.

Adonijah's bid for power divided the royal court, with some aligning with him and others remaining loyal to David. Those who supported Adonijah included Joab, the commander of David's army, and Abiathar the priest (v. 7). However, notable figures like Zadok the priest,

THE DAVIDIC CHRONICLES

Benaiah son of Jehoiada, Nathan the prophet, and David's mighty men did not join Adonijah's cause (v. 8). This division reflects the natural tendency of courtiers to align themselves with potential successors when a king is dying. With David's health failing, members of the court likely felt pressure to choose sides, anticipating the inevitable power shift. Their choices were not merely personal preferences but strategic decisions that could significantly impact their future positions and influence in the new regime.

In verses 9-10, Adonijah throws what amounts to an inaugural festival, complete with "sheep and oxen and fat cattle" (v. 9), presumably for a feast. However, his invitation list is selective. While all the leading men of the kingdom are invited, Adonijah strategically excludes "Nathan the prophet, and Benaiah, and the mighty men, and Solomon his brother" (v. 10). This confirms that Adonijah appears to be circumventing a previous announcement of Solomon as the next king, hoping to secure his coronation before David, Solomon, or anyone "in the know" can intervene.

As a reminder, recall David's readiness to believe that Mephibosheth had betrayed him during the days of Absalom. Ancient kingdoms could rise or fall based on innuendo and rumor, and fear was an almost constant companion for ancient royalty.

This situation with Adonijah bears some resemblance to events that occurred much later in Jewish history, during the reign of Herod the Great. Herod, who ruled Judea from 37 to 4 BC (traditional dates), was known for his paranoia and ruthlessness, particularly when it came to perceived threats to his throne.

In the final days of his life, Herod executed his son Antipater, whom he had previously designated as his

370

heir. This execution came after Herod had already put to death two other sons, Alexander and Aristobulus, years earlier on suspicion of plotting against him. Antipater was accused of attempting to poison Herod, leading to his swift execution just five days before Herod's own death. This tragic series of events demonstrates the extreme measures some rulers would take to protect their power, even against their own family members. In both Adonijah's and Antipater's cases, the desire for kingship and the fear of losing power led to dire consequences, highlighting the often brutal nature of royal succession in ancient times.

Nathan and Bathsheba's Intervention (1 Kings 1:11-27)

Nathan the prophet, aware of Adonijah's actions, devised a plan. This passage reveals that David was unaware of Adonijah's activities, and Nathan felt compelled to inform him, as only David could resolve the situation.

Nathan instructed Bathsheba to approach David with a rhetorical question, intended not to seek information but to convey it: "Didst not thou, my lord, O king, swear unto thine handmaid, saying, Assuredly Solomon thy son shall reign after me, and he shall sit upon my throne? why then doth Adonijah reign?" (v. 13). The strategy was for Nathan to then enter and corroborate Bathsheba's words, aiming to both inform the king and prompt him to take immediate action.

Verses 15-27 record the plan unfolding exactly as described. David is made aware of the urgent need to issue an official decree from his deathbed. This action is necessary to prevent chaos, civil war, or—at the very least— the death of Solomon and the rest of David's loyal officers.

David's Decree to Anoint Solomon (1 Kings 1:28-40)

Hearing what had happened, David decided to act decisively and quickly to make Solomon king, thus foiling Adonijah's plans. The instruction was to place Solomon on David's mule and take him to the Gihon spring (also known as Shiloah, which fed the Pool of Siloam in the New Testament).

The scene at Gihon spring was a mix of excitement and solemnity. As David's decree was carried out, a procession made its way through Jerusalem. Solomon rode at its head on King David's mule, a symbol of royal succession that drew attention from the gathering crowd.

Zadok the priest carried a horn of sacred oil from the tabernacle, with Nathan the prophet beside him. Benaiah led the Cherethites and Pelethites, protecting the young prince.

At Gihon, Zadok anointed Solomon's head with the oil. As soon as he finished, a trumpet sounded, echoing through the area.

"God save King Solomon!" The crowd cheered loudly, their approval filling the air. People began to play music, with pipes, drums, and lyres joining in celebration.

The procession back to the city was joyful. Solomon, now anointed and proclaimed, rode in the center, his face showing both wonder and resolve. Behind him, people danced and sang, their enthusiasm evident in their movements and voices.

The commotion was significant, with the combined sounds of voices and instruments carrying across

Jerusalem. As the noise spread through the city, it announced the beginning of Solomon's reign – a momentous start to a new era.

Adonijah's Fear and Submission (1 Kings 1:41-53)

The noise of the festivities reached En-rogel, where Adonijah's preparatory inaugural feast was taking place. As Joab began to ask about "the noise of the city" (v. 41), Jonathan, son of Abiathar the priest (who had followed Adonijah), entered and was welcomed as "a valiant man" bringing "good tidings" (v. 42)—which may have been wishful thinking on Adonijah's part. Jonathan immediately delivered the bad news to Adonijah: "David hath made Solomon king" (v. 43) and "they have caused him to ride upon the king's mule" (v. 44). He informed them that the city's noise was one of jubilation over their new king, Solomon. Unsurprisingly, we are told, "all the guests that were with Adonijah were afraid" (v. 49).

In response, Adonijah "caught hold on the horns of the altar" (v. 50). He made his way back to Jerusalem, into the tabernacle (compare 1 Kings 2:28), and grasped the horns of the altar as a plea for safety.

Solomon, first referred to as "King Solomon" in verse 53, accepted Adonijah's plea and sent his older half-brother home safely. However, this wasn't the end of the story. Soon after, Adonijah requested Abishag as his wife. In ancient Israelite and broader Near Eastern culture, a king's wives or concubines were closely tied to his authority and reign. By asking for Abishag—who had served King David in his final days (though the text explicitly states David did not have relations with her)—Adonijah was attempting

373

to link himself to David's legacy and, by extension, the throne. This echoes Absalom's public relations with David's concubines during his revolt (2 Samuel 16:21-22), asserting his right to rule. Solomon likely saw through Adonijah's request. His sharp reaction to this seemingly harmless appeal demonstrates his political acumen and awareness of potential threats to his newly established reign. Solomon quickly recognized that Adonijah's subtle request was a strategic move to challenge his kingship. By swiftly ordering Adonijah's execution, Solomon eliminated a potential rival, securing his rule and preventing any future claim to the throne.

Chapter 44:

DAVID'S FINAL INSTRUCTIONS AND DEATH

1 Kings 2:1-12

Having studied the life of what could easily be called history's greatest king, we now come to his death and burial. we witness King David confronting his impending death with both clarity and purpose, just as he had done with so many other issues he faced as King.

David Recognizes His Death (1 Kings 2: 1-2)

There is goodness and both emotional and spiritual health displayed when someone recognizes their impending death. In a society that often avoids discussing death, bringing it up should not be shunned for reasons of etiquette. Rather, addressing it openly demonstrates the blessing of dealing with reality head-on.

One of the most challenging aspects of dealing with dying is that often everyone knows death is near, but nobody wants to talk about it. I recently heard testimony from a dying man who was frustrated because his Christian friends wanted to avoid the subject.

Let's take from David, and many others in Scripture, a good and healthy example of how to talk about death. Face it, embrace it when it's the right time, and discuss it with your family and friends.

The Bible offers several examples of individuals who faced their impending death with clarity and purpose. Jacob (Genesis 47:29-30) requested burial in Canaan, reflecting his connection to God's covenant. Moses (Deuteronomy 31:14, 32:48-50) accepted his fate, transferring leadership to Joshua and offering final guidance. He understood his death as a consequence of his disobedience at Meribah (Numbers 20:12) and ascended Mount Nebo, embodying acceptance of God's will.

In the New Testament, Paul (2 Timothy 4:6-8) faced his likely execution with faith, reflecting on his life and ministry with satisfaction, confident in his service to Christ and the awaiting heavenly reward.

These biblical accounts illustrate how recognizing one's mortality can lead to meaningful actions, spiritual reflection, and the passing on of important legacies. They serve as powerful examples of facing death with dignity, faith, and purpose.

Not only does David discuss his impending death, but he looks to Solomon, who is only a young man of about 20 years old, and says to him, "Be thou strong therefore, and shew thyself a man" (v. 2). It's time to pass the scepter, and Solomon must quickly step up to fill some big shoes.

Just as our society struggles with speaking of death, there's also a deficiency in transitioning from boy to man. Some societies, such as Judaism and Native American cultures, have a clear transition moment. In America's past, there was a more distinct demarcation when a man left home for work, military, or school, but this is becoming less abrupt in recent times. It may be worthwhile for families to consider how to signal to their sons that it's time to become a man.

David's Spiritual Advice (1 Kings 2:3-4)

As David continues, he tells Solomon exactly how to fulfill the instruction given in verse 2, to "shew thyself a man" (v. 2), especially as the man who is king of Israel. He instructs

Solomon "to keep his statutes, and his commandments, and his judgments, and his testimonies, as it is written in the law of Moses" (v. 3). This is a reference to Deuteronomy 29, especially verse 9. By instructing Solomon to follow these commands of the Lord and the prosperity this would bring, David is essentially guiding Solomon to enter into the covenant which God made with Israel. He wants Solomon to affirm in his own life and generation that the Lord God of Abraham, Isaac, and Jacob was also Lord of Solomon and the kingdom he would inherit.

Modern readers should exercise caution when applying these verses directly to their lives. Without the principle of "rightly dividing the word of truth" (2 Tim. 2:15), misapplication could lead to disastrous consequences. For instance, one might observe this instruction in Deuteronomy 29, then again to Joshua in Joshua 1:8, and here in 1 Kings 2, concluding that there's strong biblical evidence to apply this instruction universally to all believers throughout history.

A person who rightly divides Scripture, however, would understand that covenant promises made to Israel aren't automatically applicable to individuals in the body of Christ. We, as members of this body, aren't bound by covenants. Instead, we live under God's grace, positioned between the old and new covenants, with Christ as our Mediator.

David's Practical Advice (1 Kings 2: 5-9)

David moves from the covenantal / spiritual leadership to some practical matters he wants to share with his son.

First, he deals with Joab (vv. 5-6), his nephew who had been in his service since the beginning of the kingdom, most of that time in the position of the captain of the hosts. David has, for reasons unknown, not carried out some punishment he believed Joab deserved for two infractions, each seen in verse 5, both being a similar treachery. Because of their treachery, David instructs Solomon not to let their "hoar head go down to the grave in peace" (v. 6). The term "hoar head" means "gray," but is used in a pejorative manner.

The first was Joab's killing of Abner. Abner, once captain of King Saul's army, became a "kingmaker" after Saul's death, establishing Ishbosheth as king. Abner later arranged a representative battle between his warrior and one of David's. During this encounter, Abner killed Joab's brother. Joab, waiting for the perfect timing to secure revenge, eventually caught up with Abner and killed him. This act was outside David's orders and violated the agreement of representative battle, making Joab's actions vengeful rather than righteous. (See 2 Samuel 3:27 and *The Davidic Chronicles ~ Consolidated Edition, Chapter 21*). Later, in verses 30-34, Solomon executes Joab for shedding innocent blood and bringing shame upon David's house.

The second treachery was Joab's killing of Amasa. Amasa became captain of Absalom's army during the rebellion. After Absalom's death, David surprisingly sets Amasa as his own captain, demoting Joab. Once again, Joab avenges himself, killing Amasa and being restored to his position as captain. (see *The Davidic Chronicles ~ Consolidated Edition, Chapters 38, 39*). When Solomon puts Joab to death for the killing of Abner and Amasa, he says, "Their blood shall therefore return upon the head of Joab, and upon the head of his seed for ever: but upon David, and upon his seed, and upon his house, and upon his throne, shall there be peace for ever from the LORD" (1 Kings 2:33).

378

Turning to Barzillai the Gileadite (v. 7), David desired kindness be shown to him. We first encountered Barzillai in 2 Samuel 17:27-29, where he demonstrated kindness during Absalom's rebellion. After the rebellion, David attempted to bring Barzillai to Jerusalem, but Barzillai declined, sending someone believed to be his son, named Chimham, instead. Here, David requests that care and kindness be extended to Barzillai's descendants. While we presume Solomon followed this instruction, Scripture doesn't directly record its fulfillment, unless the reference in Jeremiah 41:17 to Chimham's habitation is related (see *The Davidic Chronicles ~ Consolidated Edition, Chapter 38*).

Finally, David offers advice about dealing with Shimei's past offense, though his instructions are somewhat vague (vv. 8-9). While David leaves the specifics to Solomon's discretion, he suggests that Shimei's "hoar head" should "go down to the grave with blood" (v. 9).

David, No More (1 Kings 2:11-12)

1 Kings 2:11-12 succinctly summarizes David's reign and the smooth transition of power to Solomon. David ruled Israel for four decades—seven years in Hebron and thirty-three in Jerusalem. Upon David's death and burial in the City of David, Solomon ascended to the throne. The passage highlights that Solomon's kingdom was "firmly established," signaling the end of David's illustrious era and the dawn of Solomon's reign.

In Josephus' *Antiquities of the Jews* (7.392-394), we learn that David was buried in Jerusalem with great wealth. This treasure was so substantial that during the reign of Antiochus, the High Priest Hyrcanus robbed David's tomb to pay tribute and avoid invasion. Josephus further recounts that Herod the Great also plundered the tomb, taking a significant amount of wealth, though David's body remained untouched.

Visitors to Jerusalem, particularly the area known as Mount Zion, may have encountered the Tomb of David, a pilgrimage site since the Middle Ages. However, from a scholarly and archaeological standpoint, it's unlikely that the current Tomb of David on Mount Zion is the authentic burial place of the biblical king. The biblical text and early Jewish sources indicate the City of David as the burial location, yet no verified tomb of David has been discovered in that area. The tradition of Mount Zion as David's tomb seems to have developed later, and while it holds religious significance for many, it lacks historical and archaeological support.

Chapter 45:

DAVID'S LEGACY: THE SWEET PSALMIST OF ISRAEL

2 Samuel 23:1-7

A Strange Place For Last Words

In 2 Samuel 23:1-7, we encounter what are called the "last words" of David, but this raises an interesting question when considered in the broader context of David's life. The notion of "last words" typically carries with it the expectation of finality, a concluding moment where a person's life and influence are drawing to a close. Yet, as we read further in 2 Samuel, David's life continues with significant events still to unfold. After these so-called "last words," David orders the ill-fated census of Israel, which leads to a devastating plague. He also purchases the threshing floor of Araunah, which will later become the site of the temple. If these words were truly his last, how do we account for these subsequent actions?

This tension between what the text calls "the last words of David" and the unfinished narrative that follows suggests something deeper going on with these last words. Why would the chronicler place these final words here, when we know David still has crucial roles to play? Furthermore, the events that follow are not minor details; they include the divine judgment of Israel, personal repentance, and the foundational step toward the establishment of the Temple. These are hardly the acts of a man who has uttered his final words.

Additionally, the content of these "last words" themselves seems almost disconnected from the specific events of David's remaining life. They are lofty, poetic reflections on the nature of righteous rule and God's covenant with him, rather than personal reflections on his imminent death or preparations for succession. The placement of this passage prods us to consider the a deeper understanding of David's "last words" so that they do not leave the reader wondering why David's life seems far from finished after these supposed words have been spoken.

A Distinct Possibility For The Sweet Psalmist

Consider that these words might not be "last words" in a chronological sense, but rather an epilogue to David's Psalms. At this point in his life, David may have recognized the completion of his work on the Psalms and decided to write a summary—an afterword for the entire collection. If this premise holds true, these words could serve as a key to understanding the Davidic Psalms. They might encapsulate the themes, insights, and spiritual revelations David experienced throughout his journey as the "sweet psalmist of Israel."

The reference to David as the "sweet psalmist of Israel" in verse 1 is significant. Could these words mark the conclusion of his divinely inspired role as the composer of Israel's worship and prophecy? Are they a distillation of the prophetic themes woven throughout the Psalms? It's possible that David's "last words" encapsulate the theological and prophetic arc of his psalms, pointing toward the fulfillment of God's covenant promises. If so, these final reflections capture the essence of his worship and prophetic ministry, looking beyond his own dynasty to the eternal reign of the Messiah.

While 73 psalms are explicitly attributed to David in their titles, tradition and internal evidence suggest he may have authored up to 85. The remaining psalms were composed by various authors across different periods of Israel's history, including:

◊ Asaph (12 psalms): A Levite and chief musician in David's court (Psalms 50, 73-83).

◊ The Sons of Korah (11 psalms): Temple musicians and descendants of Korah (Psalms 42-49, 84, 85, 87, 88).

◊ Solomon (2 psalms): David's son and successor (Psalms 72, 127).

◊ Moses (1 psalm): The great leader of the Exodus (Psalm 90).

◊ Heman the Ezrahite (1 psalm): A wise man during Solomon's reign (Psalm 88).

◊ Ethan the Ezrahite (1 psalm): Another wise man from Solomon's time (Psalm 89).

The remaining psalms are either anonymous or have disputed authorship.

Our premise is that 2 Samuel 23:1-7 could serve as an overarching Davidic summary of these psalms, particularly those attributed to David. This passage, described as David's "last words," may not be his final chronological utterance but rather a concluding statement on his role as the "sweet psalmist of Israel." As such, it could encapsulate the major themes, theological insights, and prophetic elements found throughout the Davidic psalms.

This summary would provide a framework for understanding the Davidic psalms as a cohesive body of work, reflecting on God's righteousness, the ideal of righteous leadership, the Davidic covenant, and the ultimate triumph of the Messiah. By viewing 2 Samuel 23:1-7 in this

383

light, we gain a valuable lens through which to interpret and appreciate the depth and breadth of David's contributions to the Psalter.

What We Learn From These Words

There is a great deal to learn from the "last words," contained in 2 Samuel 23:2-7.

David's Recognition of Divine Inspiration:

David begins by clearly recognizing that his words are inspired by God: "*The Spirit of the LORD spake by me, and his word was in my tongue*" (v. 2). This statement holds immense significance when considered as an "afterword" for the Psalms. David acknowledges that what he wrote, particularly in the Psalms, is not merely human poetry or reflection, but is divinely inspired—what we would today call "Scripture." He is aware that his writings are the very Word of God, a profound realization that places his psalms alongside other inspired writings, even before a formal canon of Scripture was established.

This recognition ties directly to the New Testament concept of inspiration, such as in **2 Timothy 3:16**, where Paul declares, "*All scripture is given by inspiration of God*" (literally "God-breathed"). David, in this passage, acknowledges that the Spirit of the Lord "breathed" these words through him, making his psalms part of God's revelation to man. His awareness of the Holy Spirit's role in guiding his words is remarkable, showing that he knew he was a vessel for conveying God's message. This speaks to the prophetic nature of the Psalms and David's deep connection with the Spirit of God, through whom he delivered truths about righteous rule, worship, and prophecy.

384

A Description of the Ideal King or Righteous Person:

In verse 3, David describes the standard for the ideal ruler: *"He that ruleth over men must be just, ruling in the fear of God."* This sets forth the Davidic expectation for any earthly king—he must govern with justice and in reverence for God. However, while this description outlines the righteous character expected of David's descendants, it also points beyond the human ability to fully embody this ideal. The imagery in verse 4 goes even further: *"he shall be as the light of the morning, when the sun riseth, even a morning without clouds."* This beautiful image portrays the ideal king as a source of life, growth, and prosperity, like the refreshing dawn after a long night.

Yet, this level of perfection—bringing light and blessing to all—transcends the abilities of any earthly ruler. No human king, not even David himself, could truly live up to this standard. In this sense, these verses are not merely a description of what a good king ought to be, but a prophecy pointing toward the ultimate King—the Messiah—who would sit on David's throne. The coming King, Jesus Christ, perfectly fulfills this role. He is the light of the world (John 8:12), the one who brings renewal and life, fulfilling this description in a way no human ruler ever could.

Verse 4, in particular, speaks of an ideal so lofty that it is virtually impossible for any human ruler to achieve. Its language is best understood as a prophetic vision of the Messiah, the true "Son of David," who will one day reign with perfect justice and bring everlasting peace and righteousness to the world. Thus, David's description not only sets the bar for kingship in his lineage but also points forward to the coming King, Jesus Christ, who will perfectly fulfill the Davidic covenant and rule eternally in the fear of God.

385

Reflections on God's Covenant or Promises:

In verse 5, David reflects on the steadfastness of the covenant God made with him: "*Although my house be not so with God; yet he hath made with me an everlasting covenant, ordered in all things, and sure.*" Here, David acknowledges the imperfections within his own household and lineage, yet he expresses unwavering confidence in the reliability of God's promises. This "everlasting covenant" refers to the Davidic Covenant established in 2 Samuel 7, where God promises to establish David's throne and kingdom forever through his descendants.

David's reflection goes beyond his immediate circumstances, pointing toward a future fulfillment that would not depend on the righteousness of his own lineage but on the faithfulness of God. Despite the failures and shortcomings within his house, David is certain that God's word will stand—His covenant is "*ordered in all things, and sure.*" This prophetic insight reveals that David understood that the ultimate fulfillment of this promise would come through the Messiah, who would reign on his throne forever.

This confidence in God's covenant is not just a personal hope for David but a solid foundation upon which all of Israel can rest. The certainty of God's promise means that no matter how turbulent Israel's history or David's family line may become, the future Messiah will bring about the fulfillment of this eternal covenant. David's assurance in God's unbreakable word points Israel toward the coming King, in whom all God's promises will be fully realized. This eternal covenant, which transcends David's earthly reign, is a beacon of hope for the future, guaranteeing a Messianic kingdom that will endure forever.

386

The phrase "Although he make it not to grow" answers back to "*Although my house be not so with God*" and shows David's acknowledgment that, even if his sons do not fully prosper or keep God's covenant and testimony, the ultimate fulfillment of the promise is still certain. David's faith goes beyond the immediate circumstances—he knows that the everlasting covenant God made with him is "ordered in all things, and sure." While his descendants may falter, and the throne may not be continuously occupied by a Davidic king, God's messianic covenant will ultimately be fulfilled.

Judgment on the Wicked and Deliverance from Enemies:

In the closing verses (v. 6-7), David describes the fate of the wicked, using the imagery of thorns: "*But the sons of Belial shall be all of them as thorns thrust away.*" Thorns represent the wicked as being both dangerous and worthless, harmful yet ultimately destined for destruction. David emphasizes that these thorns cannot be handled without protection, displaying the uncontrollable nature of the wicked and their inevitable judgment. They will be "*utterly burned with fire,*" a vivid portrayal of the justice that awaits those who oppose God's order.

Prophetically, this image of the wicked being cast aside and burned foreshadows the ultimate fate of those who stand against God's people, Israel, in the events leading up to the Second Coming of Christ. Scripture often portrays the Day of the Lord as a time when God will pour out His wrath on the nations that rise against Israel. In Zechariah 14:2-3, we read about the nations gathered against Jerusalem, and how the Lord will fight for His people. This event culminates in the battle of Armageddon, where the forces of evil are decisively defeated by Christ (Revelation 16:16, 19:11-21).

387

David's words can be seen as prophetically pointing to this future time of judgment. The "sons of Belial" in this passage represent not just individual wicked people but those who align themselves with the enemies of God and His covenant people. Just as the nations will gather against Israel at the end of the age, these wicked forces will be met with divine destruction. The burning of thorns in 2 Samuel 23:7 foreshadows the fiery judgment that will befall those who oppose Israel during the Day of the Lord.

Thus, 2 Samuel 23:6-7 not only reflects David's understanding of justice in his own time but also prophetically points to the ultimate fate of the wicked during the Day of the Lord, when God's enemies, particularly those who stand against Israel, will be destroyed in the climactic events leading up to Christ's return.

The Psalms: A Gift of Insight

David's "last words" in 2 Samuel 23:1-7 are more than just a personal reflection; they offer a summary of the themes that permeate the Psalms. Through these final prophetic utterances, we see echoes of Messianic righteousness and justice, the enduring covenant, and the judgment of the wicked—core themes that reverberate throughout the Psalms. David's recognition of God's inspiration, his vision of the ideal king, and his understanding of God's covenant are woven into the fabric of the psalms he penned, providing believers with some of the greatest prophetic insight in all of Scripture.

The Psalms, often seen as heartfelt prayers and songs of worship, are far more than that. They are a treasure trove of prophecy, revealing God's grand plan for His people and His kingdom. Through David, God has given us one of the richest prophetic portions of Scripture. From the Messianic psalms that foreshadow the coming of Christ, to psalms that speak of His suffering and resurrection (such as Psalm 22), to those that describe His eternal reign (such as Psalm 2 and Psalm 110), the Psalms provide us with unparalleled insight into God's redemptive plan.

David, through the Psalms, has left believers with an enduring prophetic legacy. His writings do not merely offer comfort and guidance for worship; they point us toward the coming Messiah and the ultimate fulfillment of God's kingdom. In his "last words," David provides a final reminder of these great truths, echoing the themes we find throughout the Psalms, and affirming that they are not just songs of the past, but divine revelations for the future.

Prophetic Lessons from the Psalms

When viewed prophetically, each Psalm provides profound insight into the end times. The themes found throughout the Psalms align perfectly with the events of the tribulation, the rise of the Antichrist, and the establishment of Christ's eternal kingdom. Here are key prophetic lessons we learn when understanding the Psalms as revealing God's ultimate plan for Israel and the nations.

1. **The Messianic King and His Reign**
   - The Psalms declare the coming of the Messiah, His righteous rule, and His eternal kingdom.
     - **Psalm 2** reveals the rebellion of the nations against the Messiah and God's declaration of His Son's eternal reign.
     - **Psalm 110** describes the Messiah as both King and Priest, who will subdue all His enemies and rule the nations.

389

    ☐ **Lesson:** These Psalms confirm Christ's ultimate victory and His reign as King over all the earth during the Millennial Kingdom.

2. **The Antichrist and His Followers**

    ■ The singular "wicked" in the Psalms refers to the Antichrist, while the plural "wicked" represents his followers.

        ☐ **Psalm 10** describes the Antichrist as a wicked man who arrogantly defies God and oppresses the righteous.

        ☐ **Psalm 52** outlines the deceptive and destructive nature of the Antichrist.

        ☐ **Lesson:** These Psalms reveal the Antichrist's arrogance, his hatred of God's people, and his inevitable destruction by the hand of God.

3. **Israel's Prayers During the Tribulation (Imprecatory Psalms)**

    ■ The imprecatory Psalms are the prayers of Israel during the Tribulation, crying out for divine justice against their oppressors.

        ☐ **Psalm 35, Psalm 69,** and **Psalm 109** call for God's vengeance upon the enemies of His people.

        ☐ **Lesson:** These Psalms serve as Israel's cry for deliverance during the Tribulation as they plead for God's judgment on the Antichrist and his followers.

4. **The Suffering of the Righteous and the Remnant**

    ■ The Psalms reflect the suffering of the faithful remnant of Israel and believers during the tribulation, awaiting God's intervention.

- ☐ **Psalm 22** not only foreshadows Christ's suffering but also speaks of the agony of the remnant during the Tribulation.

- ☐ **Psalm 79** portrays the destruction of Jerusalem, prefiguring the devastation that will occur in the end times.

- ☐ **Lesson:** These Psalms capture the cries of the faithful remnant who endure persecution and suffering during the Tribulation, anticipating their ultimate vindication.

5. **The Final Judgment and Destruction of the Wicked**

- The Psalms clearly declare the ultimate destruction of the wicked, who will face judgment at the end of the Tribulation.

  - ☐ **Psalm 37** proclaims that the wicked will be cut off, and the righteous will inherit the earth.

  - ☐ **Psalm 9** affirms that God will judge the nations in righteousness, pointing to the Day of the Lord.

  - ☐ **Lesson:** These Psalms point to the final judgment of the wicked during the Day of the Lord, when Christ will return to establish His kingdom and destroy His enemies.

6. **The Deliverance and Salvation of Israel**

- The Psalms declare the deliverance of Israel and their ultimate salvation at the end of the Tribulation.

  - ☐ **Psalm 18** foreshadows Israel's deliverance when Christ returns to defeat their enemies and rescue His people.

- ☐ **Psalm 44** is Israel's plea for redemption and deliverance, which will be fulfilled at Christ's Second Coming.

- ☐ **Lesson:** These Psalms proclaim the moment of Israel's deliverance when Christ returns to save His people and establish His kingdom.

7. **The Restoration of Jerusalem and the Kingdom**

- The Psalms predict the restoration of Jerusalem and the reign of the Messiah from Zion during the Millennial Kingdom.

  - ☐ **Psalm 48** celebrates the future glory of Jerusalem as the center of the Messiah's reign.

  - ☐ **Psalm 102** anticipates the restoration of Zion, pointing to the establishment of Christ's kingdom on earth.

  - ☐ **Lesson:** These Psalms look forward to the time when Jerusalem will be restored and Christ will reign from His throne, fulfilling the promises of the Davidic covenant.

8. **The Nations and the Gentile Believers**

- The Psalms speak of the nations turning to God, a prophecy of the Gentile nations coming to worship the Messiah during His Millennial reign.

  - ☐ **Psalm 67** calls for God's blessing on Israel so that all nations will know Him, anticipating the inclusion of the Gentiles in the Messiah's kingdom.

  - ☐ **Psalm 72** describes the reign of the Messiah, during which all nations will bow down before Him.

□ **Lesson:** These Psalms foresee the future worship of the Messiah by all nations, as Gentiles recognize Christ as King during His Millennial reign.

9. The Refuge and Protection of the Faithful

■ The Psalms declare God as the refuge and protector of the righteous, a promise to those who seek shelter in Him during the Tribulation.

□ **Psalm 46** proclaims God as a refuge and strength, a promise to the faithful during the trials of the end times.

□ **Psalm 91** assures protection over God's people, applicable to those who remain faithful during the Tribulation.

□ **Lesson:** These Psalms promise divine protection for the faithful remnant during the Tribulation, offering hope in the midst of trials.

10. The Resurrection and Eternal Life

■ The Psalms anticipate the resurrection of the righteous and the hope of eternal life for God's people.

□ **Psalm 16** speaks of deliverance from death and resurrection, pointing to both Christ's resurrection and the resurrection of the saints.

□ **Psalm 49** contrasts the fate of the wicked, who perish, with the righteous, who are redeemed from death and given eternal life.

□ **Lesson:** These Psalms reveal the hope of resurrection and eternal life for those who trust in God, which will be fully realized at the return of Christ.

The Davidic Chronicles

The Psalms, when read prophetically, offer tremendous insight into the end times. They foretell the rise of the Antichrist, the suffering of the faithful, the cries of Israel during the Tribulation, and the ultimate deliverance through the Messiah. The Psalms reveal the final judgment of the wicked, the restoration of Jerusalem, and the reign of Christ, providing a comprehensive picture of God's redemptive plan for Israel and the world. Through these ancient songs and prayers, David has left us with one of the most powerful and detailed prophetic records in all of Scripture.

Chapter 46

Biblical Personalities in the Davidic Account

Abi-albon the Arbathite

Abi-albon, an Arbathite, is listed among David's mighty men (2 Samuel 23:31; 1 Chronicles 11:32). He likely hailed from Beth-arabah, near the Jordan Valley. His presence in this elite group underscores his bravery and loyalty to King David.

Abiezer the Anethothite

Abiezer, from Anathoth in Benjamin, served as one of David's mighty men (2 Samuel 23:27; 1 Chronicles 11:28). His inclusion highlights his valor in battle, contributing to David's military successes.

Abinadab

Abinadab was one of Jesse's sons and David's older brother. He was passed over when Samuel anointed David as king (1 Samuel 16:8). Another Abinadab is noted as the guardian of the Ark of the Covenant for a time (1 Samuel 7:1).

Abner

Abner, Saul's cousin and commander of his army, played a key role in the transition of power to David. Initially an adversary, Abner later pledged loyalty to David but was murdered by Joab (2 Samuel 2-3).

Abiathar

Abiathar, a priest and descendant of Eli, served David during his reign. Loyal during Absalom's rebellion, Abiathar later supported Adonijah over Solomon, leading to his exile (1 Samuel 22:20-23; 1 Kings 2:26-27).

Adino the Eznite

Adino, leader of David's mighty men, was known for slaying 800 enemies at once (2 Samuel 23:8). His extraordinary feat demonstrates his unmatched combat prowess.

Adoram

Adoram, also known as Adoniram, oversaw forced labor under David, Solomon, and Rehoboam. His role made him a controversial figure, and he was killed during a rebellion (2 Samuel 20:24; 1 Kings 12:18).

Ahithophel

Ahithophel, a counselor to David, betrayed him by siding with Absalom. His wisdom was legendary, but after his advice was ignored, he took his own life (2 Samuel 15-17).

Ahiam, son of Sharar the Hararite

Ahiam, listed among David's mighty men, is noted for his valor in combat (2 Samuel 23:33). He likely hailed from a region known for producing skilled warriors.

Amnon

Amnon was David's firstborn son who violated his half-sister Tamar. This crime led to his murder by Absalom, Tamar's full brother, setting off a chain of family and political strife (2 Samuel 13).

Araunah the Jebusite

Araunah owned the threshing floor where David built an altar to the Lord, stopping a plague. This site later became the location of Solomon's temple (2 Samuel 24:18-25).

Asahel, brother of Joab

Asahel, known for his speed, was a commander in David's army. He was killed by Abner during a pursuit, sparking a feud between their families (2 Samuel 2:18-23).

Azmaveth the Barhumite

Azmaveth, from Bahurim, was one of David's mighty men (2 Samuel 23:31). His valor contributed to the military achievements of David's reign.

Bani the Gadite

Bani, a Gadite warrior, joined David during his time in the wilderness. He exemplified loyalty and skill among the men who supported David early on (1 Chronicles 12:8).

Chapter 46 ~ Biblical Personalities in the Davidic Account

Barzillai

Barzillai was an elderly Gileadite who supported David during Absalom's rebellion by providing food and supplies. He declined David's invitation to the palace, preferring to live his remaining days at home (2 Samuel 17:27-29; 19:31-39).

Bathsheba

Bathsheba, wife of Uriah and later of David, is central to one of David's most famous sins. She became the mother of Solomon, continuing David's royal lineage (2 Samuel 11-12).

Benaiah the Pirathonite

Benaiah, a renowned warrior, was captain of David's bodyguard and later of Solomon's army. His exploits included killing a lion and a giant Egyptian (2 Samuel 23:20-23; 1 Kings 2:34-35).

David

David, the shepherd-turned-king, is celebrated as Israel's greatest monarch. Known for his psalms, military victories, and deep relationship with God, his reign established Jerusalem as Israel's capital and laid the foundation for the Davidic covenant (1 Samuel 16-1 Kings 2).

Eleazar, son of Dodo the Ahohite

Eleazar, one of David's top three mighty men, defended a field of barley against the Philistines, achieving a great victory with God's help (2 Samuel 23:9-10).

Eliab

Eliab was David's eldest brother. He was rejected by God as king due to his heart, not his stature, and is known for belittling David when he visited the battlefield before defeating Goliath (1 Samuel 16:6-7; 17:28).

Eliam, son of Ahithophel the Gilonite

Eliam, a mighty man, was the father of Bathsheba and son of Ahithophel. His family ties are intricately linked to David's court and his eventual betrayal (2 Samuel 11:3; 23:34).

Elhanan, son of Dodo of Bethlehem
Elhanan, a mighty man from Bethlehem, is credited with killing a giant Philistine in David's service (2 Samuel 21:19; 1 Chronicles 11:26).

Eliphelet, son of Ahasbai the Maachathite
Eliphelet is listed among David's mighty men, highlighting his role in defending the kingdom during David's reign (2 Samuel 23:34).

Gad
Gad, a prophet during David's reign, advised the king on spiritual matters and played a role in averting God's judgment through sacrifice (1 Samuel 22:5; 2 Samuel 24:11-19).

Gareb the Ithrite
Gareb, an Ithrite warrior, was one of David's mighty men (2 Samuel 23:38). His inclusion underscores his valor and loyalty.

Goliath
Goliath, the giant Philistine warrior, was defeated by David with a sling and a stone, showcasing God's power through the faith and courage of a young shepherd (1 Samuel 17).

Heleb, son of Baanah the Netophathite
Heleb, a Netophathite, served as one of David's mighty men, contributing to the military successes of his reign (2 Samuel 23:29).

Helez the Paltite
Helez, a Paltite from the tribe of Ephraim, was one of David's mighty men (2 Samuel 23:26). His bravery earned him a place in this elite group.

Hezrai the Carmelite
Hezrai, from Carmel, served as one of David's mighty men (2 Samuel 23:35). His exploits, though not detailed, were significant enough to be recorded.

Hiddai of the Brookes of Gaash

Hiddai, from the region of Gaash, is listed among David's mighty men for his bravery in combat (2 Samuel 23:30).

Igal, son of Nathan of Zobah

Igal, a warrior from Zobah, served among David's mighty men. His inclusion signifies his role in defending Israel (2 Samuel 23:36).

Ira, son of Ikkesh the Tekoite

Ira, from Tekoa, was one of David's mighty men, celebrated for his courage in battle (2 Samuel 23:26).

Ira the Ithrite

Ira, an Ithrite, was a member of David's elite warriors, signifying his importance in David's military campaigns (2 Samuel 23:38).

Ishbosheth

Ishbosheth, Saul's son, briefly ruled Israel as a rival king to David after Saul's death. His reign ended when he was assassinated by his own captains (2 Samuel 2-4).

Ittai, son of Ribai of Gibeah

Ittai, a warrior from Gibeah, served among David's mighty men. His loyalty and skill are noted in his service to the king (2 Samuel 23:29).

Jehoshaphat

Jehoshaphat served as a recorder in David's administration, chronicling the king's reign and aiding in the governance of Israel (2 Samuel 8:16).

Jesse

Jesse, David's father, was a Bethlehemite from the tribe of Judah. He is best known for presenting his sons to Samuel, leading to David's anointing as king (1 Samuel 16).

Jonathan, son of Saul

Jonathan, Saul's son, was David's closest friend and ally.

Despite his loyalty to his father, he recognized David's anointed kingship. He died in battle alongside Saul (1 Samuel 18-20; 31:2).

Jonathan, son of Shammah the Hararite
Jonathan, a mighty man, was known for his bravery and skill in David's service (2 Samuel 23:32).

Joab
Joab, David's nephew and commander of his army, was instrumental in many of David's victories. Though fiercely loyal, his ambition often led to conflicts with David (2 Samuel 2-24).

Maharai the Netophathite
Maharai, a Netophathite, served as one of David's mighty men and was a commander over a division of the army (2 Samuel 23:28; 1 Chronicles 27:13).

Mebunnai the Hushathite
Mebunnai, a mighty man, is noted for his valor in defending Israel during David's reign (2 Samuel 23:27).

Mephibosheth
Mephibosheth, Jonathan's crippled son, was shown kindness by David, who restored Saul's land to him and invited him to eat at the king's table (2 Samuel 9).

Nathan
Nathan, a prophet, was a trusted advisor to David. He delivered God's promises of the Davidic covenant and confronted David over his sin with Bathsheba (2 Samuel 7; 12).

Naharai the Beerothite
Naharai, Joab's armor-bearer, is listed among David's mighty men for his contributions to the kingdom's defense (2 Samuel 23:37).

Paarai the Arbite
Paarai, an Arbite, was among David's mighty men,

celebrated for his bravery in defending the kingdom
(2 Samuel 23:35).

Samuel

Samuel was a prophet, judge, and priest who anointed
both Saul and David as kings. He guided Israel through a
critical period of transition from judges to monarchy
(1 Samuel 1-16).

Saul

Saul, Israel's first king, began well but was rejected by
God due to his disobedience. His jealousy of David led to
his downfall and tragic death in battle (1 Samuel 9-31).

Shammah, son of Agee the Hararite

Shammah is renowned for defending a field of lentils
against the Philistines, earning him a place among David's
top three mighty men (2 Samuel 23:11-12).

Sheva

Sheva served as a scribe in David's administration,
playing a critical role in maintaining the records of the
kingdom (2 Samuel 20:25).

Shimei

Shimei, a relative of Saul, cursed David during Absalom's
rebellion but later sought forgiveness. He was ultimately
executed under Solomon's rule for breaking an oath (2
Samuel 16:5-13; 1 Kings 2:36-46).

Solomon

Solomon, son of David and Bathsheba, succeeded David
as king. Known for his wisdom and the construction of the
temple, he marked the height of Israel's power (1 Kings 1-11).

Uriah the Hittite

Uriah, one of David's mighty men, was betrayed by David
after his wife Bathsheba became pregnant by the king. He
was sent to his death in battle (2 Samuel 11).

The Davidic Chronicles

Zadok

Zadok, a priest during David's reign, remained loyal through Absalom's rebellion and anointed Solomon as king. He established the Zadokite priestly lineage (2 Samuel 15; 1 Kings 1:39).

Zalmon the Ahohite

Zalmon, from Ahoah, was one of David's mighty men. His bravery is commemorated in the list of warriors (2 Samuel 23:28).

Zelek the Ammonite

Zelek, an Ammonite, served as one of David's mighty men, demonstrating loyalty and valor despite his foreign origin (2 Samuel 23:37).

About the Author

Dr. Randy White is a pastor, theologian, and author with a deep commitment to teaching the Bible verse-by-verse and encouraging readers to question long-held assumptions about Scripture. With years of pastoral experience, Dr. White focuses on helping believers develop a literal understanding of the Word of God, emphasizing its clarity and consistency.

Randy White on the Sea of Galilee

As the founder of Dispensational Publishing House, he works to provide resources that uphold biblical inerrancy and promote careful, independent study of Scripture. He is also the host of *Ask the Theologian*, a program dedicated to addressing theological, biblical, and worldview questions.

Dr. White's writing reflects his love for biblical history and his desire to help readers engage with Scripture on a deeper level. His works often explore the historical and theological dimensions of biblical figures, including his study of King David in *The Davidic Chronicles*.

Dr. White lives in Taos, New Mexico, with his wife, Shelley, where he continues to teach, write, and explore the rich truths of the Bible.

Dispensational Publishing House is striving to become the go-to source for Bible-based materials from the dispensational perspective.

Our goal is to provide high-quality doctrinal and worldview resources that make dispensational theology accessible to people at all levels of understanding.

Visit our blog regularly to read informative articles from both known and new writers.

And please let us know how we can better serve you.

Dispensational Publishing House, Inc.
PO Box 3181
Taos, NM 87571

Call us toll free 844-321-4202

www.DispensationalPublishing.com